I BEAR
WITNESS

I BEAR WITNESS

ECKHARTZ
PRESS

Dan McNeil

I dedicate this book to the three most important coaches in my life.

Dave Shelbourne and Al Holok were terrific football coaches, but they also are men of integrity. From them, I learned there are practices and habits that always are essential, never negotiable — preparation, commitment, sportsmanship, unity and living in an upstanding manner. I learned being a leader requires a willingness to be unpopular. They taught me I could make myself better than I was born. Through the weight room, I discovered self-esteem I never knew before. We remain connected.

Barbara Mayer was not a football coach at Highland High School. She was about five feet tall, an ex-nun and "recovering Catholic" who taught journalism. And more. She was the light when my world went dark. Ms. Mayer mothered me when my mom was unavailable. She trained me, developed me and pushed me. Barbara passed away four years ago but she was with me every time I sat down with this project. "The key to good writing is re-writing." Teacher, advisor, spiritualist, writer, poet. Namaste, my dear mentor.

FOREWORD

Walter Payton was the apple of my eye when I played high school football in the 1970s. Payton came to the Bears in '75 and, by his MVP season of '77, Sweetness was the main ingredient in the mix I called my conversational arsenal. Did you see Walter do *this*? Did you see my guy do *that*? It did little to break the ice with girls.

Fast forward to '93, Payton, who remained my favorite athlete of all time, called my radio show on his own accord. He was listening. Pinch me. Shortly after, we wore the same radio uniform when he joined the staff at the Score, then on AM-1160. Just before Payton fell ill with the liver disease that took his life, we had a misunderstanding. It never was resolved, and it haunted me. Details are within.

I was stoked when the Bears drafted Dan Hampton in the spring of '79. Hampton was a badass defensive lineman from Arkansas, where he played for Lou Holtz. My father was roped into being a sports fan by his oldest son. Roy McNeil was an Arkansan, too, so he immediately took to Hampton. I spent Thanksgivings in Benton as a teenager. Hamp came from Cabot, which was a half-hour east.

Very quickly, Hampton's play overshadowed his roots. He was a ferocious football player and quickly became my favorite Bear defender. I got to know Dan a bit through the years and enjoyed his company. Then, in 2009, I stole his job. The Score hired me to do the midday show, along with Matt Spiegel, and reassigned midday hosts Hamp and Laurence Holmes. To his credit, Hampton never took it personally. I think he was unfulfilled talking about baseball anyway, but it's meant something that he's remained an ally.

In the movies, we find all the answers to life's riddles. In *Broadcast News*, the late William Hurt plays *Tom Grunick*, a rising star network anchor whose accomplishments exceed his skills. Colleague Albert Brooks is *Aaron Altman*, a competent reporter vying for the network's affection but not getting it. Altman is jealous of Grunick. And honest with him. As the two converse at a party, Grunick asks Altman "How are you supposed to act when your real life exceeds your dreams?" Says Altman: "Keep it to yourself."

I can't do that. My desire is to shout it from a mountain top. I am a lucky man. I've made a meaningful living — for a few years, absurdly generous — talking about sports. It was what I wanted to do when I was 7 years old.

On August 19 of '69, I punched in my first by-line. Kenny Holtzman of the Cubs no-hit Henry Aaron's Braves at Wrigley Field. After dragging my mother's old Smith-Corona manual typewriter from her closet, I played the hunt-and-peck game and punched out 20" of red-hot postgame copy. On August 19 of '85, I started an internship at WGN, which had just reacquired rights to Bears rights. I should buy an extra lottery ticket every year on August 19.

They say timing is everything. You better believe it. Nobody who worked a minimum wage job anywhere in America in '85 had more fun or got more out of a $3.85 an hour job than I did. As a football fan and as burgeoning radio talent, I was on top of the world. The 1985 Chicago Bears were the biggest thing to hit Chicago since the cow kicked over the lantern. My wild, mercurial ride was emerging from the cocoon. Just a baby. And the '85 Bears were the team that cut the ribbon. Boo yah.

During the past 40 years, I've been clocking the Bears and the NFL with more enthusiasm and intensity than anything I ever did professionally. I could have found happiness and esteem coaching high school football and teaching English but I'm thankful I had this. I've had more pinch me moments than one should be allowed. Details are within. In Chicago, the Bears rule the roost. This is a Bears market. But few have been bullish on the Bears until this past offseason. Quickly, with some perseverance and a little good fortune, Ryan Poles seemingly has his team primed for a renaissance. What's taken the Bears this long? Is it more than quarterback play? Bad coaching? Poor personnel decisions? Why has Green Bay enjoyed such a long stretch of dominance over the Monsters of the Midway? Details are within. What you'll learn is the Bears, despite those occasional little peaks like in '10 and '18, are a most dysfunctional organization. Maybe the most bizarrely operated outfit in the league. The McCaskeys should have purchased apple orchards. Fruit doesn't need the maintenance humans do, and people skills never were the family's strong suit. Dating to George Halas, the original grumpy Bear, the team has been stalled by an odd ownership group with clunky interpersonal relationship habits.

Get ready for the games people played that dropped your jaw and raised your spirits. And those that made your head sag and put you in bed on a Sunday afternoon as soon as the sun set. Get ready to reboard the roller coaster. It hasn't all been a picnic and some of the laments of Bears fans have been the same since the Eisenhower administration. But you and I keep coming back, regardless how dire the times. Is this blind faith or loyalty? Lemmings or true blue?

I hope you enjoy taking the tour with me. From Payton to Caleb Williams, from Mike Ditka to Matt Eberflus, these are the stories of your Chicago Bears over the last 40 years. Thanks for buying a ticket. Welcome. Make every page clear the way to clarity.

CHAPTER 1

The Poles Position
FAST REBOOT TO CONTENTION?

> *"We're gonna be gettin' rid of these people here. First, Mr. Samir Naga... Naga... Na... not gonna work here anymore, anyway."*
> *– one of The Two Bobs (Paul Willson) in the 1999 film Office Space.*

The Ryan Poles we observed on HBO's *Hard Knocks* or heard after the 2024 NFL draft is a decidedly more confident, more polished executive than when he joined the Bears in January of '22. Not surprising. Poles deftly navigated his way through storms and quickly garnered the attention and respect of peers and colleagues. The 39-year-old general manager also is accessible and transparent, rare traits in Lake Forest. The fast roster turnover he orchestrated was impressive. Relentless effort sprinkled with a little fairy dust and *poof!* The Bears earned the incessant stir they created in the offseason and finally the enthusiasm going into a season felt merited.

There's good reason to be suspicious, however, Poles may lack one critical component so many were hopeful for when the Bears pressed reset on GM and coach again in '22 — freedom. The kind of power the Bears never have granted to a personnel man or coach since George Halas. Further, the head coach Poles retained wasted another August. Now in his third season, Matt Eberflus still has decision making deficiencies. Early returns on new offensive coordinator Shane Waldron weren't good and September of '24 was a replay of '23's. Finally in Week 3, with nine minutes remaining in the game in Indianapolis, the Messiah threw his first NFL touchdown pass. A chronic need for self-preservation stunted Caleb Williams' third start. The Colts won 21-16 and Eberflus' upstarts fell to 1-2. Back to the GM.

The perception of Poles and president Kevin Warren creating radical change at the top of the food chain is an illusion. The new Bears front office faces the same obstacles as its predecessors. Anybody who hasn't felt the continued looming of chairman George McCaskey hasn't been paying attention. It wasn't difficult to connect the dots and arrive at the conclusion that Poles' union with Eberflus was an arranged marriage. First, more recent meddling from the top.

Boy George stiff-armed Warren and Poles on front office changes the tandem desired long ago. Finally, the chairman caved in mid-April when the Bears hired Ted Crews as an advisor to the president and chief of communications. Chicago first heard Crews' name when Poles was introduced in late-January of '22. Their circles intersected in Kansas City. Mutual respect and trust were established, and Crews was on Poles' list of Chiefs staffers he thanked at the introductory news conference.

Instead of recognizing the upside of wisdom Poles gained in the scouting department of a Super Bowl champion, McCaskey protected the old guard. Family loyalist Scott Hagel, once a fine publicist before the transfusions kicked in, finally was reassigned to a peripheral position in a distant location on campus. Hagel's presence as the "third suit in the room" during coaching interviews was off-putting to some and a real red flag for Bruce Arians when the Bears were wooing him several coaching hires ago. Public relations director Brandon Faber, hired in '16, was fired once Crews finally was McCaskey-approved.

The McCaskeys want you to think they've retreated and are affording this administration total space command. Instead, Warren's already full plate with the eternal stadium dilemma was overloaded with a tug-of-war this past winter and spring. Two hires for positions clearly were within the president's and the GM's jurisdiction became a wrestling match for several months. G-Mac just can't help himself.

Rewinding to the winter of '22, Eberflus was announced as the 17th coach in team history less than 36 hours after the Bears hired Poles. Whoa. Fast search and decision on the headmaster. I believed Poles was authentic when he described a "love at first sight" dynamic with Flus but insiders insist McCaskey and outgoing president Ted Phillips were pushing the Colts defensive coordinator. It wasn't a quantum leap to believe Poles when he said Eberflus was one of three candidates on his short list long before the Bears named him the GM. The Colts were the No. 1 team in the league in turnover differential and Flus was getting rave reviews. In any business, however, when one receives that first opportunity to sit in the big chair, a sip of company Kool-Aid is sometimes necessary. Poles *wanted* to buy in and believe they had the right man.

It sure smacked of an arranged marriage. The timeline just didn't jibe.

Poles got snippy with *Sun-Times* veteran Mark Potash at the news conference when Potsy persisted. He asked a second question about "a more extensive search" for Matt Nagy's successor and Poles fired back defensively. "It *was* an extensive search. I found him," as he nodded toward his new football soulmate.

The Bears also interviewed Cowboys defensive coordinator Dan Quinn, now the head man in Washington. Quinn got to Chicago in a sour mood after flying to O'Hare in coach. The Bears have an estimated worth of near $7 billion and they welcomed a qualified candidate for one of the most 'important positions in the organization like minor leaguers. It's a bad optic, one they haven't been able to shake since George Halas refused to pay for George Blanda's special kicking shoe in the '50s.

Since their union, Poles and Eberflus have created a palpable symmetry and comfort level, both behind the scenes and when seated side-by-side at news conferences. Frick and Frack. On the heels of a 7-10 finish, the two answered questions together again in a January 10 season-review news conference. Many were surprised Eberflus was retained after '23's 0-4 start and other mishaps along the way. The Bears blew a 26-14 lead with less than four minutes remaining in a 31-26 loss to the Lions in Week 11. With an opportunity to play spoiler in Green Bay on the final Sunday, the Bears were lifeless and lost to the Packers more convincingly than the 17-9 final indicated. Eberflus took the ball after winning the coin toss, giving Jordan Love a shot at one extra possession.

But there was Flus, seated to Poles' left, listening to the GM sing his praises.

When asked why he didn't make a change, Poles reiterated his opening remarks about leadership Eberflus provided to calm the storm when the team was reeling. Asked if he has autonomy, Poles said "Yes, it's my call.

I give my input to George and Kevin and the nice thing is we're all on the same page."

There was no follow up on "giving input" constituting autonomy. Or if Jim Harbaugh was a non-starter for Warren, with whom Harbaugh collided in '20 during the pandemic. Warren was quick to postpone the Big 10 season when he was commissioner and Harbaugh mocked him for it publicly and privately. Harbaugh, Bill Belichick, Pete Carroll and Mike Vrabel all were available, but the Bears stood pat.

Those desirous of a change couldn't believe the NFL world in which they were living. Two Super Bowl winning coaches and a freshly crowned national champion college coach with Bears roots couldn't get in the door for an interview. Flus had gone from dead man walking to trusted general. His defense did improve and ultimately overcame the unexplained firing coordinator Alan Williams following the loss to the Packers on opening day. After an 0-4 start, the Bears regrouped slowly and, with Eberflus calling the defense, finished second in the NFL in interceptions with 22 (Tampa Bay, 25). The Bears went 5-3 down the stretch and were among the top scoring defenses in the league in the second half of the season.

I was among those still underwhelmed. The Bears only could play the team lined up across from them, but six of their seven wins came at the expense of quarterbacks Sam Howell, Brian Hoyer, Bryce Young, Joshua Dobbs, Kyler Murray and Taylor Heineke. In Week 14, the Bears defeated Jared Goff and NFC North champ Detroit, 28-13. That was the only bright feather in the plume.

DEJA VU, ALL OVER AGAIN

The first month of the '24 season opened with more of the same Eberlusian gaffes. Third-year man return man Velus Jones oddly needed to prove one more time he couldn't be trusted to catch a punt without misadventure. His muff on opening day resulted in a Tennessee touchdown and the Bears needed gifts from an unseasoned Will Levis to avert disaster. Again, the offense looked as if it didn't spend time together in August.

Waldron didn't have answers for the Texans in Week 2, a 19-13 loss.

It wasn't a game many expected the Bears to win, but nobody thought they'd look like the '23 Bears. Williams was sacked seven times. After two games, the splashy new Chicago offense had one touchdown. D'Andre Swift, who played all of two snaps in the preseason, was a non-factor. The Bears averaged 2.3 yards per carry in the loss to Indy, which was the worst run defense in the league.

The offensive line was, in a word, terrible. And the *can't-miss* No. 1 pick in the draft looked unsettled. Pressing. It wasn't expected to be *that* bumpy out of the chute. Before Week 4's game against the Rams, former Mike Martz told me Poles needed to deal for *two* offensive linemen to turn around a shaky commencement to the Caleb era.

THE NFL'S CAVE OF WONDERS

The ramp-up to September of '24 hadn't produced Bears fever that burned this hot since Ronald Reagan was in office. It was earned by these Bears, as it was by the *Shufflin' Crew* in the '80s. The overhaul required courage, constitution and patience by Poles, top lieutenant Ian Cunningham and the staff to the city all lathered up again.

That was fast. When Poles arrived, the roster was uninspiring, and the Justin Fields dream remained alive after a wobbly but not condemning rookie season. Poles didn't panic and band-aid it with overpriced veterans with too much tread. He traded Roquan Smith, the best player. That's bravado for a rookie GM on a team often regarded as untrustworthy and unwilling to reward their own with second contracts. Poles was willing to grind with the mess he inherited and presided over a team-record 10-game losing streak in a 3-14 season. A silver lining appeared as Week 18 concluded, however, when Houston beat Indianapolis in overtime in a bizarre, improbable finish. It put the Bears in the pole position with the first pick.

Poles then found the NFL's *magic lamp*. He gave it a rub and out emerged Carolina Panthers owner David Tepper. Poles is *NFL Aladdin*. Tepper is the Genie. His generosity is boundless. Carolina swapped the No. 9 pick and D.J. Moore and two more draft picks for the No. 1 overall. Moore exceeded high expectations in '23, catching 96 passes for 1,364 yards and eight touchdowns.

Rookie first-round tackle Darnell Wright was a hit. Cornerback Tyrique Stevenson, also part of the harvest in the fourth round, made 16 starts. There's one last puzzle piece coming in the second round of the '25 draft.

You likely knew these things, but the gravity of all contributing factors that led to Caleb Williams is just beginning to unveil itself. The stars never were aligned so perfectly for the Bears before.

Tepper's bobbles coming into the '23 season, and how they benefited the Bears, kept coming. He rolled dice on Young, who wasn't the consensus No. 1 quarterback. The Ohio State product flopped conclusively. Tepper already had hired the wrong coach, Frank Reich. The word was Reich and Tepper battled over Young, and it drove a wedge between them. Reich, a questionable hire anyway after the Carson Wentz-led Indianapolis fizzle in '21, was dumped after a 1-10 start. The Panthers finished 2-15, gifting the first pick of the draft to the Bears.

Apologies for good fortune are unnecessary. Luck is where hard work and patience meet opportunity. Position by position, the rapid reconstruction of the roster and in the front office legitimized the buzz. They're going to be *very, very good soon*. Whether Poles lands the Bears in the winner's circle with Eberflus as ringleader is murky.

NO HISTORY, PLEASE

Poles is fatigued by reliving Bears history. I'm sad to lose him as a reader but it's my job to be your tour guide for four decades of Bears explorations. Two years ago, Poles' predecessors Ryan Pace and the peculiar Phil Emery left behind only Fields, Cole Kmet and a few reliable special teamers. They also left him without a first-round pick, the price of the trade-up with the Giants to get Fields in '21. Nagy's fingerprints were on that one, too. The budget for free agents also was light in Poles' first go-round so beatings were inevitable. The following offseason, however, the Bears had near $120 million in cap space with which to work. Poles distributed it generously but not recklessly.

The youthful Bears have catching up to do in the NFC North, expected to be the best division in the league in '24. Defending champion Detroit and the omnipresent Packers also have young players who've earned more than their first varsity letters. The Lions outplayed the 49ers in the NFC title game, but Dan Campbell chose guts over smarts twice and San Francisco went to the Super Bowl. Green Bay also had the 49ers buckling but couldn't close. The schedule seemingly fell in the Bears' favor with nine straight non-divisional games to tune up for the first divisional date on November 17 against the Packers. That afforded the offense ample time to get tuned up for the next border war. They weren't prepared for the curtain to open against the Pack last September, just as Nagy's Bears weren't in his second year in '19.

As the '24 season neared, the biggest threat to the offense was the uncertainty of the line. Defensive tackle also was a concern, although second-year man Gervon Dexter had a great offseason and training camp. Dexter has rotated with Andrew Billings, a consistent performer in '23. Zacch Pickens wasn't a lock to make the roster despite the DT void after Justin Jones took a bloated deal with the Cardinals. Until the Montez Sweat trade, Jones, Billings and DeMarcus Walker were the only productive D-linemen but none were elite.

The secondary is the team's strength and it's a good one to have in a stacked division. Eberflus' defensive backs won't be compared to Seattle's *Legion of Boom* for their physical style, but this is the most talented, deepest and youngest group most can recall. Cornerback Jaylon Johnson, freshly rewarded with a four-year, $76 million deal, is the prize piece. He's 25. Draft classmates of '22 Jaquan Brisker and Kyler Gordon are core players and trending toward earning second contracts.

One last look at the how the long shot road to Williams was paved. In Week 18 of the '22 season, Lovie Smith knew he was gone in Houston and won a game he was supposed to lose. Owner Cal McNair was expecting a lie-down in Indianapolis to secure the Texans the top pick. Lovie wanted the win and in doing so, flash a middle finger to McNair on his way out the door. You likely know the Texans beat the Colts 32-31 in overtime. Exactly how Houston pulled it off deserves illumination.

Lovie's Last Stand was engineered by the never-say-die spirit of quarterback Davis Mills. On fourth and goal from the Indy 28, Mills threw a touchdown pass to tight end Jordan Akins. *Fourth and goal from the 28.* A few plays earlier, Mills connected on a fourth and 12 with a 30-yard completion to Brandin Cooks. Houston also converted on a third and 13. And on a third and 10. The game-winning drive, which concluded with a two-point conversion to Akins, took 2:43 in 14 plays.

If the Caleb-led Bears ever win a Super Bowl, Chicago should declare January 8 a city holiday and call it *Lovie Appreciation Day*. Every year, Mills or Akins could be toastmaster. Maybe a statue of Akins' touchdown, the eighth of his career. Start sculpting, here in the land of few trophies but many monuments.

DRAFT DAY CORONATION

Poles didn't get cute. He could have played percentages and traded down at either the top spot, the ninth or both to accrue more picks. Instead, he remained convicted on Williams and Odunze. In a draft class that produced a record six QBs to go in the top 12, Poles got the consensus No. 1 and the receiver he never thought would slip to ninth. On paper, the offense looks like it won't be needing Nagy's trick bag or anything Luke Getsy may have left behind.

The rookie draft class of '24:

1 (1)	Caleb Williams	QB USC
1. (9)	Rome Odunze	WR Washington
3. (75)	Kiran Amagadjie	OT Yale
4. (122)	Tory Taylor	P Iowa
5. (144)	Austin Booker	DE Kansas St.

The question isn't "which receiver breaks the team record of 5059 career receiving yards?" It's *"which one gets there first,"* Moore or Odunze? Both should have Johnny Morris' team standard in the rear-view mirror by early in the '28 season. Moore got a 1364-yard head start in '23. Morris played for the Bears between '58 and '67 season. Yeah. 19-f'ing-67.

The selection of Amagadjie in the third eased some concerns about depth at tackle. Amagadjie is a Hinsdale Central product, who played in just four games his final year at Yale after having surgery to repair a quad tear. His progress has been slow. Tory Taylor, the thunder-footed Australian, averaged an astounding 43.8 yards net in '23 and has a knack for kicking to the boundary (if you prefer, the "coffin corner"). Booker was expected to go in the third and could be a pleasant surprise. He's light in the caboose but has a fast first step and uses his hands well. He made a big impression in a preseason game and suited up when they began playing meaningful games.

2023 Bears' draft class:

1. (10)	Darnell Wright	OT Tennessee
2. (53)	Gervon Dexter	DT Florida
2. (56)	Tyrique Stevenson	CB Miami
3. (64)	Zacch Pickens	DL South Carolina
4. (115)	Roschon Johnson	RB Texas
4. (133)	Tyler Scott	WR Cincinnati
5. (148)	Noah Sewel	LB Oregon
5. (165)	Terell Smith	CB Minnesota
7. (218)	Travis Bell	DT Kennesaw State

After flipping one spot with Philadelphia (took DT Jalen Carter), Poles secured the tackle he believes will anchor the O-line for years. Wright had a terrific start to his career at RT and played all 1133 offensive snaps. He was flagged for just six pre-snap penalties and five holding calls and the expectation is an ascent to stardom. Dexter flashed late in the season but was not as disruptive as the Bears hoped. He played 39% of the defensive snaps, rotating with fellow rookie Pickens and Billings.

Stevenson was rushed into the lineup by injuries. He had two picks, four PDs and five tackles and earned NFC defensive player of the week honors in Week 17 against Atlanta, a 37-17 victory. Smith, also a corner, was the surprise of this class. Smith made four starts and gives the Bears depth and an additional nickel. Neither Johnson nor Scott provided much spark to a listless offense in '23 and have been obscured further by a handful of offensive additions.

2022 Bears' draft class:

1. no pick (Fields trade in '21)		
2. (39)	Kyler Gordon	CB Washington
2. (48)	Jaquan Brisker	S Penn State
3. (71)	Velus Jones Jr.	WR Tennessee
5. (168)	Braxton Jones	OT Southern Utah
6. (186)	Zachary Thomas	OL San Diego State
6. (203)	Trestan Ebner	RB Baylor
6. (207)	Doug Kramer	OL Illinois
7. (226)	Ja'Tyre Carter	OL Southern
7. (254)	Elijah Hicks	S California
7. (255)	Trenton Gill	P North Carolina State

The absence of a first-rounder will keep this class from "great," but Poles scored with both choices in the second. Gordon plays big at the line of scrimmage for 6-0, 200 and is a reliable open-field tackler. He missed five games early in '23 after playing 97% of the defensive snaps as a rookie. Brisker, who started 15 games in each of his first two seasons, isn't the "hammer" some of us grew up with (think Doug Plank or Gary Fencik) but he's an asset. Braxton Jones started all 17 games and didn't miss a snap in his first year but slipped in '23 and missed six games with a neck injury.

YEAR 3 FOR THE FLUS

Hard to believe Eberflus was the favorite to win coach of the year on most gaming sites. I saw +900 on the BetRivers app in late August. Last November, he was on the endangered species list, a certainty to be fired. His role in the early stumbles was blurred by wins against lousy teams and an unprecedented thrill ride of an offseason.

The truth is the Bears had one impressive win in '23, the 28-13 win over Detroit in Week 14. The mid-season acquisition of Sweat produced a renewed enthusiasm and better performances from the defense but the level to which Eberflus' defense improved was overstated. With Harbaugh available, as well as the crusty ones who won Super Bowls, the Bears stayed the course with the head coach who oversaw consecutive bad starts. And now, a third sluggish first month. Getsy's offense opened last year with no identity and Green Bay shelled the Bears 38-20 at Soldier Field. Wasting August with divisional opponents on the card for opening day has become an all-too-familiar calling card from Bears coaches.

After an 0-3 start — with losses to the Packers, Tampa, 27-17, and Kansas City, 41-10 — the Bears hosted Denver, which had just given up 70 points to the Dolphins. The Bears blew a 28-7 late third-quarter lead at Soldier Field and lost to the Broncos, 31-28. Jonathan Cooper's strip and return of former Ohio State teammate Fields was the backbreaker.

In Week 15, the Bears led Cleveland 17-7 early in the fourth quarter and lost 20-17.

In Week 18 at Lambeau Field, the Bears failed to score a touchdown the defense couldn't solve Love on third down. The Packers quarterback completed 84% of his passes and Green Bay snagged the seventh wild card spot. Johnson didn't suit up. The Packers won their 10th straight in the series.

In the first meeting with the Vikings, a 19-13 loss at Soldier Field in Week 6, Justin Jefferson didn't play. Minnesota's best offensive threat also missed the Week 12 rematch at U.S. Bank Stadium, as did quarterback Kirk Cousins. The Bears muscled out a 12-10 win behind four Cairo Santos field goals.

The Bears beat Howell 40-20 in Week 5 win at Washington, the *win one for Dick Butkus* game. Moore had a breakthrough game, catching eight balls for 230 yards and three TDs. Howell also got the job done for the Commanders, throwing for 388 yards and two TDs against a Chicago defense that was still struggling to tread water through the first half of the season.

The Bears walked all over Hoyer when the journeyman and his Raiders came to the lakefront in Week 7, 30-12. Hoyer carded a 37.1 rating. The Raiders were sleepwalking, already checked out on Josh McDaniels, who was fired a week later.

The Bears beat Young in a 16-13 taffy pull in Week 10 at Soldier Field. The skittish rookie posted a 68.4 rating and Carolina fell to 1-9.

They beat Dobbs (Cousins' backup) in the Week 12 win in Minneapolis.

Dobbs threw four picks.

Murray came up short in a Week 16 win over Arizona, 27-16.

Poor Heineke didn't have a chance in Week 17, when the Bears thrashed Atlanta 37-17. Heineke's rating was 26.1.

Winning is never an easy proposition in the NFL and there is enormous value in experiencing success, regardless of the opponent. Cherish those events. Collect them and keep stacking them. That's how confidence is born. Just pump the brakes on this "elite" stuff. Not yet.

There's no gentle way to say it. Eberflus doesn't give off the vibe of a bright guy. In the heat of the moment, he gets rattled. The coach burned a timeout to deliberate going for two or kicking the PAT in the loss to the Colts. In Houston, he wasted a challenge, succumbing to the plea of Gordon, who thought he had both hands under the ball for an interception of C.J. Stroud. Flus buckled to placate a gesticulating player. He didn't ask his staff in the coaches' box to look at the replay and ask if it warranted a challenge. These things shouldn't happen in a coach's third season.

He's user-friendly enough, seems to be a likeable guy, in a goofy uncle kind of way. He confuses easily and fumbles between thought and speech. Flus doesn't look like a man brimming with confidence. Even with new threads, a more stylish coiffe and a neatly trimmed beard. Is that a quality one can develop or an intrinsic quality? It's tough to imagine a room full of virile young men who believe *this* is the guy who's going to lead them through NFL minefields.

In my mind's eye, Eberflus is a long shot to succeed as an NFL headmaster. Players typically respond best to leaders who teach well and provide a compass, but an element of fear also is an attribute. There's a ruthlessness to coaching football at the highest level and the guys who hoist trophies invariably have that edgy side. Eberflus doesn't appear to have it.

THE BEARS' HISTORY OF BUILDERS

Before moving on to Williams and the ghosts of *Bearsmas* past, a masthead for those who preceded Poles and handled personnel. GM history (post Halas):

Ryan Poles	2022-present
Ryan Pace	2015-2021
Phil Emery	2012-2014
Jerry Angelo	2001-2011
Mark Hatley	1997-2000 *official title was VP of personnel
Dave Wannstedt	1994-1996 *Wannstedt director of player personnel
	*Graves director of scouting
Rod Graves	
Dave Wannstedt	1993 *de facto GM
Bill Tobin	1987-1992 *director of player personnel
Jerry Vainisi	1983-1986
Jim Finks	1974-1982

Over the next four chapters, a deeper dive into the quarterback position, Poles' body of work and we'll plow through the team's history in the draft, trades and free agency markets.

Right now, pour one and raise your glass to the present. Nothing shy of catastrophic injuries can undo a bright future. Right? There ain't no way they got this one wrong. The expectation is for Super Bears, and I'll hold them to that regardless of '24's final report card. No.18 contends he lives to rewrite history. This is a village that's overdue for it. My fear is Williams may need new co-conspirators. Eberflus and Waldron didn't debut as magically as Jagger and Richards.

If Williams *does* author the book he plans to write, Poles might feel like talking history again.

CHAPTER 2
New Kid in Town (again)
CALEB & THE LEGACY HE FOLLOWS

> *"Let's talk about the draft. What do we need? I hear a quarterback is a good thing to have." – fictional Cleveland Browns owner Anthony Molina (Frank Langella) in the 2014 film Draft Day.*

The 2024 calendar slowly oozed into September and opening day against Tennessee couldn't get here fast enough. Fatigued from a year of erroneous rumors and distortions of the truth about Caleb Williams, it was finally time to witness the first pick in the draft take a chokehold on his job as quarterback of the Bears. Arriving at the football part of the burgeoning megastar was an arduous exercise.

One by one, Williams quashed perceptions. A clearer picture of his parents, Carl Williams and Dayla Price, vanished suspicions of their "over-involvement" in Caleb's business. It turned out Carl is not Marv Marinovich, the overbearing father of USC star quarterback Todd Marinovich. In '91, Todd burst out of USC as a first-rounder, then busted out of the NFL a few years later as an absolute mess. Caleb's father is a real estate developer and owner of an upscale athletic performance training center in Washington, D.C. Caleb attended D.C.'s Gonzaga College high school, a private Catholic prep school. Annual tuition is $31,500.

In his Heisman trophy acceptance speech in '22, Williams vividly described his parents' positive qualities. He thanked them for being providers and a support system for what *he* wanted, not what they wanted. Carl's training center became the home gym for Caleb and his Gonzaga teammates. Dayla is a nail technician and planted the seeds for her son's fondness for manicures and cuticle stylings when he was a child.

Williams shot down the notion he would pull a John Elway and snub Chicago the way Elway did to the Baltimore Colts in '83. At the combine, Williams appeared to be at complete ease just being one of the fellas. Once he arrived, the No. 1 pick did everything the Bears asked him to do. Ballgames and boat tours. Promotional videos and digital media. The suspicion Williams might be *too cool for school* disintegrated. Jaylon Johnson had been on that train, too, but later backpedaled on his "Joe Hollywood" warning to the flamboyant quarterback.

The last item on the check list before getting to work was hammering out a contract. That's where the bigness of Williams' star was evidenced.

Caleb Williams is a corporation. To his credit, Williams removed himself from negotiations and hired a team of labor attorneys to investigate his contract. It didn't sit well with the Bears, however, because they couldn't get in a room with the lawyers. Williams' team wasn't NFLPA certified. It muddied the water more than the Bears admitted but on July 17, three days before training camp opened, Williams signed for $39.5 million. The future and *the now* was in the fold.

The language and legality of the CBA as it pertains to rookie contracts were items Carl Williams and Dayla were asking questions about last fall. Good for them, bad for the Bears, who had no appetite for a discussion about removing the fifth-year option or forfeiting their right to put the franchise tag on Williams. There also were inquiries made about paying Williams as an LLC.

Neither GM Ryan Poles nor Williams offered details, but a relieved Williams noted the experience will be valuable for "the next one and things like that." The current CBA doesn't expire until March of 2031 and it's a certainty the first contract's restrictions and limitations are going to be high on the union's to-do list.

Right now, it's show time.

CENTRAL CASTING QB

From head to toe, Williams looks the part. It's more than the measurables like size, agility and arm strength. He's 6-1, 215. He moves with purpose and his gait is confident and seamless. Williams drips youthful exuberance. He often is smiling and his desire to fit in when the rookie class convened for workouts in May seemed authentic. When he answers questions, he makes eye contact and typically offers a thoughtful reply. Williams possesses a presence, and he always appears to be *present*.

The Caleb buzz intensified when teammates, coaches and experts defined his qualities. The Bears had to get one right finally. *This* is the guy, a Bears quarterback who lifts his team to greatness. Consistently. No more game balls for a game manager. Gone are the days of saluting quarterbacks only because they rifled a third-and-goal throw into the second row to get the field goal. Or applause for the guy with the dreaded "thorough understanding of the system" highest on his list of qualities.

Williams exudes confidence. You see a leader, by example, with the words he chooses and how he comports himself. You see a guy with star qualities.

The flowing robes. The grace. Striking.

It's Year One with the new Savior. Most observers were convinced this time, they found *the One*. Count me among them. To ease Williams' transition to the NFL and the enormous expectations of him, he was welcomed by an embarrassment of riches. The trademark of the Bears for 104 years may have been a tenacious defense but for the next four years, Caleb, Rome Odunze, Darnell Wright, Cole Kmet and D.J. Moore are all under contract. Points, points, points, points. Points, points, points, points.

When quarterback-starved Chicago initially heard the '22 Heisman trophy winner likely would say *"don't do it because I won't come,"* some used the perceived threat to build a case against Williams. I don't remember hearing more predictions of NFL doom after one bad game the way Williams' detractors barked after three picks in USC's 48-20 loss at Notre Dame in mid-October. That was enough in some corners. Some naysayers bemoaned his demeanor. Perish the thought the quarterback of the hard scrabble Chicago Bears weeps in front of cameras and, Halas forbid, polishes his nails.

On the Friday morning of the combine's final weekend, Williams coolly put rumors to rest. "If I get drafted by the Bears, I'll be excited." For those rooting for the Bears to get him, it breathed hope in earnest for the first time. Bursting from of the Dark Ages of offensive football was in the

Bears' grasp. When Poles subsequently spoke of "doing right by Justin," the arrival of Williams appeared imminent. At his pro day at USC, the video bytes of Williams and his dad interacting with Poles and Matt Eberflus were compelling. Caleb was greeted warmly by new Bears wide out Keenan Allen, his pal for a year already in Los Angeles.

The images brought it home. This thing was ordained. On April 25th in Detroit, when his name was called, Williams walked with bounce in his stride, emerging from the green room and onto the stage. He grinned, then belted out *"WOOOOO!"* And there was one last primal urge to yelp as he approached Roger Goodell's embrace — *"YEAHHHHH!"*

It delivered. In a stylish but not opulent navy suit, Williams sent a euphoric shot of adrenaline to a fan base deprived of a quarterback for most of 104 years. *Sportsgasm.*

Chicago's most important 22-year-old drew raves as soon as OTAs began. The *pink cloud* phase all over again. There's room here for the analytical and intellectual components. Pocket awareness and arm slots. Drop backs and check downs. I asked several A-list quarterbacks for their early reads on Williams and they're on deck. *Fire and passion* come first, however. It's an emotional game and many of us are emotional consumers of it. To get the picture painted comprehensively, one needs to get be reminded of the depths of suffering. What follows are four new millennium exhibits that encapsulate quarterback hell in Chicago.

QB HELL VARIETALS

It was Thanksgiving of '04 and the Bears were in Dallas. Lovie Smith was reduced to bullpen arms most of the year with Rex Grossman's second season quashed from a broken ankle suffered in a preseason game. The lifelessness displayed by Terry Shea's offense in a 21-7 loss morphed to helplessness. It's a microcosm of the misery, missing only a left-handed passer. Or a former first-rounder who flopped. Or a guy completely uninterested in succeeding at professional football. Or in the case of Cade McNown, all three.

I don't remember who earned the drumstick on the turducken, but Cowboys quarterback Vinny Testaverde was the best quarterback after erupting for 92 passing yards and a touchdown. The Bears didn't compete. It was Jonathan Quinn's third and final start of the season and the sixth and last of his career. Quinn was so bad in Week 12, Smith gave him the hook and Craig Krenzel got a chance to dust off the old cannon. Quinn, a Jacksonville third-rounder in '98, went 10-of-21 for 86 yards. Dallas intercepted him twice and sacked him four times. He posted a 19.2 rating. Krenzel, a low-risk gamble in the fifth-round of '04, went 5-of-10 for 46 yards and was sacked twice. For both QBs, '04 was their last year in the league. A veteran who can't play dead and an overmatched rookie — Bear traditions.

The Bears punched out only 10 first downs and 140 total yards. They converted 2-of-14 on third down and lost two fumbles. The only highlight was a 45-yard interception return for a touchdown by R.W. McQuarters shortly before halftime. It kept the Bears alive and kept the offense off the field. It was the longest three hour, seven-minute game ever played, a real endurance test for anybody who hung with it. Perhaps it was this stinker that's behind my disproportionate dislike for the ridiculous orange jerseys. I shiver anytime they wear it, just like the suspicions of another sullied Thanksgiving when the schedule is released. And the Bears are in Detroit for it again in '24.

Let's go to the '15 season, when the John Fox retirement fund tour stopped in Seattle in Week 3. It was Jimmy Clausen time against Pete Carroll's vaunted defense. Clausen completed nine passes for 63 yards. The Bears were 3-for-13 on third down and mustered only 146 yards offense. The Seahawks, who were 14.5-point favorites, cruised to a 26-0 win — without a takeaway.

Even on rare occasions when a Bears passer clears 300 yards, results underwhelm. Jay Cutler is peerless in junk stats. In his unsatisfying first year in '09, the Bears were in San Francisco for a *Thursday Night Football* scrap with Mike Singletary's 49ers. With the nation's eyes on Cutty, he passed for 307 yards. It was the *five* interceptions that undermined the effort. Robbie Gould kicked two field goals, and the Bears lost 10-6.

Even in victory, the Bears can stuff offensive football in a time machine to get the win. Carolina was at Soldier Field in '17 for Mitch Trubisky's second start. Call it *The Eddie Jackson Game*. Fox was in save-his-own-ass mode and Trubisky attempted only seven passes the entire game, completing four for 104 yards. The Bears berthed a litter of five first downs. Jackson returned a fumble 75 yards to give the Bears a 7-0 lead in the first. Before halftime, he took a Cam Newton pick 74 yards to the house. The Bears won it 17-3. A burn-the-tape game for most. A real work of art for anybody who took the Bears and laid the 2.5 points.

It's unfathomable when you pause to really digest it. How could the Bears perform at quarterback so far below the standard for so long? The quarterbacks who've piled out of the clown car after the '80s Bears stretch to infinity. Will Furrer. Peter Tom Willis. Dave Krieg. Henry Burris. Steve Stenstrom. Moses Moreno. Chris Chandler. Shane Matthews. Cade McNown. Kordell Stewart. Chad Hutchinson. Jonathan Quinn. Rex Grossman. Kyle Orton. Brian Griese. Jeff Blake. Jason Campbell. Todd Collins. Caleb Hanie. Jimmy Clausen. Brian Hoyer. Josh McCown. Matt Barkley. Chase Daniel. Nick Foles. Mike Glennon. Mitch Trubisky. A clown car indeed, but no colorful baggy pants, painted faces, or light bulb noses. Men wearing navy blue jerseys numbered between 2 and 19 are the highly paid athletes who keep emerging and tripping all over their big blue shoes.

FIRST HISTORY TO WRITE: 4000 YARDS AND 30 TOUCHDOWNS

While Chicago was enduring Fields' farewell campaign, Brock Purdy was setting San Francisco's single-season standard with 4280 passing yards. Purdy was the last player taken in the '22 draft and last year was his first full season at the helm. In Green Bay, Jordan Love was in his third year but his first as the starter after Aaron Rodgers was moved to the Jets. Love didn't set the Packers' one-year mark, but he threw for 4159 yards and 32 touchdowns. In 15 games with the Texans, offensive rookie of the year C.J. Stroud passed for 4108 yards. Sam Howell of the Commanders was just shy of 4000 yards.

The one-year passing standard in Chicago is an attainable goal for Williams *now*. Given good health and with the cast assembled for Caleb, it should be *the expectation* he bests Erik Kramer's team mark of 3838 yards this year. If he starts all 17 games and doesn't, he and the Bears did some things terribly wrong. It's not damning but dispiriting when you consider the volume of quarterbacks who clear the 4000-yard bar every year.

I was aware Kramer's 3838 yards in '95 was the one-year mark and the lowest of all 32 teams, but curiosity grew while scrolling recent 4000-yard seasons. Even before a 17-game schedule, there were quarterbacks who weren't respected — punchlines even — who threw for more than 3838 yards in a season. Buckle up, it's going to be a bumpy read.

A dozen years ago, when fantasy football owners combed the waiver wire for QB reinforcement, Tampa's Josh Freeman was an option. Nobody in America punched in his name and felt good about it. The '09 first-round pick threw for 4065 yards in a 7-9 season. Freeman played seven years and posted a career rating of 77.6. That would be the best year in Bears history. He threw 27 TD passes, which would be tied for third most for the Bears. Kramer fired 29 in '95 and Cutler's best was 28 in '14.

Jacksonville's Blake Bortles cleared the Kramer bar *twice*. Matt Schaub of the Texans did it *three times*. How Cutler didn't jump it just once in eight years with the Bears is hard to understand. He was healthy for most of his tenure in Chicago.

During the Packers' 32-year stranglehold on the rivalry, Aaron Rodgers and Brett Favre both topped Kramer's standard 11 times. Favre also did it with the Vikings. Peyton Manning beat it with the Colts 11 times and three more with the Broncos. Tom Brady had the most seasons with more passing yards than Kramer's mark — 15 — a dozen with the Patriots and three more with the Bucs.

Here are single season passing yards bests for all 32:

1. 5477 Broncos, Peyton Manning, 2013
2. 5476 Saints, Drew Brees, 2011
3. 5316 Buccaneers, Tom Brady, 2021
4. 5250 Chiefs, **Patrick Mahomes**, 2022
5. 5235 Patriots, Tom Brady, 2011
6. 5129 Steelers, Ben Roethlisberger, 2018
7. 5084 Dolphins, Dan Marino, 1984
8. 5038 Lions, Matthew Stafford, 2011
9. 5014 Chargers, **Justin Herbert**, 2021
10. 4924 Falcons, Matt Ryan, 2016
11. 4933 Giants, Eli Manning, 2011
12. 4917 Commanders, Kirk Cousins, 2016
13. 4903 Cowboys, Tony Romo, 2012
14. 4886 Rams, Matthew Stafford, 2021
15. 4823 Texans, Deshaun Watson, 2020
16. 4804 Raiders, Derek Carr, 2021
17. 4761 Colts, Andrew Luck, 2014
18. 4717 Vikings, Daunte Culpepper, 2004
19. 4690 Titans, Warren Moon, 1991
20. 4671 Cardinals, Carson Palmer, 2015
21. 4673 Packers, Aaron Rodgers, 2011
22. 4611 Bengals, **Joe Burrow**, 2021
23. 4544 Bills, **Josh Allen**, 2020
24. 4436 Panthers, Steve Beuerlein, 1999
25. 4428 Jaguars, Blake Bortles, 2015
26. 4317 Ravens, Joe Flacco, 2016
27. 4282 Seahawks, **Geno Smith**, 2022
28. 4280 49ers, **Brock Purdy**, 2023
29. 4132 Browns, Brian Sipe, 1980
30. 4039 Eagles, Carson Wentz, 2019
31. 4007 Jets, Joe Namath, 1967
32. 3838 BEARS, Erik Kramer, 1995

Almost all those standards were set in the 16-game season era. Namath's 4007 yards for the Jets in '67 was amidst a 5-8-1 season and is the most antiquated. Browns quarterback Brian Sipe, a one-year superstar, hit 4132 yards in his MVP season in '80.

Adding insult to injury, Kramer's season was only fourth-best in the NFC Central. Favre won the MVP in '95 with 4413 yards and 38 TDs. Detroit's Mitchell was 4338 and 32 TDs and Minnesota's Moon went 4228 and 33 TDs. All three topped E.K. in yards and TD passes. Atlanta's Jeff George, Denver's John Elway and the Rams Jim Everett also threw for more yards.

The single season standards for TD passes:

1.	55	Broncos, Peyton Manning, 2013
2.	50	Patriots, Tom Brady 2007
		Chiefs, **Patrick Mahomes**, 2018
4.	49	Colts, Peyton Manning, 2004
5.	48	Dolphins, Dan Marino, 1984
		Packers, Aaron Rodgers, 2020
7.	46	Saints, Drew Brees, 2011
8.	41	Lions, Matthew Stafford, 2011
		Rams, **Matthew Stafford**, 2021
10.	40	Seahawks, Russell Wilson, 2020
11.	39	Vikings, Daunte Culpepper, 2004
12.	38	Chargers, **Justin Herbert**, 2021
		Falcons, Matt Ryan, 2016
14.	37	Bills, **Josh Allen**, 2020
		Cowboys, **Dak Prescott**, 2021
16.	36	Titans, George Blanda, 1961
		Giants, Y.A. Title, 1963
		Ravens, **Lamar Jackson**, 2019
		49ers, Steve Young, 1998
20.	35	Jaguars, Blake Bortles, 2015
		Cardinals, Carson Palmer, 2015
		Bengals, **Joe Burrow**, 2022

23.	34	Raiders, Daryl Lamonica, 1969
		Panthers, Steve Beuerlein, 1999
		Steelers, Ben Roethlisberger, 2018
26.	33	Eagles, Carson Wentz, 2017
		Buccaneers, Jameis Winston, 2019
		Texans, Deshaun Watson, 2020
29.	31	Jets, Ryan Fitzpatrick, 31, 2015
		Commanders, Sonny Jurgensen, 1967
31.	30	Browns, Brian Sipe, 1980
32.	29	BEARS, Erik Kramer, 1995

The Jets and Cleveland are the only two teams that rival the Bears lifetime in quarterback hell. A century at the shallow end of the gene pool. The Jets weren't launched until the AFL's arrival in '60.

What follows is what qualified observers told me about Caleb Williams.

Kurt Warner, HOF Class of '17, NFL Network studio analyst:

"What I like is I've seen him have the capability of doing everything. To me that's what you want from a quarterback. We often fall in love with the physical traits. The creativity... a lot of people have compared him to Patrick Mahomes already. I don't ever like to jump to those levels, but I see why because there is a creativity. There is a unique ability to throw the football on the move. To me, it's more that I've seen him have the capabilities of playing inside the pocket, being patient, making big time throws down the field. I've seen aspects of everything I want in a quarterback. That's what excites me about the possibilities.

"What I want to see here in his first year is them homing in on him playing from inside the pocket. Playing the game, becoming a passer, seeing the field, getting the ball out and then allowing the creative piece to become secondary and not just throwing him in and giving him the ball and letting him run around and be creative, but not developing him as a quarterback."

Erik Kramer, Bears' QB '93-'98:

"What I haven't seen enough of yet is where he decides to take what the defense gives him and makes the game simple. There's too many times where read 1 is open but read 1 doesn't get the ball. Read 4 or 5 isn't open and then all chaos breaks loose. And then he finds somebody. The game needs to be simpler than that. Here's what scares me a little bit — it's the drop back. You want a nice, efficient, smooth, almost 'liquid' pass drop. You play with that fluidness. Often times, he looks kind of like a whirling dervish in that backfield, but it really isn't that difficult."

Rodney Peete, USC alum, 15-year NFL QB:

"You got the right guy. He's got the right temperament, the right attitude, the right work ethic. He will bring so much to this team to make everybody better. The more he's there, the more you're going to like him. He's a special kid. I'm excited to see what he does, this year and beyond.

"I was actually critical of him at USC at times for trying to do too much, trying to put the team on his back — which he did often-times because he had to. They struggled on the offensive line and in some other areas and had to rely on Caleb doing everything for them. There are going to be times where he doesn't need to run out of the pocket. He needs to be patient, especially in the NFL. Completions matter. Sometimes you've got to take that three-yard completion and not go for the big play every time. There were times when he went big-play hunting more often than not and that's something he's going to have to work through, within the system, now that he's in the NFL.

"I think the Mahomes comparison is a very good comparison. He can make every single throw and that's why people make the comparison. He can throw it to his left, to his right, side-arm, over the top, anything you ask him to do, he can make the throw. That's a talent we haven't seen a lot of."

SHANE WALDRON'S TURN

No marriage in Chicago is more important than Williams' union with offensive coordinator Shane Waldron. The early returns were shockingly unsatisfying. Waldron was the OC in Seattle the past three seasons and held the same title for a year under Sean McVay with the Rams. Warren Moon, HOF class of '06, did Seahawks radio for almost 20 years and keeps a critical eye on Seattle, as well as college football on the West coast. Two things he said about Waldron struck me as requisite for a coordinator. Waldron insists on spreading the ball around, which shouldn't be a tall order for Williams, given the skilled players assembled. Of greater relevance was a comment about what Waldron did with Seahawks quarterback Geno Smith when the former Jets second-round pick of '13 won the '22 comeback player of the year award. Smith finished in the top five in the most meaningful metrics. Waldron's method begins with allowing his quarterbacks do what they do best, not shoehorn them into *his system*. Novel.

"He did a great job of putting an offense together that played to Geno's strengths," said Moon, who also gave a ringing endorsement to the trio of Chicago wide receivers. He's a Washington alum and watched every game Odunze played for the Huskies. "Geno has a really good arm and he's really good in rhythm. And he had a lot of really good rhythm type throws where he got to his back foot and let the ball go. There wasn't a lot of sitting there and holding the football, which was something he had done a lot earlier in his career. He was going to make the read, a simple read, and get the ball out quickly. That not only helped the receivers as far as the timing was concerned, that helped his offensive line because they didn't have to protect as long because the ball is out of there in rhythm. That's something Shane brought to the offense, along with the running game. A very successful running game. I think for every quarterback to be successful, you've got to be able to run the football and make the defense play the run. That's when the passing game and particularly play action pass becomes more valuable because now the defense is looking run and you play action. That's when you get some bigger windows to throw the football into the secondary."

Waldron turned 45 before the season and appeared to be tracking toward a head coaching opportunity. That was said of Luke Getsy, too. Historically, the lack of progress on the field, combined with incompatible OCs and QBs, made for fast divorces. The Bears would love to be looking for a new OC in two years because Waldron gets a chance somewhere. That's only happened only once with a Bear assistant. Adam Gase was given a chance to front an NFL team, first with the Dolphins and then the Jets. In Gase's first year in Miami in '16, he won 10 games and earned a wild card berth (lost to

Pittsburgh 30-12), but it was downhill from there. He was whacked after three years with a 23-25 record (.479). The Jets went 2-15 in '20 and the salty Gase got curbed after two years, going 9-23 (.281).

Since '85, the Bears have finished in the Top 10 in scoring offense only eight times. In the past 40 years, they're in the bottom halfway too often. Here's a look at the offensive coordinator history and how they ranked among their NFL peers:

	Points Scored	Points Per Game	Ranking
2023 Luke Getsy	360	21.2	18th
2022 Luke Getsy	326	19.2	23rd
2021 Bill Lazor	311	18.3	27th
2020 Bill Lazor	372	23.3	22nd
2019 Mark Helfrich	280	17.5	29th
2018 Mark Helfrich	421	26.3	9th
2017 Dowell Loggains	264	16.5	29th
2016 Dowell Loggains	279	17.4	28th
2015 Adam Gase	335	20.9	23rd
2014 Aaron Kromer	319	19.9	23rd
2013 Aaron Kromer	445	27.8	2nd
2012 Mike Tice	375	23.4	6th
2011 Mike Martz	353	22.1	17th
2010 Mike Martz	334	20.9	21st
2009 Ron Turner	327	20.4	19th
2008 Ron Turner	375	23.4	14th
2007 Ron Turner	334	20.9	18th
2006 Ron Turner	427	26.7	2nd
2005 Ron Turner	260	16.3	26th
2004 Terry Shea	231	14.4	32nd
2003 John Shoop	283	17.7	23rd
2002 John Shoop	281	17.6	27th
2001 John Shoop	338	21.1	11th
2000 Gary Crowton	216	13.5	28th
1999 Gary Crowton	272	17.0	25th

1998 Matt Cavanaugh	276	17.3	25th
1997 Matt Cavanaugh	263	16.4	28th
1996 Ron Turner	283	17.7	26th
1995 Ron Turner	392	24.5	8th
1994 Ron Turner	271	16.9	24th
1993 Ron Turner	234	14.6	24th
1992 Greg Landry	295	18.4	16th
1991 Greg Landry	299	18.7	14th
1990 Greg Landry	348	21.8	10th
1989 Greg Landry	358	22.4	10th
1988 Ed Hughes	312	19.5	18th
1987 Ed Hughes	356	23.7	9th
1986 Ed Hughes	352	22.0	13th
1985 Ed Hughes	456	28.5	2nd

It's a mathematical high probability at least two of the six quarterbacks taken in the first 12 picks will be an abject failure. It's likely a couple of them will be reduced to scratching and clawing their way to serviceable. From a metrics standpoint, those outcomes are smarter wagers than one of them ultimately wearing a yellow jacket in Canton. The Vikings were the first of the six clubs that went QB hunting to get burned by injury. J.J. McCarthy went on IR after knee surgery, not ACL reconstruction however, and yielded to the well-traveled Sam Darnold. Here they are... the 2024 franchise saviors:

1. Caleb Williams, BEARS, USC
2. Jayden Daniels, Commanders, LSU
3. Drake Maye, Patriots, North Carolina
8. Michael Penix Jr., Falcons, Washington
10. J.J. McCarthy, Vikings, Michigan
12. Bo Nix, Broncos, Oregon

Fingers crossed for Andrew Luck comparisons. It's not possible to think JaMarcus Russell, is it? Ask Steven A. Smith, who was projecting bust for Williams after three games. Recent evidence suggests how tenuous NFL life is for top prospect quarterbacks. A rewind to the Fields year, also quarterback heavy. It's not gone as planned. The '21 QB class:

1. Trevor Lawrence, Jacksonville, Clemson
2. Zach Wilson, NY Jets, BYU
3. Trey Lance, San Francisco, North Dakota State
11. Justin Fields, BEARS, Ohio State
15. Mac Jones, New England, Alabama

Only Lawrence emerged with potential superstar hopes. Of these five top 15 picks, Lawrence is the only one who remains with the team that drafted him. The arrow for the top pick in the '21 draft, however, isn't pointing up as it did when the former Clemson star concluded his rookie season. After an enormous bed wetting with four picks in the first half of the wild card game against the Chargers, Lawrence regrouped and engineered a 27-point comeback and dumped Los Angeles, 31-30. The '22 and '23 seasons, however, didn't produce marked growth for Lawrence. The Jaguars opened '24 stuck in neutral and Doug Pederson's future looked murky. Lawrence now has Jones to caddy for him. The Patriots dumped Jones for a sixth-rounder.

Lance, who produced shockingly ugly results after the 49ers were so high on him, is in his second year on the bench in Dallas. If there's a better recent example of the unpredictable nature of NFL quarterbacks, I can't think of it. San Francisco was wrong on Lance, the third-overall pick in '21, but struck gold with the last pick in '22, Purdy, *Mr. Irrelevant*.

My expectations for Fields in Pittsburgh were temperate and then Mike Tomlin named him the starter. The Steelers then had a solid start. Most thought they traded for Fields as a lifeboat if expected starter Russell Wilson played poorly. In '23, Wilson found some redemption for his flame out in Seattle and bumpy start in Denver. The Broncos ate money but were delighted to rid themselves of the quirky two-time NFC champion. Pittsburgh got bargains on both. Relinquishing only a conditional pick — a fourth- to sixth-rounder for Fields— his $2.7M salary was more than worth the risk for an expected backup who's 25. Fields remains one of the NFL's all-time best scramblers. Offensive coordinator Arthur Smith began the year looking like a genius. Fields was playing with confidence and the Steelers played clean offensively in September.

If single season passing standards for all 32 teams weren't enough evidence of the Chicago drought, the career passing marks might be even more dispiriting. Cutler's 23,443 yards are the team record. He was with the Bears for eight years. Only the Texans, who arrived in '02, and the Buccaneers, born in '76, are below the Bears. These numbers were entering the 2024 season. It's worth noting Patrick Mahomes leapfrogged Len Dawson in Kansas City (the guy the Bears passed on for Trubisky). Here are all career leaders, beginning with the 21st century's highest standard for excellence in any sport. Some teams have more than one who cleared Cutler's bar for career passing yards of 23,443:

1.	New England	
	74,571 Tom Brady	
	29,657 Drew Bledsoe	
	26,886 Steve Grogan	
2.	New Orleans	
	68,010 Drew Brees	
3.	Pittsburgh	
	64,088 Ben Roethlisberger	
	27,989 Terry Bradshaw	
4.	Green Bay	
	61,665 Brett Favre	
	59,055 Aaron Rodgers	
	24,718 Bart Starr	
5.	Miami	
	61,361 Dan Marino	
	25,092 Bob Griese	
6.	Atlanta	
	59,735 Matt Ryan	
	23,470 Steve Bartkowski	
7.	L.A. Chargers	
	59,271 Philip Rivers	
	43,040 Dan Fouts	
	26,938 John Hadl	

8.   N.Y. Giants
        57,023 Eli Manning
        33,462 Phil Simms

9.   Indianapolis
        54,828 Peyton Manning
        39,768 Johnny Unitas
        23,671 Andrew Luck

10.   Denver
        51,475 John Elway

11.   Detroit
        45,109 Matthew Stafford

12.   Baltimore
        38,245 Joe Flacco

13.   Seattle
        37,059 Russell Wilson
        29,434 Matt Hasselbeck
        26,132 Dave Krieg

14.   Buffalo
        35,467 Jim Kelly
        27,590 Joe Ferguson

15.   Las Vegas
        35,222 Derek Carr

16.   San Francisco
        35,124 Joe Montana
        31,548 John Brodie
        29,907 Steve Young

17.   Arizona
        34,639 Jim Hart

18.   Dallas
        34,183 Tony Romo
        32,942 Troy Aikman
        29,459 Dak Prescott

19.   Tennessee
        33,685 Warren Moon
        27,141 Steve McNair

20. Minnesota
33,098 Fran Tarkenton
24,775 Tommy Kramer

21. Philadelphia
32,873 Donovan McNabb
26,963 Ron Jaworski

22. Cincinnati
32,838 Kenny Anderson
31,594 Andy Dalton
27,149 Boomer Esiason

23. Carolina
29,975 Cam Newton

24. Kansas City
28,507 Len Dawson
28,424 Patrick Mahomes

25. N.Y. Jets
27,057 Joe Namath

26. Jacksonville
25,698 Mark Brunell

27. Washington
25,206 Joe Theismann

28. L.A. Rams
23,258 Jim Everett

29. Cleveland
23,713 Brian Sipe
23,584 Otto Graham

30. BEARS
23,443 Jay Cutler

31. Houston
23,221 Matt Schaub

32. Tampa Bay
19,737 Jameis Winston

Caleb Williams, the world is yours. Tear it up, man. Tyson Bagent, stay close.

CHAPTER 3
Cold Draft Bears
HIGHS & LOWS IN THE DRAFT

"I've listened to you tell those parents 'When I know, I know. And when it comes to your son, I know.' And you know what? You don't. You don't."
– Oakland Athletics GM Billy Beane (Brad Pitt) in the 2011 film Moneyball.

There is no offseason activity that produces more anxiety than the declaration *"the Bears are on the clock."* Too many boulevards of broken dreams traveled. Expectations unmet. The first round haunts every NFL town, but the Bears consistently whiff at the most critical positions on the field — quarterback, pass rusher, offensive tackle and wide receiver.

There was a decidedly different vibe this past April. The writing was on the wall with Caleb Williams at the top but debate on what Ryan Poles should do with the ninth pick was compelling and exciting. Whichever direction Poles went, the roster was going to be upgraded meaningfully. The only question was *at which position* would the Bears improve dramatically.

The highlight reels of 15 or 20 players at impactful positions were intoxicating and at least five receivers resembled video games. Ohio State's Marvin Harrison Jr. was ticketed to Arizona at four, but Poles likely would get a shot at Texas speedster Xavier Worthy or at least one of the LSU kids, Malik Nabers or Brian Thomas. And the dude with the cool name from runner up Washington stood out, too.

Rome Odunze can go up there and get it, yes. Odunze has good size at 6-3, 212 and runs a 4.45 with a 39" vertical leap. He had 10 games with 100+ receiving yards last year and the Huskies finished runner up to Michigan. He's willful and has strong hands. In his senior year, the Las Vegas native accrued 1640 receiving yards, most ever by a Huskie wide out and he finished second in school history (behind only Reggie Williams).

Now Odunze is Chicago's guy. Rome isn't going to rewrite the record book in a day but it's there for the taking if he stays on the trajectory he crafted at UW. The ninth pick in the '24 draft has *future franchise record holder* written all over him. He doesn't have to rival Jerry Rice to get there.

As they've done with quarterbacks, the Bears historically have gone shopping for gently used wide receivers after their draft picks underwhelmed or busted. D.J. Moore, Brandon Marshall, Muhsin Muhammad and Jeff Graham all began their pro tours elsewhere. Alshon Jeffrey, albeit briefly, was a productive second-round pick. By default, Jeffrey is the Bears' draft standard in the post-merger NFL.

Odunze was in disbelief when the Score's Danny Parkins informed him of Johnny Morris' career receiving record of 5059 yards the day after the Bears took him. "That's it?" Odunze puzzled. "That's all?" Yep.

Plausible arguments can be made the receiving standards in McCaskeyville are more embarrassing than the unimpressive quarterback records. Morris retired after the '67 season. His 5059 yards represent the lowest team record in the league. Bemoaning the absence of great receivers is no revelation but the depths of receiver misery need to be defined more thoroughly to grasp the full scope of the famine. That sobering unveiling will precede my picks for the best and worst draft picks in team history.

PACE & NAGY'S DRAFT BANKRUPTCY

It handicaps a team, sometimes cripples it, when forfeiting first-round picks for veteran help becomes habitual. Ryan Pace, Poles' boyish-faced predecessor, moved three first-round opportunities over four years. The price for Mack in '18 was two first-rounders (and record money soon after). Pace and Matt Nagy were so hell bent on getting Justin Fields, they parted with their first-round pick in '22 to slide up nine slots.

Teams grind over everything with the draft. Where does he fit? He does *this* well, but can we get him to do *that*? Can we live with the back issues? Is he mature enough? How fast does he process? Is he explosive enough? Personnel and coaching staffs pore over game "tapes" and even practices. They talk to a player's college coaches and opposing coaches. Wherever there's intel, they're on it. The hours and resources invested in the draft process is staggering, considering a "good year" leaves you with one All

Pro and another two or three contributing pieces. One "blue player" (scout speak for elite) three core players and two contributors is a great draft. The Packers Hall of Fame general manager Ron Wolf outlined his philosophies in *The Packer Way*, published in '99. Roster construction was the central theme in Wolfe's *nine stepping stones to building a winning organization.*

In a perfect world, an NFL roster is sprinkled with a team's own first-round picks but stocked with *your guys,* chosen from the second round and beyond, now in their third-to-seventh years. The prime beef you inspected meticulously from every angle, then drafted and developed. With that in mind, a look at what Pace and his guys left to their successors.

2021 draft class:
1. (11)   Justin Fields, QB, Ohio St.
2. (39)   Teven Jenkins, G/T, Oklahoma St.
5. (151)   Larry Borom, T, Missouri
6. (217)   Khalil Herbert, RB, Virginia Tech
6. (221)   Dazz Newsome, WR, North Carolina
6. (228)   Thomas Graham, CB, Oregon
7. (250)   Khyiris Tonga, DL, BYU

After 38 pro starts and many questions still unanswered, the Bears cut bait with Fields. You know the story. Jenkins, when healthy, has been a solid piece on the O-line. Borom has been a mixed bag, as has Herbert, whose ineffectiveness in '23 necessitated the signing of D'Andre Swift. Herbert hurt his ankle when Fields turned him around on a short circle route early in the year. Justin Newsome appeared in three games for the Bears in '21, his only NFL season. Graham suited up four times before joining Cleveland for one season in '22. Tonga started two of the 15 games for which he dressed in '21, then spent two years in Minnesota before signing with Arizona.

Grade: D

2020 draft class:

1.   no pick (Mack trade)
2. (43)   Cole Kmet, TE, Notre Dame
2. (50)   Jaylon Johnson, CB, Utah
5. (155) Trevis Gipson, DE, Tulsa
5. (163) Kindle Vildor, CB, Georgia Southern
5. (173) Darnell Mooney, WR, Tulane
7. (226) Arlington Hambright, T, Colorado
7. (227) Lachavious Simmons, T, Tennessee St.

Kmet and Johnson are examples of how the core should look but the Bears needed to bag two more contributors with so many at-bats in this class. Wolf's objective was to stack players ultimately deserving of second contracts. Eluding the constant reboot at the same position via draft, trade or free agency is paramount. Unfortunately, that's been the exception to many draft classes of Bears GMs the last 30-some years. Gipson appeared in all 17 games (started 10) in '20 before going to Tennessee and Jacksonville. Vildor gave the Bears depth and help in nickel coverage and appeared in 44 games before splitting '23 between Detroit and Tennessee. Mooney showed upside in his second year, catching 81 passes for 1055 yards and four TDs, but underwhelmed in '22 and '23. Atlanta signed him to a puffy deal this offseason. Hambright made one start as a rookie, then was out of the league for two years before signing with Indianapolis in '23. He appeared in two games. *Pig* Simmons was out of football after one year.

Grade: C

2019 draft class:

1.   no pick (Mack trade)
3. (73)   David Montgomery, RB, Iowa St.
4. (126) Riley Ridley, WR, Georgia
6. (205) Duke Shelley, CB, Kansas St.
7. (222) Kerrith Whyte Jr., RB, Florida Atlantic
7. (238) Stephen Denmark, CB, Valdosta St.

Pace found value with Montgomery, whose best season was '20 (247-

1070-8 as a ballcarrier and 54-438-2 as a receiver. The Bears didn't pick up his fifth-year option and he split for Detroit. Monty topped 1000-plus rushing yards and posted a career-best 4.6 ypc in '23. Ridley lasted two years, appearing in 10 games with 10-108-0. Shelley gave the Bears secondary depth for three years, appearing in 30 games before defecting to Minnesota, then to LAR. Whyte didn't make the roster but did in Pittsburgh for one season. Denmark was in training camps for four NFL teams but never dressed for a game. It's tough to grade this class too harshly, given that Pace didn't have a pick until the 73rd. Then again, he caused it.

Grade: C-

2018 draft class:

1. (8)   Roquan Smith, LB, Georgia
2. (39)   James Daniels, C, Iowa
2. (51)   Anthony Miller, WR, Memphis
4. (115) Joel Iyiegbuniwe, LB, Western Kentucky
5. (145) Bilal Nichols, DT, Delaware
6. (181) Kylie Fitts, DE, Utah
7. (224) Javon Wims, WR, Georgia

Smith is a great tackler, but Poles let the Ravens overpay for a linebacker who didn't make enough splash plays or destroy game plans (20 career sacks, two career FFs, one FR, nine INTs). That said, Smith has been first-team All Pro the past two years. Daniels started every game in two of his four years in Chicago but couldn't nail down either center or guard spots and the Bears gave up on him. He made 15 starts for the Steelers in '23 and all 17 the previous year. Miller made 17 starts over three years before splitting his last pro season between Houston and Pittsburgh in '21. Iyiegbuniwe was a special teams contributor for four seasons and last played for Carolina in '22. Bilal Nichols was a terrific pick at 145. He was miscast as a rookie on the edge but jumped into the DT rotation in '19 and provided dependable depth. Nichols started all 34 games with the Raiders before signing with Arizona in '24. Fitts appeared in six games his rookie year before three equally uneventful seasons in Arizona. Wims had good size and made the roster for three years, starting six games in '19, before one last NFL breath in Arizona. His untimely unsportsmanlike conduct penalty in '19 is his lasting footprint.

Grade: C+

2017 draft class:

1. (2)   Mitch Trubisky, QB, North Carolina
2. (45)   Adam Shaheen, TE, Ashland
4. (112) Eddie Jackson, S, Alabama
4. (119) Tarik Cohen, RB, North Carolina A&T
5. (147) Jordan Morgan, G, Kutztown St.

Forever to be regarded *the one that got away*. That requires another list. Pace passed on Patrick Mahomes and Deshaun Watson and took Trubisky, despite only one year as a starter at North Carolina. The Bears GM also forfeited a third-round pick to flip with the 49ers to move up *one slot* to get him. To encore the boner, Pace had to be the smartest guy in the room when he took Shaheen, a project from tiny Ashland University (it's in Ohio). In three seasons, Shaheen recorded 13 starts and caught 26 passes for 249 yards and four TDs. He played in Miami in '20 and '21, then retired. If Pace wanted a project TE, he could have gone with a scrappy, undersized Iowa Hawkeye named George Kittle. He went in the fifth round and San Francisco's choice paid a handsome return. Jackson started all 16 games as a rookie and set an NFL record for turnover return yardage in one game (76-yard fumble return; 75-yard Pick 6 vs Carolina). Jackson was first-team All Pro in '18, but an assortment of injuries and a lack of assertiveness rendered him a subpar tackler. After 100 career starts, 16 INTs (three TDs) 10 FFs and six FRs, the Bears released Jackson to make cap space. He signed with the Ravens in late July. Ahh, Tarik Cohen. Never forget Mighty Mouse. Cohen was a muscular, mercurial little guy who earned first-team All Pro as a punt returner in '18. He appeared in 51 games before injuries truncated his '20 season and career. Morgan never secured an NFL roster spot. Despite my fondness for Cohen, Pace must suffer.

Grade: F

As it is with the sexy positions, the Bears also spray tee shots in the lumber yard when they take a whack at anchor tackles and pass rushers. The optimism for Darnell Wright, Poles' first shot at a first-round pick, is warranted. History, however, is littered with way more Gabe Carimis than Jimbo Coverts. And the most effective edge rushers — Montez Sweat, Robert Quinn, Khalil Mack, Julius Peppers — all were acquired via trade or free agency.

It may *feel* like your Bears are the worst ever, but the truth is even the most decorated franchises pick lemons. Colossally and consistently. Green Bay has demonstrated a high success rate picking quarterbacks, but the Packers are imperfect, too. They've struck out on a bunch of high draft choices in the last 20 years. So have the 49ers, Chiefs, Patriots and Ravens. Nobody hits for a high percentage. Wolf's philosophy was to find those diamonds in the rough in the later rounds to salvage contributors, at the minimum, in every draft.

CATCH THIS

Many words have been written and spoken about the rookie quarterback, so I want to dial in on first-round wide receivers. Between '10 and '19, via research compiled by ESPN's Paul Hembo, the *hit rates* for wide receiver are extremely low. Only 12% of the 34 receivers who went in the first round were "worth" a first-round investment. Only four of those 34 were voted first-team All Pro. Receivers earned second contracts with the team that drafted them only 27% of the time.

Here's the list of wide receivers drafted in the first round in the last 10 years. Three possible Hall of Famers — Mike Evans, Justin Jefferson and Ja'Marr Chase — headline a group that also includes several players who were out of football in three years. Don't feel bad for not recognizing every name. It's a study of the first round of the NFL draft, not Super Bowl MVPs. There's no correlation between the two.

2023: Jaxson Smith-Nijgba (20) Seattle; Quentin Johnston (21), LAC; Zay Flowers, (22), Baltimore; Jordan Addison (23), Minnesota. 2022: Drake London (8) Atlanta; Garrett Wilson (10) NYJ; Chris Olave (11) New Orleans;

Jameson Williams (12) Detroit; Jahan Dotson (16) Washington; Treylon Burks (18) Tennessee. 2021: Ja'Marr Chase (5) Cincinnati; Jaylen Waddle (6) Miami; DeVonta Smith (10) Philadelphia; Kadarius Toney (20) NYG; Rashod Bateman (27) Baltimore. 2020: Henry Ruggs (12) Las Vegas; Jerry Jeudy (15) Denver; CeeDee Lamb (17) Dallas; Jalen Reagor (21) Philadelphia; Justin Jefferson (22) Minnesota; Brandon Ayiuk (25) San Francisco. 2019: Marquise Brown (25) Baltimore; N'Keal Harry (32) New England. 2018: D.J. Moore (24) Carolina; Calvin Ridley (26) Atlanta. 2017: Corey David (5) Tennessee; Mike Williams (7) LAC; John Ross (9) Cincinnati. 2016: Corey Coleman (15) Cleveland; Will Fuller (21) Houston; Josh Doctson (22) Washington; Laquon Treadwell (23) Minnesota. 2015: Amari Cooper (4) La Vegas; Kevin White (7) CHICAGO; DeVante Parker (14) Miami; Nelson Agholor (20) Philadelphia; Breshad Perriman (26) Baltimore; Phillip Dorsett (29) Indianapolis. 2014: Sammy Watkins (4) Buffalo; Mike Evans (7) Tampa Bay; Odell Beckham Jr. (12) NYG; Brandin Cooks (20) New Orleans; Kelvin Benjamin (28) Carolina.

This book is a record of the Chicago Bears so it's unnecessary to go deeper on the wide outs lister above. A casual perusal of the list will lead one to conclude wide receiver is a high-risk position in the first round. Other noteworthy nuggets: the rookie class of '23 failed to dazzle but second-rounders like Green Bay's Reed, Kansas City's Rice and Denver's Mims are on a higher trajectory than the four players who went in the first. The Bears got a taste of one of the two receivers who went in the first round in '19, N'Keal Harry. The Patriots bailed quickly on Harry, uninspiring in his brief stint here. Overlooked in the '19 draft: Deebo Samuel went in the second (36), as did A.J. Brown (51). Michael Thomas of New Orleans (47) was more productive than all five receivers who went ahead of him in '15. In '14, neither Tampa nor the Giants regretted picking Evans and Beckham, respectively. The Bills, Saints and Panthers, conversely, would love a do-ever. Davante Adams went in the second (53) to the Packers and Buffalo took Watkins with the fourth. New Orleans took Cooks at 20 and Carolina grabbed Benjamin at 28.

Odunze is only the fourth receiver the Bears drafted in the first round since '93 when they took Curtis Conway sixth overall. Michigan's David Terrell was their first-rounder in '01 (eighth overall) and they used the seventh overall on West Virginia's Kevin White in '15.

While never elite, Conway stayed upright and made 81 starts in seven seasons in Chicago. He caught 329 passes for 4498 yards (13.7 ypr) and 31 touchdowns before spending three seasons with the Chargers and a year with both the Jets and 49ers. *C-Way* was Dave Wannstedt's first pick as head coach/*de facto* GM in '93. Conway's slow start — 19 catches in '93 and only 39 in '94 — is what precludes him from "hit" status. It wasn't a wasted pick, but it wasn't a good one, either. Call it a wash. More on White and Terrell soon.

The Bears career leader, former CBS-2 sports anchor Morris, began his 10 years with the Bears in '58. He was a running back the first three seasons before moving to flanker. He had one terrific year. In '64, Morris had 93 catches, 1200 yards and 10 touchdowns. The rest of his PFR page looks like Darnell Mooney's. And Morris is the standard bearer in Chicago. Johnny even thinks it's embarrassing 5059 hasn't been topped. He admitted as much on my radio show *almost 30 years ago.*

A few zingers to warm up an icy topic.

I often the confused the pass catching Smiths. Was it Jerry or Jackie Smith who choked in a Super Bowl and dropped a would-be game winner? Which played for Washington and which for the Cardinals? Both played a long time ago and I still can't commit it to memory. What I do retain is they both accrued more yards than Morris did. And both Smiths *were tight ends.*

- The 49ers boast *three tight ends* who bested Morris' 5059: Kittle, 6274, Vernon Davis, 5640, and Brent Jones, 5195.

- The Bengals have had *three tandems* of wide receivers *with overlapping careers* whose yardage exceeded Morris. Sharing the wealth didn't stop these pairs from topping 5059: Chad Johnson, 10,783, and T.J. Houshmanzadeh, 5782; Carl Pickens, 6887, and Darnay Scott, 5975; Issac Curtis, 7101, and Cris Collinsworth, 6698.

- Think '90s football in Detroit and Barry Sanders is where we all go.

It might surprise you to learn *all three Lions receivers* — Herman Moore, 9174, Johnnie Morton, 6499, and Brett Perriman, 5244 — would be the Bears' career yardage leaders. *"Mitchell back to pass and why not?"* — Wayne Larrivee, Bears' radio, frustrated by the unstoppable Detroit passing game in '95.

- The Packers have *four combinations* of receivers/tight ends with overlapping careers who all exceeded 5059. Boyd Dowler, Carrol Dale and Max McGee; Sterling Sharpe and Antonio Freeman; Greg Jennings and James Jones; Jordy Nelson and Randall Cobb.

- There are 201 players who bested Morris' career record. One did it for two teams — Derrick Mason, Tennessee, 6114, and Baltimore, 5777. Given good health, Tyreek Hill likely will be the second to do it this year. The Cheetah had 6630 yards in six seasons with Kansas City and is at 3509 in just two seasons in Miami.

Here are the career receiving yards leaders for all 32 teams:

1. Jerry Rice, San Francisco, 19,247
2. Tim Brown, Las Vegas, 14,734
3. Larry Fitzgerald, Arizona, 17,492
4. Marvin Harrison, Indianapolis, 14,580
5. Isaac Bruce, LAR, 14,109
6. Andre Johnson, Houston, 13,597
7. Andre Reed, Buffalo, 13,095
8. Steve Largent, Seattle, 13,089
9. Jason Whitten, Dallas, 12,977
10. Julio Jones, Atlanta, 12,896
11. Cris Carter, Minnesota, 12,393
12. Jimmy Smith, Jacksonville, 12,287
13. Steve Smith, Carolina, 12,197
14. Art Monk, Washington, 12,026
15. Hines Ward, Pittsburgh, 12,083
16. Antonio Gates, LAC, 11,841
17. Don Maynard, NYJ, 11,732

18. Mike Evans, Tampa Bay, 11,680
19. Calvin Johnson, Detroit, 11,619
20. Rod Smith, Denver, 11,389
21. Travis Kelce, Kansas City, 11,328
22. Chad Johnson, Cincinnati, 10,783
23. Stanley Morgan, New England, 10,352
24. Donald Driver, Green Bay, 10,137
25. Marques Colston, New Orleans, 9759
26. Amani Toomer, NYG, 9497
27. Harold Carmichael, Philadelphia, 8978
28. Mark Duper, Miami, 8869
29. Ozzie Newsome, Cleveland, 7980
30. Ernest Givins, Tennessee, 7935
31. Derrick Mason, Baltimore, 5777
32. Johnny Morris, BEARS, 5059

With Morris so far behind the pack, I couldn't help but seek a refresher on who follows good ol' No. 47 in the Halas-McCaskey scrapbook of pass catchers. How many of these guys did you watch play?

1. Johnny Morris, 5059 ('58-'67)
2. Harlon Hill, 4616 ('54-'61)
3. Alshon Jeffrey, 4549 ('12-'16)
4. Walter Payton, 4538 ('75-'87)
5. Mike Ditka, 4503 ('61-'66)

Only Jeffrey played in this century. Who says the NFL is a passing league these last 30 years. Do a little contrast and compare with the Bears' fab five and the other 31 teams' receivers. A stiff drink might be required. By team, here are *all of the players* who beat Morris' 5059 with one franchise:

Arizona (10) Larry Fitzgerald, 17,492. Roy Green, 8496. Jackie Smith, 7918. Anquan Boldin, 7520. Pat Tilley, 7005. Mel Gray, 6644. Frank Sanders, 6579. Bobby Joe Conrad, 5828. Sonny Randle, 5438. Rob Moore, 5110.

Atlanta (5) Julio Jones, 12,896. Roddy White, 10,863. Terance Mathis, 7349. Alfred Jenkins, 6267. Andre Rison, 5633.

Baltimore (2) Derrick Mason, 5777. Todd Heap, 5492.

Buffalo (5) Andre Reed, 13,095. Eric Moulds, 9096. Lee Evans, 5934. Stefon Diggs, 5372. Elbert Dubenion 5294.

Carolina (4) Steve Smith, 12,197. Muhsin Muhammad, 9255. Greg Olsen, 6433. D.J. Moore, 5201.

Cincinnati (9) Chad Johnson, 10,783. A.J. Green, 9430. Isaac Curtis, 7101. Carl Pickens, 6887. Cris Collinsworth, 6698. Eddie Brown, 6134. Tyler Boyd, 6000. Darnay Scott, 5975. T.J. Houshmandzadeh, 5782.

Cleveland (6) Ozzie Newsome, 7980. Dante Lavelli, 6488. Mac Speedle, 5602. Ray Renfro, 5508. Gary Collins, 5299. Paul Warfield, 5210.

Dallas (8) Jason Whitten, 12,977. Michael Irvin, 11,904. Tony Hill, 7988. Drew Pearson, 7822. Dez Bryant, 7459. Bob Hayes, 7295. Frank Clarke, 5214. CeeDee Lamb, 5145.

Denver (10) Rod Smith, 11,389. Demaryius Thomas, 9055. Shannon Sharpe, 8439. Lionel Taylor, 6872. Ed McCaffrey, 6200. Steve Watson, 6112. Riley Odoms, 5755. Vance Johnson, 5695. Haven Moses, 5450. Emmanuel Sanders, 5361.

Detroit (5) Calvin Johnson, 11,619. Herman Moore, 9174. Johnnie Morton, 6499. Brett Perriman, 5244. Gail Cogdill, 5221.

Green Bay (14) Donald Driver, 10,137. James Lofton, 9656. Sterling Sharpe, 8134. Davante Adams, 8121. Don Hutson, 7971. Jordy Nelson, 7848. Boyd Dowler, 6918. Antonio Freeman, 6651. Greg Jennings, 6537. Max McGee, 6346. Randall Cobb, 6316. Billy Howton, 5581. Carroll Dale, 5422. James Jones, 5195.

Houston (2) Andre Johnson, 13,597. DeAndre Hopkins, 8602.

Indianapolis (8) Marvin Harrison, 14,580. Reggie Wayne, 14,345. T.Y. Hilton, 9691. Raymond Berry, 9275. Lenny Moore, 6039. Jimmy Orr, 5859. Bill Brooks, 5818. John Mackey, 5126.

Jacksonville (2) Jimmy Smith, 12,287. Keenan McCardell, 6393.

Kansas City (10) Travis Kelce, 11,328. Tony Gonzalez, 10,940. Otis Taylor, 7306. Dwayne Bowe, 7155. Tyreek Hill, 6630. Henry Marshall, 6545. Carlos Carson, 6360. Stephone Paige, 6341. Chris Burford, 5505. Eddie Kennison, 5230.

Las Vegas (4) Tim Brown, 14,734. Fred Biletnikoff, 8974. Cliff Branch, 8685. Todd Christensen, 5872.

Los Angeles Chargers (9) Antonio Gates, 11,841. Keenan Allen, 10,530. Lance Alworth, 9584. Charlie Joiner, 9203. Gary Garrison, 7533. Kellen Winslow, 6741. Wes Chandler, 6132. Anthony Miller, 5582. Malcom Floyd, 5550.

Los Angeles Rams (8) Isaac Bruce, 14,109. Torry Holt, 12,660. Henry Ellard, 9761. Cooper Kupp, 7066. Elroy Hirsch, 6299. Jack Snow, 6012. Tom Fears, 5397. Flipper Anderson, 5246.

Miami (5) Mark Duper, 8869. Mark Clayton, 8643. Nat Moore, 7546. Chris Chambers, 5688. O.J. McDuffie, 5074.

Minnesota (9) Cris Carter, 12,383. Randy Moss, 9316. Anthony Carter, 7636. Adam Thielen, 6682. Jake Reed, 6433. Sammy White, 6400. Steve Jordan, 6307. Justin Jefferson, 5899. Ahmad Rashad, 5489.

New England (7) Stanley Morgan, 10,352. Rob Gronkowski, 7861. Wes Welker, 7459. Julian Edelman, 6822. Troy Brown, 6366. Irving Fryar, 5726. Ben Coates, 5471.

New Orleans (4) Marques Colston, 9759. Eric Martin, 7854. Joe Horn, 7622. Michael Thomas, 6569.

New York Giants (4) Amani Toomer, 9497. Odell Beckham Jr., 5476. Frank Gifford, 5434. Tiki Barber, 5183.

New York Jets (5) Don Maynard, 11,732. Wesley Walker, 8306. Wayne Chrebet, 7365. Al Toon, 6605. Laveranues Coles, 6605.

Philadelphia (8) Harold Carmichael, 8978. Pete Retzlaff, 7412. DeSean Jackson, 6512. Mike Quick, 6464. Zach Ertz, 6267. Pete Pihos, 5619. Tommy McDonald, 5499. Bobby Walston, 5363.

Pittsburgh (7) Hines Ward, 12,083. Antonio Brown, 11,207. John Stallworth, 8723. Heath Miller, 6569. Louis Lipps, 6018. Lynn Swann, 5462. Elbie Nickel, 5131.

San Francisco (9) Jerry Rice, 19,247. Terrell Owens, 8572. Dwight Clark, 6750. Gene Washington, 6664. George Kittle, 6274. Billy Wilson, 5902. Vernon Davis, 5640. John Taylor, 5598. Brent Jones, 5195.

Seattle (6) Steve Largent, 13,089. Tyler Lockett, 7994. Brian Blades, 7620. Doug Baldwin, 6563. Darrell Jackson, 6445. D.K. Metcalf, 5332.

Tampa Bay (2) Mike Evans, 11,680. Chris Godwin, 6690.

Tennessee (6) Ernest Givins, 7935. Drew Hill, 7477. Kenny Burroughs, 6906. Charley Hennigan, 6823. Haywood Jeffires, 6119. Derrick Mason, 6114.

Washington (9) Art Monk, 12,026. Charley Taylor, 9110. Gary Clark, 8749. Santana Moss, 7867. Bobby Mitchell, 6492. Ricky Sanders, 5854. Jerry Smith, 5496. Terry McLaurin, 5283. Hugh Taylor, 5233.

Now for the best of — and the messes of — *the Bears on the clock.*

BEST DRAFT PICKS SINCE '85:

1. **Brian Urlacher**, linebacker, New Mexico. 2000, 1st round, 9th overall. HOF Class of '18. DROY in '00, DPOY in '05, Urlacher also finished fifth in MVP voting in '05. He played in 182 games in 13-year career, all with the Bears. Spectacular tackler with closing speed. Unrivaled ball skills and terrific deep middle 'backer in Lovie Smith's *Tampa 2* scheme. The late Mark Hatley was the scout who had the courage to pull the trigger on a "project." Draftniks buzzed about two Penn State defenders, Courtney Brown and Lavar Arrington, usually debating which the Browns should take with the first pick. Cleveland chose Brown, a disruptive pass rusher. Washington followed the script and drafted Arrington, a linebacker who could run. Arrington had a much more productive career, but neither validated his draft position. Urlacher was an unknown and NFL scouts weren't certain what he was. A huge safety? Strong-side linebacker? Where do you put this tall, muscular gazelle from a non-football factory? Bears' coach Dick Jauron wasn't sure,

either. They figured it out. Urlacher landed in Canton in '18. Details in Chapter 13, *Demolition Man*.

2. **Charles Tillman**, cornerback, Louisiana. 2003, 2nd round, 35th overall. Once GM Jerry Angelo was out of the first round, Tommie Harris excepted, he was terrific. *Peanut* Tillman, who was the sixth cornerback taken in the '03 draft, quickly fit in and demonstrated sticky coverage skills and, by modern standards, was a physical tackler. *The Peanut Punch*, of course, is what endeared Tillman to Bears fans. Turnovers change games and Tillman did that. Tillman should have been more recognized nationally. He forced 42 fumbles in 12 Bears seasons, including a league-high 10 in '12, his lone All Pro selection. Tillman recovered 40 fumbles and accrued 36 interceptions. Nutty is a borderline Hall of Famer. If Packers safety Leroy Butler is Canton-worthy primarily for the *Lambeau Leap*, why not a guy whose signature move actually impacts outcomes of games, not just how many fans get a free handful of tight glutes.

3. **Olin Kreutz**, center, Washington. 1998, 3rd round, 64th overall. Kreutz never threw or caught a pass, but he is, to date, the team's most productive offensive draft pick since.... man.... tackle Jimbo Covert in '83, I suspect. Other cities get sexy. Chicago gets street fighters. Kreutz was an iron man. Missed only one start between '01 and '10. Logged 183 starts, 191 appearances in 13 seasons with the Bears. A weight room animal and vocal team leader. The Big O could frustrate with unsportsmanlike penalties and occasionally the shotgun snap caught a piece of his ass cheek and didn't get there but damn, I want that guy on my side. So did his teammates.

4. **Lance Briggs**, linebacker, Arizona. 2003, 3rd round, 68th overall. Briggs was a valuable piece on the Super Bowl 41 defense. The 6-1, 245 lb. Briggs was a life-long Bear, spending all of his 12 seasons here. Started all 16 games seven times and 15 games twice. Briggs made 170 starts as an outside LB, excelling more in coverage (16 INTs and 16 FFs) than as a pass rusher (15 sacks). He was great in run support and

accrued 97 TFLs. Briggs was a sure-handed, physical tackler. A perfect complement to Urlacher.

5. **Mike Brown**, safety, Nebraska. 2000, 2nd round, 39th overall. Another Hatley find. Brown was tracking toward greatness before injuries slowed his career. Undersized at 5-11, 205, Brown immediately grasped Greg Blache's defense and was a first-team All Pro in his second year. Brown and Urlacher, taken 30 picks apart, anchored a defense that consistently was among the NFL's best for five years. Urlacher called Brown the smartest teammate he ever played with. Brown played nine seasons for the Bears, two of them as a corner. He collected 17 INTs and 8 FFs.

Second-round gems include **Devin Hester**, KR, Miami, 2006, 57th overall, **Matt Forte**, RB, Tulane. 2008, 44th overall.

Hester couldn't settle in at the University of Miami as a receiver or corner. A great athlete with absurdly swivel hips and change of direction burst. Angelo rolled dice and Hester made him glad he did. The '24 enshrinee in Canton was the most electrifying return man in history. In his rookie year, he immediately made his presence felt with three punt returns for TDs and two kickoff returns. In his career, he authored 14 punt return TDs and five kick return TDs. Like no specialist before him, Hester was the human highlight reel.

Forte was a versatile back and stayed healthy enough to start all but five games in his first seven years with the Bears. The sleek back carried an astounding (now) 316 times for 1238 yards and eight TDs as a rookie. His most productive year as a ball carrier was '13, (289-1339-9). In '14, Forte hauled in 102 receptions for 808 yards (7.9 ypr) and four TDs. Forte started 120 games in eight years, twice making the Pro Bowl. Forte was fit, but one of the leanest 20+ touch-per-game guys in the league. No. 22 finished his career with the Jets in '16 and '17.

Diamond in the Rough third-rounder **Jim Flanigan**, DT, Notre Dame, 1994, 74th overall. Among the highlights of the Dave Wannstedt/Rod Graves era. Flanny was the *anti-combine* pick, underwhelming in the gym (comparatively) and a tick undersized at 6-2, 280. In the fourth round of '94, the Bears again doubled off the wall with Ohio State running back **Raymont Harris**, who starred down the stretch in the playoff hunt of '94 and the New Year's Day '95 playoff win the Metrodome.

BUSTER BARS

It's impossible to pare the list of draft disasters to five. If there has been a defining consistency from the war room, it's whiffing at the same position. Positions like, well... quarterback, disruptive pass rushers, play-making receivers, anchor offensive tackles and top-tier running backs. Because they've fumbled so consistently at those positions, I've doubled up and dropped a deuce on each critical position.

When assessing the most crippling choices — those that retard the growth of the franchise and get coaches and GMs fired — I looked exclusively at first-round picks. By position, my choices for the worst choices since '85.

1. Quarterback: **Mitch Trubisky**, 2017, 2nd overall, North Carolina. **Cade McNown**, 1999, 12th overall, UCLA.

    So tough declaring one worse than the other. Trubisky at least hung around for a bit and broke a sweat. Still, he went second, and the Bears passed on Patrick Mahomes. Pace and Nagy had to have Mitch with his one year as a starter under his belt. It wasn't Trubisky's fault he was over-drafted, but he took the wrath and the louder it got, the more he seemed to buckle. Trubisky didn't possess the requisite qualities of leadership and confidence. He threw 64 TDs and 37 INTs. His career rating as a Bear was 87.2. It seemed much worse. Maybe I still recall the Christmas sweater. Or how a guy from the Cleveland area could come off as such a vapid rube. It's on Pace, not the player.

    McNown took the beatings he deserved in Chicago, but the country didn't flinch at his failure as only the 12th player drafted. There was Tim Couch, an all-time bad No. 1 overall candidate. Akili Smith went third to the Bengals and barely got on the field. He threw five TD passes in his career. McNown's reputation was stained before his arrival. Stories circulated about the quarterback using a handicapped parking placard in his sports car so he could enjoy preferred parking at UCLA. He was one of just seven left-handed quarterbacks to go in the first round (Michael Pennix Jr., Atlanta, just did it) and lasted only two years before he was out of football. The cocky redhead went 3-12 in his two years, throwing 16 TD passes with 19 INTs and a rating of 67.7. He wasn't a mope. He just didn't care. Teammates speak candidly of his lack of preparation for a date in San Francisco later. One quarterback too challenged mentally, the other too lazy. Bear Down.

2. Wide receiver: **Kevin White**, 2015. 7th overall, West Virginia. **David Terrell**, 2001, Michigan, 8th overall.

White was in Pace's first draft class and the first exhibit of the young GM's acute case of numb-nuttedness. Eyebrows raised across the country when White was the second receiver to go (Amari Cooper, Raiders, fourth) in the first round. It wasn't a great crop of receivers in '15, as evidenced by the some of the selections of teams starved at the position. The Dolphins took Devante Parker 14th. *Just a guy.* Nelson Agholor went to the Eagles at 20. Serviceable player at best, still touring the league. The Ravens used the 26th pick on Breshad Perriman, a physical specimen but pedestrian, who also played for the Browns, Bucs and Jets. So, you wanna draft a receiver in the first round, do you? White rarely got on the field. Chronic feet and ankle problems. The seventh pick in the draft made only five starts in three seasons with the Bears, catching 25 passes for 285 yards. And those were the most "productive" years of White's six-year career. White, now 32, also toiled in New Orleans and San Francisco for three more years. He averaged one reception a year. He never scored an NFL touchdown. Minnesota took Stefon Diggs in the fifth. Seattle took Tyler Lockett in the third.

Continuing the *"what we could have had"* game, played annually by fans of all 32 teams, the Bears took Michigan receiver David Terrell with the eighth pick in '01. The Colts grabbed Reggie Wayne 30th. It was a perfect situation for Wayne, playing opposite HOFer Marvin Harrison with Peyton Manning slinging it. Wayne prospered. His career dwarfs the collective resumes of fellow first-rounders Terrell, Koren Robinson (ninth, Seahawks), Rod Gardner (15th, Redskins), Santana Moss (16th, Jets) and Freddie Mitchell (25th, Eagles). A big, strong guy at 6-3, 215 lbs., Terrell was a regular in only one of his four years. As a rookie, he snagged a career-high four TDs, His best year was '04 when he caught 42 passes for 699 yards, a healthy 16.6 yards per catch. He finished his modest career in Denver and appeared in only one game. Biggest detriment to Terrell's game: he didn't catch very well. Typically, that's problematic.

3. Tackle: **Chris Williams**, 2008, 14th overall, Vanderbilt. **Stan Thomas**, 1991, 22nd overall, Texas.

Angelo rolled dice on Williams, who came with lower back problems. Few people with chronic LBP get better over time, especially in physically demanding professions. Williams spent training camp in the tub his rookie season and suited up for nine games. In '09, the Vandy man stayed upright but was ineffective. It wasn't long before the Bears committed resources to the O-line in the first round again, drafting Kyle Long in '14. The Rams were next for Williams before his candle burned out in Buffalo in '14.

The selection of Thomas' in '91 was more evidence personnel boss Bill Tobin was slipping. A super scout for a decade, Tobin found *slightly above average* in the first round too often — Brad Muster, Wendell Davis and Mark Carrier. He said pass rusher Ron Cox, a second-rounder out of Fresno State in '90, was "a Lawrence Taylor type." I don't know about his habits off the field, but Cox never flirted with Taylorian skills on it. The talent and staying power of the Super Bowl O-line finally was dissipating and Thomas busted. He made just seven starts in two years before the Bears cut him. A few years later, Mike Ditka washed his hands of Thomas. "That one wasn't on me. I didn't want that loser." Thomas spent two more equally sleepy years with the Oilers before retiring.

4. Edge/ OLB: **Shea McClellin**, 2012. 19th overall, Boise State. **John Thierry** 1994, 12th overall, Alcorn State.

"Who?" was the universal response around Chicago and the NFL when Phil Emery plucked McClellin off the potato farm at least 15-20 picks higher than expected. The mistake was evident immediately. The Boise Stater appeared blinded by the bright lights of Bourbonnais. Overwhelmed in his first camp, physically in position group drills, understanding the hybrid position, even socially. Pass rushers who were misses have been taken much higher than 19, but that's where Military Phil grabbed him. Chandler Jones still was on the board. In four years with the Bears, McClellin had five more sacks than you did. But he did knock Rodgers out of a game at Lambeau Field in '13. And the Bears actually won a game in Titletown on *MNF*, 27-20.

Thierry is a great example of impressive measurables not telling the whole story. A specimen who dominated against lesser college competition, relying on size and speed. At 6-4, 250, he ran well, but J.T. had no feel for reading and reacting. Thierry was not an instinctual player and struggled to understand what coaches wanted. He made only 28 starts in five years and accrued 12.5 sacks. Thierry moved on to Cleveland in '99 before two forgettable years as a starter in Green Bay. He finished his nine-year career in Atlanta. Thierry was 46 when he suffered a fatal heart attack in '17.

5. Running Back: **Curtis Enis**, 1998 5th overall. Penn State. **Cedric Benson**, 2005, 4th overall, Texas.

Enis went fifth in '98, the last dance for Wannstedt and Graves. When the Bears took him, there was uncertainty about his quickness for tailback in the NFL. Maybe he was a fullback with good speed. He proved to be neither and a variety of injuries precluded him any tenure. Enis played only three seasons — all with the Bears — the best of which was '99 (287 carries, 916 yards, 3.2 ypc and three TDs). Fred Taylor (ninth overall, Jacksonville) and Robert Edwards (18th overall, New England) were on the board, but the Bears chose the more physically imposing Enis after many loud and sometimes heated debates.

Benson's plight was tragic. The Heisman trophy winner out of Texas was an enormously talented player but packed a lot of baggage. Following a lengthy holdout his rookie year, Benson was treated as an interloper. The '05 Bears were understandably ardent fans of veteran Thomas Jones. Ced's fondness for altered states were well documented and arrest reports mounted until the Bears gave up on him after the '06 season. He was off to Cincinnati, where he found some success, topping 1000 yards in three straight seasons. In '09, Benson he ripped the Bears for 189 yards and a touchdown. Behavioral problems continued to plague Benson up until his fatal motorcycle accident in '19.

The 2003 Draft, Michael Haynes, DE, 14th overall, Penn State. **Rex Grossman**, QB, 22nd overall, Florida.

Angelo had the fourth pick in Round 1 but traded it to the Jets and moved down to accrue more picks. I campaigned for Terrell Suggs, who racked up 22.5 sacks his last year at Arizona State. The Bears were among a handful of teams bothered by Suggs' subpar 40 time. Baltimore took him as an edge rusher/OLB with the 10th pick and Suggs validated it. He was to Ray Lewis what Briggs was to Urlacher. Haynes, meanwhile, was a disaster. When he got to training camp in Bourbonnais, he claimed he was put off by foul language used by Bears coaches. That was a new one. Haynes didn't earn a start as a rookie and started only four games in three years in Chicago. The Bears were his only NFL stop. He had 5.5 sacks in his career.

Grossman survived nine NFL seasons, the first six with the Bears. He was game manager personified in the Super Bowl year of '06, starting all 16 games, completing 54.6% of his passes for 3193 yards and 24 TDs vs. 20 INTs and a QB rating of 73.9. Grossman wasn't big at 6-1, 220 and he wasn't fast. He didn't extend plays and had difficulty with ball security. Not first-round material. Say it with me in Lovie's Texas drawl: *"Rex Is Our Quarterback."*

Did the Bears win the Khalil Mack sign and trade? It's on the table next, as well as Poles' activity as a wheeler-dealer. Plus, ranking the historically good and bad moves when the Bears go horse tradin'.

CHAPTER 4
Don't Sweat the Trade Market
POLES THE DEALER, BEARS TRADE HISTORY

> *"Ten oughta do it, don't you think? You think we need one more?*
> *Okay, we'll get one more. Who do you got in mind?"*
> *– Danny Ocean (George Clooney) in the 2001 film Ocean's Eleven.*

Jaquan Brisker's potential to help make Chicago's defense great again was evident his rookie season in 2022. As advertised, the Penn Stater was smart, fast and willing to engage physically. Brisker made 73 solo tackles, second only to linebacker Nicholas Morrow (83). He started 15 games as a 23-year-old rookie free safety. One Brisker distinction was dubious, however. His four sacks were tops on the Bears. Ryan Poles couldn't stomach it much longer. The '23 Bears started 2-6 and after muscling out a league-low 10 sacks, it was time to fill a glaring need that didn't make the shopping list in the '23 offseason.

The timing of Washington Commanders' tank-job fire sale was perfect. Poles moved on Montez Sweat for a second- round pick in '24. The Bears then had to *pay that man his money*. Like Khalil Mack before him in '18, Sweat was on an expiring contract and the Bears had to ante up for the most essential defensive component. The price for Sweat was $98 million, $42M of which is guaranteed. The former Mississippi State star will average $24.5M per season over the next four years.

If you can't grow apples, go buy 'em. The *kill-the-quarterback* strain is sweetest. Sweat made an impact immediately. He led the Bears in sacks with six and became the first player in league history to lead two teams in sacks in the same year. The Commanders also moved oft-injured Chase Young and Sweat's road to a unique distinction was unimpeded.

It speaks volumes on where a team goes without a destructive pass rusher — right back to near the top of the draft. The Commanders took quarterback LSU quarterback Jayden Daniels with the second pick after going 4-13. And Carolina's 2-15 season wasn't all on rookie quarterback Bryce Young. The Panthers were last in the league in sacks with 27 and forced the fewest turnovers, 11. The combination of a challenged offense and limp pass rush lined up perfectly for the Bears to get right back to the top of draft and get their franchise quarterback.

Sweat is 28. His reputation is clean, and all accounts report he's a tireless worker. I don't suspect his impact will rival the effect Charles Haley had in Dallas in '92, likely the bar for trades involving edge rushers. Haley transformed the Dallas defense when they were constructing their '90s dynasty. The Bears are hopeful Sweat receives a better rhythm section from supporting bandmates in '24. Conversations at Halas Hall will be much different in February if they don't.

KEENAN ALLEN

On March 14, Poles sent a fourth-round pick to the Chargers for wide receiver Keenan Allen. Chicago was drunk on the Bears for six weeks before the commissioner ultimately called Caleb Williams' name. Allen is a pro's pro. He understands the slot position as well as any receiver in the league and Shane Waldron's offense is rigidly "position specific." Allen stays after practice to work with younger players and is reported to be a genuinely willing tutor for younger players. He's a crisp, seamless route runner and compensates for lack of speed with experience and a strong will. He's 6-2, 215. Last year, in his 11th pro season, Allen caught a career-high 108 balls and carded his second-highest total receiving yards with 1243.

Allen's mettle was recognized when he earned the NFL comeback player of the year in '17. He caught 102 passes for 1394 yards (13.7 ypr). The CPOY sometimes is given to the player who shows the most dramatically improved performance, like Geno Smith did in Seattle in '22. Typically, however, voters favor a player who overcame a traumatic injury and performed among the elite at his position. Allen blew out his knee in the Week 1 against Kansas City and lost the '16 season.

The comeback award is meaningful in my NFL world, even more so when a player whose position requires explosion, running and making fast cuts is coming off ACL reconstruction. Allen was only 25 when he returned in '17, but already experienced orthopedic issues, including a broken ankle before his junior year at Cal.

Allen gets hurt a lot. He didn't even get to October before standing on the sideline in civilian clothes. It's not a character assassination. It's truth. He was inactive for the last four games in '23 with a heel problem. K.A. was on the injury report for three other games with a quad, a hamstring and a shoulder. He's 32, which is old for a healthy receiver. Listening to Bears fans and media fawn over the trade in the spring was a reminder of a town that often suffers from premature adulation over a recognizable name. Allen's background is steeped in accomplishments but the label "injury prone" was earned.

It was a terrific idea by Poles, regardless of Allen's production. The Bears don't need a 108-1243-7 slash line from him with D.J. Moore, Rome Odunze, two good tight ends and D'Andre Swift. If K.A. evens flirts with those numbers with whatever time he has with Bears, something went terribly wrong with the others. The Bears didn't extend Allen's contract, which is in its final year. For only the tariff of a fourth-rounder, it was worth it. Even if his role already has morphed into a player-coach dynamic. Well done, Ryan Poles.

CAROLINA TRADE BUZZ STILL HUMMIN'

Before the Bears arrived at their final OTAs in the spring, I heard the sports opinion factory churning out content on how the deal with Carolina already is the best trade in team history. It was posited the '22 pick swap in the first round, Moore and two additional picks probably will leapfrog the Herschel Walker deal in '89 as the most impactful in NFL history. Maybe in all of team sports. Brad Biggs of the *Tribune* emptied his Bears mailbag on the topic. Poles' thievery as "the greatest ever" gained steam.

Too much, too soon.

Writing the obit for Young after one year, as terrible as it was, is premature. The rookie was on an island on a bad roster and Carolina did nothing to facilitate the growth of their 21-year-old quarterback. Maybe

Dave Canales and his staff won't fix Young — if the second-year man unseats Andy Dalton, who got the Week 3 start and led the Panthers to a convincing romp over the Raiders.

Moore was terrific in '23, but Williams hadn't experienced his first NFL test. Against the Texans in Week 2, Williams was all over the map in the 19-13 loss in Houston. The Texans play a role in the Chicago-Carolina trade's final evaluation, too. The deal won't sparkle so much if C.J. Stroud's star keeps ascending, and Caleb isn't the Bear we though he was. And you can bet on at least two of those six QBs taken in the top 12 falling on their asses. If the Texans win a Super Bowl driven by Stroud, look out. The Bears needed a quarterback in '23 and passed. They also passed on Will Anderson, who Houston took right after Stroud at No. 2. The Bears also lacked a disruptive pass rusher. Anderson was the defensive rookie of the year and he's cheap for three more years. The Bears exhausted a huge chunk of cap space on Sweat.

Corner Tyrique Stevenson was pressed into action by injury and started 16 games his rookie year. Stevenson was the fourth-rounder who came in the Carolina trade and has a high ceiling. He plays opposite Jaylon Johnson, however, and will be targeted heavily. There's an additional second-rounder coming in April of '25. Dave Tepper really did appear from a magic lamp.

When bubbly Bears voices were taking it to the "Herschel Walker trade level," somebody needed to suggest easing back on the throttle just a bit. A quick review of what Minnesota gifted to Dallas would provide clarity. The Cowboys used first-round picks on running back Emmitt Smith, safety Darren Woodson and Chicagoan Russell Maryland. Smith is the league's all-time rushing leader. Woodson was a hammer and earned three first-team All Pro selections. Maryland, who went to Whitney Young high school, was a gap-stuffing defensive tackle and great athlete. No need to reel off the veterans the Cowboys also swiped from the Vikings. The fleecing already is evident.

Williams must win at a high level and sustain it before the Carolina trade receives its final report card and its place in history. Caleb opened the '24 season with much to prove just to jump over Jared Goff and Jordan Love in the division. Dallas won three Super Bowls in four years to validate the slam dunk on the Walker deal. Eberflus is winless against the Packers in four tries and the Bears haven't won the North since '18. Slow your roll, Sparky.

KHALIL MACK

Best-ever and worst-ever conversations are mental masturbation personified, but we *are* discussing the history of a pro football team, not current events or those in history that shaped the world in which we live. I had to give it much consideration because no trades made in this millennium jumped out as "best ever" territory. In fact, it's not easy pulling nominees. Some are screaming *"Mack, you idiot"* or *"Mac, you're an idiot."*

Sorry, but I can't call the Khalil Mack trade in '18 a win. They needed more to justify the weighty costs. They won one division title. They never won a playoff game.

It was a bold move from general manager Ryan Pace. He took a swing, and it was extremely *unBearslike* to trade for an elite pass rusher and subsequently pay him record money. Pace parted with two first-rounders and then signed Mack to a $141M deal, at the time the richest deal for any defender in NFL history. Aaron Donald jumped it shortly after. The Rams defensive tackle was the '18 DPOY and Mack finished second. No. 52 in blue made a big splash in '18 and racked up 12.5 sacks, forced six fumbles and was first-team All Pro.

The Bears went 13-3 and won the North, but Cody Parkey's double doink sealed the Bears' fate and Philadelphia escaped Solider Field with a 16-15 wild card win. All fingers pointed at Parkey afterward, but it was another underwhelming effort by the offense that undid Team Nagy. Mitch Trubisky didn't throw an interception, but the Bears didn't find the end zone for the first 51 minutes. They went 6-of-15 on third down.

The Nagy train stalled in the second year and Mack went several multiple-game stretches without hitting a quarterback. He wasn't forcing turnovers. He had four fewer sacks and only 12 QB hits. The '19 Bears were fourth in scoring defense, but Roquan Smith, Danny Trevathan, Akiem Hicks and Kyle Fuller consistently graded highest. They went 8-8 and finished third. After another lousy start in '20, the Bears regrouped and grabbed a wild card berth in the first year of Super Wildcard Weekend. New Orleans dumped them 21-9 at Soldier Field in a playoff loss that's only vaguely memorable. In '21, Mack appeared in just seven games. It was his last year in Chicago, and he was moved to the Chargers so the Bears could wiggle out of some of the contract.

Pace parted with two first-round picks and a committed a big hunk of cap space to an edge rusher who was *occasionally* impactful. They needed more of the '18 Mack to call it a "great" trade. I can't even get to "good." The ROI dipped precipitously after one terrific season. The end game left the Bears looking to reload and without elite or even good players they might have found with picks they burned to acquire Mack. They didn't have much of a budget for free agency and the roster lacked a heartbeat when Poles and Matt Eberflus arrived in '22. There weren't players who could flip a game with one splash play. Unless Justin Fields jumped out of a phone booth and sprinted 60 yards for a touchdown.

The Mack deal was a wash. It helped manufacture one memorable season, ultimately sullied by a Trubiskian offense that wallowed in the mire. Poles and Flus bit down hard on their frustration and weathered the worst season since Jim Dooley's Bears went 1-13 in '69.

The Jay Cutler deal also was a wash. Jerry Angelo swung for the fences in '09 when he traded with Denver for Jay Cutler, and it sent a jolt of hope into a city starved for a franchise quarterback. It cost the Bears their first-round pick in '10 and Kyle Orton. The Bears never achieved expectations with Cutler at the wheel. Much more on the sour-faced Cutler in Chapters 13 and 14.

BEST DEALS AND MESS DEALS

Picking which trade is the best in team history is a challenging assignment. As evidence still is being collected on the '22 deal with Carolina's Genie, it's not an obvious answer, especially with this book's mission statement to chronicle only the last 40 years. The most common answer by Bears enthusiasts is a trade I didn't live — the one George Halas made with Pittsburgh in '64 that led to Dick Butkus in the '65 draft. It wasn't surprising when I discovered very few football enthusiasts in their early 60s only vaguely recall Butkus being a pick from a trade. Most admitted they never knew that.

If you're fatigued by war stories about the Bears of yore, stand in line. In less than a decade, nobody will be talking about Sid Luckman anymore. I welcome that too and Luckman actually was kind to me once. The Bears legend of the '40s sent Christmas sweaters to sports yapper Chet Coppock and his staff in the late-'80s. It was perk for being the lead lackey in the Godfather of Chicago sports talk's *boyquarium*. Chester, this diet Coke's for you.

To give this section on trade history any teeth, I reluctantly rewound beyond '85. There just weren't enough deals afterward that set up the Bears for years. The internet reintroduced me to Luckman and other Bears none of us ever watched. *"Storied tradition"* they still say of the Bears on network promos. Sure, it is. I was unaware Halas traded for the pick that led to Luckman. At this point I don't care. No Bears from the '40s, sorry and no burning desire to herald Doug Atkins, the ferocious pass rusher on the '63 championship team. George McAfee, anybody? Keep it. My list, my rules. I'll accept the majority opinion and keep the Butkus trade alive, but that's where the line gets drawn.

Since 1964, the best and worst trades:

THE BEST

1. **Dan Hampton** (via Tampa Bay) 1978-79

   Before the '78 season, the Bears traded veteran defensive tackle Wally Chambers to Tampa for the Bucs' first-round pick in '79. It wound up the fourth-overall pick. Jim Finks took Hampton, a defensive lineman from Arkansas. Chambers, a first-team All Pro and runner up to Jack Lambert for DPOY in '76, was a fan favorite on bad Bears teams. Good ol' No. 60 was running out of steam so Finks moved him to Tampa, where he had only three sacks in '78. Chambers played only one more year.

Hampton's success was immediate. He started all 16 games his rookie season and finished third in DROY voting. *Danimal*, aka *The King*, was a versatile, relentless and fearless player for most of his 12-year HOF career. He was enormous, 6-5, 265 and he cut a Hollywood cowboy-type handsome veneer. Hamp played defensive end for most of his first nine years, then moved to tackle exclusively for the last three. His most prolific season was the coming-of-age year in '84, when he accrued a career-high 11.5 sacks and was voted first-team All Pro. Despite numerous orthopedic issues and surgeries, most notably knees, Hampton went to the post for 157 NFL games, all with the Bears. He was inducted in Canton in '02.

2. **Brandon Marshall** (from Miami) 2012.

Labeled a malcontent and discarded after four years in Denver, Marshall's second team, the Dolphins, were ready to punt after only two years. It was on the heels of his Marshall's first Pro Bowl selection. His reputation was sullied by an attitude, in addition to a rap sheet 17 or 18 arrests deep, I forget. The Bears got Marshall at the right time and for the right price — a pair of third-round picks. In his first year here, B-Marsh caught 118 passes for 1508 yards (still single-season records) and 11 touchdowns. He was first-team All Pro. Marshall produced again in '13 with 100 receptions for 1295 yards and a team-record 12 TD catches.

Marshall did things no Bears receiver did before, like get his hands to the top on contested catches and rip the ball into this body to secure it. He was a quarterback's dream on the fade. Marshall blocked like he *wanted* to block. Off the field, Marshall was rehabilitating his image and became a mental health awareness pitchman, regularly confessing some of his own bad wiring and bad decisions. Teammates, however, either grew tired of, jealous of, or both, with Marshall and he fell out of favor in his third year with the Bears. He caught 61 balls for 721 yards and eight TD and was off to the Jets for two more years.

3. **Dick Butkus** (via Pittsburgh) 1964-65

Before the '64 draft, Halas traded his second- and fourth-round picks to the Steelers for their first-round pick in '65. That pick was fourth and with it the Bears took Dick Butkus, Chicago Vocation High School and the University of Illinois. Butkus was an overnight sensation and earned first-team All Pro as a rookie after gathering five interceptions, seven fumble recoveries and a highlight reel full of bone-jarring tackles. A ruthless tackler, Butkus finished in the top five in MVP voting four times. Despite chronic knee issues (for which he later sued the Bears and disentangled from Halas for several years), Butkus missed only two games in his first eight seasons. He was the most violent player in an era littered with rules benders. Now, back to a world that included not only colored television but a remote control in every home.

4. **Jeff Graham** (from Pittsburgh) 1994

For the cost of only a fifth-round pick, the Bears got one of their most trustworthy receivers in my lifetime. Graham, who was in his fourth NFL season, lightened the load for second-year wideout Curtis Conway, the first-rounder in '93 who had a slow first two seasons. With Erik Kramer and Steve Walsh running the offense, Graham prospered, catching 68 passes for 944 yards and four touchdowns in his first season. He set career highs with 82 catches for 1301 yards in '95. The offense jumped to eighth in scoring in a 30-team league, averaging 24.5 ppg. Graham, unfortunately, was a cap casualty and the Bears had to let him walk. He played six more years, the first two with the Jets, one with Philadelphia and the final three with San Diego.

5. **Roquan Smith** (to Baltimore) 2022-2023

The Roquan Smith deal was covered in *The Poles Position* so little left to say. I was an enormous Smith fan a few games into his first year in '18. In October of '22, he was dealt to Baltimore after talks on a second contract stalled. The Bears got second- and fifth-round picks and linebacker A.J. Klein. The picks were used on defensive tackle Gervon Dexter and tackle Noah Sewell. Not sure how they'll contribute meaningfully but Poles salvaged something out of Smith's imminent departure. Bruised feelings already existed between management and Smith, who didn't have an agent. The trade took the Bears off the hook for an enormous contract. Baltimore paid Smith $100M ($45M is guaranteed). The Bears are better offer with the linebackers they bought a year ago — Tremaine Edmunds and T.J. Edwards.

Honorably mentioned: In '81, the Bears traded a fifth-round pick to San Francisco to move up two spots — 40th to 38th — in the second round. They took inside linebacker Mike Singletary out of Baylor. It was a good move. Singletary was the captain of the '85 Bears, defensive coordinator Buddy Ryan's first lieutenant. Singletary was enshrined in Canton, HOF class of '98.

THE WORST

1. **Rick Mirer** (from Seattle) 1997

   In Mirer's rookie season with the Seahawks, the second-overall pick led the NFL in one category — he was sacked 47 times. That was his best year, one that offered only occasion flickers of hope. The next three were dreadful. So, the Bears just had to go get him.

   The Bears sent a first-round pick to Seattle for a quarterback who never would throw a touchdown pass in their uniform. Mirer appeared in seven games and went 0-3 as the starter. He threw six interceptions and carded a 37.7 rating. Dave Wannstedt took the heat for it and never ducked his critics. Wannstedt, however, never signed off on compensation for Mirer. He pleaded guilty to coveting Mirer, but Wanny was informed by one of the suits they parted with a first-round pick for him. More on Mirer in *He's Got a Knee.*

2. **Greg Olsen** (to Carolina) 2011

   Jerry Angelo wasn't bashful after trading Olsen — 26 at the time — to Carolina for a third-round pick. The fiery GM implied Olsen didn't want to do what the Bears wanted from their first-round pick from

Miami. "He wanted to be Kellen Winslow. We were looking for Mike Ditka." The translation for those who never purchased vinyl recordings: Winslow, HOF class of '95, was among the first TEs to move away from the tackle and occupy the slot. The nomenclature today calls the position the "U" tight end. The U role requires a more diverse arsenal — agility, deception and speed. The "Y" is the traditional tight end who lines up next to the tackle. The Y essentially is a sixth O-lineman in the running game. He needs size, strength and the neanderthal gene. Ditka was a Y. Travis Kelce plays both roles better than anybody in the game today.

Angelo and Olsen could have met in the middle. What Olsen saw in himself, however, was spot on and he proved it in Carolina, He carved out a borderline Hall of Fame resume. And if the Bears were steamed Olsen didn't want to hit the weight room to put more junk in the trunk, they weren't wrong. In the biz, they call it "an anchor." If you're light in the ass, it's a detriment to any player whose position requires straight-forward run blocking skills. The powerful trunk fuels the process. Keeping the shoulder pad level down, firing out and exploding into a defender with the shoulder, head up and driving until the whistle is expected of the Y. George Kittle's stay-with-it block on Aidan Hutchinson in the NFC Championship game is textbook quality. At the apex of his finish, Kittle even used his neck for leverage. Olsen never wanted to do those things.

3. **Justin Fields** (via NY Giants) 2021, (to Pittsburgh) 2024

For those new to the club, the Bears liked Fields so much in '21 they traded with the Giants to move up nine slots to get him. The Giants got the Bears' first rounder in '22, and the Bears picked 11th instead of 20th. It was a bizarre three years. Wouldn't it be a thing if only the Bears got *a running back* who could average a league-leading 7.1 yards per carry. In his second year, Fields was a video game. In 15 games, he updated and upgraded NFL standards for running quarterbacks. It was exciting in a Devin Hester kind of way. Fields rushed for 1143 yards in '22. His breakaway speed, coupled with lighting quick change of direction made tacklers look foolish.

He didn't improve as a passer. Getting the ball out quickly. Seeing the field. Taking check downs. Throwing the ball away. Feeling pressure. Fields went 10-28 in three years. His 60.3% completion rate is well below today's standards. Offensive coordinator Luke Getsy left a stain on Fields, too. Lots of blame to go around but the bottom line is the trade to slide up to get him cost the Bears a first-round pick. Bad trade.

Many also believe the return Poles received from Pittsburgh for Fields in the spring should be considered an all-time bad deal. A fourth- to sixth-round conditional pick was salvaged, but the market for starters evaporated with Fields on the outside looking in. Poles got what he could and cut the losses. Fields appeared quite comfortable early in Steel Country. If the Bears had an experienced coaching staff with a strong-willed leader, it would have been a shrewd move to keep him on the roster. He was inexpensive at $2.7M and would have provided an additional threat with the ball in his hands. Of course, there was no need for a Williams insurance policy. He's a can't-miss.

4. **Mitch Trubisky** (via San Francisco) 2017

Giving away two third-rounders and a fourth-rounder won't cripple a team but because *giving* those picks to the 49ers is what Pace did, it earns a place here. Refresher: the Bears and 49ers flipped successive picks, second and third. The price for moving to No. 2 to get Mitch Trubisky was Chicago's third-round pick for two years and a fourth-rounder. All based on the fear San Francisco would draft him second if Pace didn't move for him. How many demerits for Pace? Had Pace traded *down* and gained additional picks, he *still* could have claimed the jittery kid in Carolina blue. John Lynch proved early in his career he can be as ruthless as a GM as the HOF safety was on the field. I wondered how much laughter filled the San Francisco war room that night in '17. Trubisky did a year in Buffalo, backing up Josh Allen before two years as Kenny Pickett's understudy in Pittsburgh. He's back with the Bills this year.

5. **Thomas Jones** (to NY Jets) 2007

The respect and affection Thomas Jones gets from teammates today rivals what the '80s Bears express for HOF DT Steve McMichael. It's the proverbial "first guy in the weight room, last guy to leave" thing. And it's real. Captaincy isn't gifted. T.J. was more valuable than his very good numbers indicated. It's tough to be too harsh on Angelo for breaking it up after three years. Jones was turning 29 before the '07 season and he endured hard miles in three years in Chicago. Those were the prices paid for hiding Rex Grossman. The Bears took Cedric Benson fourth in '05 and although teammates didn't take to him, it was time to cut Jones loose and unlock what seemed enormous potential for Benson. Angelo dealt T.J. to the Jets for a second-round pick.

Benson flopped with the Bears while Jones crushed it in New York. He averaged 310 carries in his first three seasons in green and in '08, his ninth season, he made his first Pro Bowl. He set career-highs in '09 with 331 attempts for 1402 yards and 14 touchdowns. T.J. spent the final two seasons of his 12-year NFL career with the Chiefs. When he was done, he accrued more 10,500 rushing yards and 68 rushing TDs. Thomas Jones - Warrior.

Dishonorably mentioned....

In '95, the Bears traded Trace Armstrong to Miami for second- and third-round picks. Armstrong had a down year in '94 and was a locker room lawyer, but the cat went on to accrue 56.5 more sacks in his career and played until he was 38. With '94 first-rounder John Thierry not developing, Armstrong's departure left Alonzo Spellman as the best edge rusher for a couple of years.

In October of '09, the Bears traded a second-round pick to Tampa Bay for pass rusher Gaines Adams, the fourth-overall pick in the '07. Adams appeared in 10 games for the Bears. He went sackless. Never registered a quarterback hit, as a matter of fact, but Adams did force a fumble. In January of '10, Adams died of a coronary condition previously undetected. He was 26. Tragedy, one that makes football irrelevant, but the Bears weren't at fault.

It's worth noting, in Adams brief NFL career, he scored one touchdown. It was with the Bucs in Week 3 of the '08 season. Adams took a Kyle Orton interception 45 yards for a score, giving Tampa a 14-6 lead over the Bears. Gruden's Bucs prevailed in overtime, 27-24.

Let's go shopping next and explore one more way to stack that roster with stallions. Or not.

CHAPTER 5
Help Wanted
(some experience required)

> *"I got a good deal on those boys.*
> *The scouts said they showed a lot of promise."*
> *– fictional Charlestown Chiefs general manager Joe McGrath*
> *(Strother Martin) on the Hanson Brothers, in the 1977 film Slap Shot.*

Julius Peppers *is* football in North Carolina. Lawrence Taylor earned more plaudits and collected more trophies, but Peppers won the most hearts.

Peppers grew up in West Central Carolina in Bailey, which boasted 566 denizens in the 2020 census. At 6-5, 225 coming out of Southern Nash high school, Peppers had college options but stayed home and went to UNC. He also played basketball for two years for the Tar Heels. In '02, Peppers was drafted second overall by the Carolina Panthers, behind only quarterback David Carr of the expansion Houston Texans.

On August 2, Peppers' enshrinement in the Hall of Fame was a reason for celebration for every sports fan in North Carolina. There was cause for a victory dance in Chicago, too. Peppers symbolizes the fall of *McCaskeyism*.

The historic *White vs. the NFL* antitrust case verdict launched free agency in '93. It was 17 years, however, before the Bears finally swung for the fences in the open market. General manager Jerry Angelo signed Pep to a $91 million deal, $42M of which was guaranteed. On the same day, March 5 of '10, the Bears announced two other signings — running back Chester Taylor, Adrian Peterson's caddy in Minnesota (Taylor still owed him for poker debts), and tight end Brandon Manumaleuna, a nine-year veteran. For 16 years, Taylor and Manumaleuna had been the garden variety Bears free agency bounties. The Bears just never had an appetite for being big players in the free market.

"I don't think we were even in the top 25 (spending) in the Super Bowl year ('06)," Angelo said. The 75-year-old Angelo brimmed with pride when he detailed Peppers' attributes — the ability to read and react fast, agility, speed, the long arms, fitness level, heart. It was Pep's work ethic that put the most lift in Angelo's voice when we reconnected in July. Oddly, even after eight successful years with Carolina, Angelo said there remained hesitance with Peppers. He was already 29 but coming off a career-high 14.5 sacks and was healthy most of his career.

"There were some snakes in our head," Angelo said. "You hear things and reputations and perceptions of people are out there. 'Does he play hard all the time? Does he care enough?' Julius is a shy guy and doesn't say much. His first love was basketball. Our coaches, Lovie (Smith) and Rod Marinelli did a great job investigating it and what we found out was that not only was Julius Peppers a great athlete and a great football player, he's also a great teammate and human being. Nobody worked harder. I've been around some great players who never stopped grinding, Randy White with the Cowboys, the four Hall of Famers in Tampa with Warren Sapp, Derrick Brooks, John Lynch and Ronde Barber. That's the kind of player and person Julius Peppers is."

Three weeks before his induction in Canton, a 36-second video of Peppers receiving his jacket hit social media. He grinned as he slowly opened the stylish box. To his left, Peppers' long-time fiancé, Claudia Sampedro, was equally stoked. Peppers and Sampredro, a Cuban-born reality television personality and fashionista, have been together since '14. The box is hinged from its outsides and Peppers opened both doors. A leather back top has a sharply-stamped salutation and Claudia provided enthusiastic play-by-play. "Welcome to the Pro Football Hall of Fame."

Pep wanted the prize inside, eager to blow right by greetings as he did offensive tackles. "There it us," gleamed Peppers, almost in a whisper. Low decibel levels typically accompanied his deep, bass voice. N.C.'s pride and joy grabbed the hanger and pulled out the garment for its unfurling. Claudia continued. "Class of 2024, No. 377," adorned the inside pocket where designer labels usually are stitched. She clapped, then quickly happy-slapped the counter on the island in their home's kitchen. Peppers held the jersey in front of him. "Nice, baby," she gushed. "It's nice, isn't it," Peppers confirmed, still just above a whisper.

Nice is Carolina barbecue. The paths Peppers chose to earn that jacket, the care with which he approached his craft, treated coaches and teammates, and played, exceeded *nice* by a country mile.

Peppers was a fast study and earned defensive rookie of the year in '02. Most effective as a pass rusher, he had the smarts, agility and speed to play in coverage as well and honors poured in during his first eight years. Two first-team and a pair of second-team All Pro selections and five Pro Bowls. He copped another first-team All Pro nod in '10 with the Bears. And another second-team selection. And three more Pro Bowls. Peppers moved on to Green Bay for two years before the bashful, now gray-bearded Baileyian punctuated his HOF career with two more seasons in Panthers' blue, black and silver.

His record with the Bears sparkled but it was a mere four-year stop in a 17-year epic career. Widening the focus, it's bigger than that here. Angelo stripped the shackles of free agency oppression off Team McCaskey. At least for a four-year term. Peppers remains the only elite player the Bears acquired in free agency.

The Bears just didn't spend money on talent after meeting the salary cap's floor. And how closely those minimum requirements are tracked, reported and enforced is unclear, even to coaches and personnel departments. Some have no recollection of the league's "89% rule."

SWIFTLY SPEAKING

Turning over the roster almost entirely is not a one-year proposition and Ryan Poles had more shopping to do after a 7-10 finish in '23. After executing a fast reload on defense the previous offseason, March and April of '24 produced a flurry of free agent buys, as well as trades, up and down the offense. Shane Waldron possesses an embarrassment of riches and Caleb Williams was welcomed with an arsenal to facilitate a smooth entry. Shiny, sparkling toys in every direction. If the big fellas can keep him vertical. In September, they couldn't.

Running back D'Andre Swift didn't flourish, either.

In March, the Bears signed Swift to a three-year, $24M deal, $15.3M guaranteed and a $4M signing bonus. Swift is coming off his most productive season, his only in Philadelphia, after three years with Detroit. Green Bay went big with Josh Jacobs, four-years, $48M, $12.5M guaranteed, and the Vikings were convinced enough by Aaron Jones' strong finish in '23 to bring him in for a year and guarantee all his $7M with a $4M signing bonus.

Swift is a cost-efficient player in an era that values touches more than carries. Heavy-load backs are an endangered species. Waldron's history isn't a rigid "this is my system" guy but backs are expected to catch the ball. Fullbacks on occasion, too, when you spot one. The Bears have one in Khari Blasingame, rostered again in '24, his sixth NFL season and third in Chicago. He had 13 career receptions and 11 rushing attempts coming into the year.

Swift collected a career-high 268 touches last year. It's curious he didn't garner more attention in Detroit, which drafted him 35th overall in '20. As a rookie, he failed to unseat a 35-year-old Adrian Peterson and, in subsequent years, shared time with replacement-level former Packer Jamaal Williams. Swift carried only 99 times in his third season in '22, but was targeted 70 times and caught 48 balls. For what it's worth, HBO's *Hard Knocks* depicted Swift as too passive for fire-and-brimstone backs coach Duce Staley. The price for Swift was a tick more than what Detroit paid David Montgomery in '23. Monty's deal was for four years with a little more than half of $16M guaranteed after the Bears hung out the *not interested* sign.

Neither of Montgomery's successors in the Bears' backfield, Khalil Herbert nor fourth-rounder Roschon Johnson, stole the running back job in '23. So, Poles then targeted Swift. In '23, Herbert didn't get many touches in the first three games but got rolling in Week 4 when he rushed 18 times for 103 yards in a 31-28 loss to Denver. He incurred an ankle injury the next week in Washington, however, and missed five games. Scrambling to his left, Justin Fields' dump off to Herbert was badly errant. Herbert twisted abruptly and awkwardly to his right, trying to get his hands in position for the short pass. He didn't suit up again until Week 11, a 31-26 loss in Detroit.

Poles also added depth to the offensive line, which was expected to be a "pardon our dust during reconstruction" scenario, a chronic problem for most NFL teams. *Musical Bears*, as I started calling it many camps ago, has reared its ugly head again. Center/guard Coleman Shelton signed a one-year deal and was slated to battle Ryan Bates for the starting center job in camp. Bates began the year on IR and Shelton struggled terribly in September. The former Ram started all 17 games last year, his fifth with LAR. Tackle Matt Pryor also took a one-year deal. The Bears are Pryor's fourth team in six years. He was forced into duty at right guard in Week 3 when the consistently unavailable Nate Davis wasn't right. It didn't go well.

Barring the '05-'06 seasons. when Angelo's fix-on-the-fly O-line clicked, *Musical Bears* has been playing since the '80s *Black and Blues Brothers* disbanded.

Tight end Gerald Everett signed a two-year, $14M, $6M guaranteed deal. Cole Kmet's production has increased consistently but depth anywhere on the roster hasn't been a luxury the personnel department produced for some time. Everett is an effective red zone target at 6-3, 245 lbs. The Bears are his fourth team. He was a second-round pick of the Rams in '17 and produced his career bests, 58 rec. 558 yds and four TDs, two years ago with the Chargers. Marcedes Lewis, now 40, also was in camp for depth at TE. Lewis is expected to be the best option when the Bears go to "12" personnel" with two tight ends, typically deployed in short yardage.

Defensively, safeties Kevin Byard and Jonathan Owens were added to support the young and talented back end. Owens made a fast impression, scoring the Bears' first touchdown of the year after taking a blocked punt 21-yards to the house in the opening day win over Tennessee. Byard is 31 and has 28 career picks, top 10 among active players. He signed a two-year deal for $15M, $3M bonus. Almost half is guaranteed. Owens, 29, did a two-year deal for $4.75M, $1.5M guaranteed. The husband of gymnast Simone Biles spent '23 with Green Bay after four years in Houston. His most productive year was '22 when he started all 17 games and made 84 solos. Before camp started, Owens said he was shutting down all social media after facing criticism for joking about being "the catch" in his marriage to the globally-revered Biles. The Bears gave him a hall pass in August to be with Biles in Paris as the 27-year-old Texan racked up more gold.

THE EDMUNDS AND EDWARDS SHOW
SEASON 2

Some Clevelanders opted for coffee instead of a Dog Pound Brew at the halftime break in Week 15 of the '23 season. The Bears and Browns malingered their way to a 7-7 deadlock. Luke Getsy's offense opened the third quarter with a quick three-and-out. Nothing says *"this is gettin' good"* quite like the jog of a Bears punter. In this case, Trenton Gill.

On Cleveland's first snap, eventual comeback player of the year Joe Flacco tried to rifle the ball in a tight window to Cedric Tillman in the middle of the field. As the ball met Tillman's hands, he was drilled at chest level by linebacker T.J. Edwards. The ball popped up and fell into the hands of linebacker Tremaine Edmunds. The former Buffalo first-rounder raced down the sideline, discarded a diving Flacco at the 15, and the Bears jumped up top with a 45-yard pick 6.

It's the kind of bang-bang play coaches show several times in film review. It illuminates *team*. It's the tip drill coming to life and swinging a game in your favor, in this case only temporarily. Edwards delivered the stick to send the ball airborne and Edmunds finished with the catch and return. The *Edwards and Edmunds Show*. Before Eberflus' crew gets to the grind of NFC North opponents in November '24, most will know who wears 49 — Edmunds — and who wears 53 — Edwards. Poles zoomed in and signed the FA linebackers to rebuild the front seven in the eventful '23 off-season. It took time for newcomers to mesh and function cohesively as it does in football. In the end, the sum of Edmunds and Edwards are a big part of why the Bears feel chesty about their defense.

Edwards played all 17 games, logged more than 1000 snaps (97%), and led the team in tackles. His FA deal for was for three-years, $40.5M, $24.25M guaranteed. The former Eagle grew up in Lake Villa and idolized Bears linebacker Lance Briggs. Edwards was undrafted out of Wisconsin in '19. Edmunds missed two games in '23 with a knee injury suffered when he collided with Gervon Dexter at full speed in the loss to the Chargers. His four interceptions shared the team lead with Jaylon Johnson and Tyrique Stevenson. Edmunds, Buffalo's first-rounder and 16th-overall pick in '18, is guaranteed $50M of a $76M, four-year deal.

The tandem is expected to collaborate on a highlight reel of splash plays over the next few years. Edmunds and Edwards were the biggest prizes for the Bears when they started free agency in '23 with a league-high $120M of cap space. The '24 season began in fine fashion for the duo.

THE HOME DEPOT FOR NFL GMs

Two years ago, Bears fans cracked wise about Poles' decision to re-sign Equanimeous St. Brown. *"We've got the wrong St. Brown."* Amon-Ra St. Brown ascended to stardom in Detroit and the Lions rewarded him with a four-year, $120M contract in April. Equanimeous St. Brown, three years older than his brother, was a perfect and inexpensive asset ($1.25M) for the Bears. He landed in New Orleans. E.S.B. was a consistent special teams performer for two years and, as a bottom of the depth chart receiver, he could be trusted to remember the snap count and understand the passing tree.

That's what free agency is. Roster construction includes very few tape measure home runs. Whether through the draft, trades or in free agency, it's targeting the best possible pieces for their specific place in the system. And while practicing safe salary cap management. Fans and media demand the long ball, but the most complete rosters are laced with solid, supporting cast "singles hitters." Pieces in a puzzle. Smart, versatile, cost-efficient players.

Free agency is being willing to lose, too. It's Lucas Patrick, the center who was better than Bears fans thought the last two years. If you believe the data and conclusions drawn by *Pro Football Focus* are gospel, *PFF* rated Patrick as the No. 2 run-blocking center in the league in '23. Injuries bit him regularly and the former Packer was a mixed bag in his two years. Now in New Orleans, Patrick cost the Bears $8M.

Free agency is Byron Pringle, the former Kansas City fourth-option target. Poles took a flyer on Pringle in '22, a one-year deal for $4M, and a few weeks after doing the deal, Pringle was arrested for reckless driving and driving on a suspended license. He'd been doing donuts in a school parking lot with his infant son in the back seat. Ever sit behind the wheel of a high-performance vehicle with 500+ horsepower under the hood? Unwise idea for an untrained pilot, child on board or not. Pringle made four starts and appeared in 11 games in his one year before scooting along to the Commanders.

Diving into free agency means taking risks, like Poles did when he signed Larry Ogunjobi as his first FA acquisition in March of '22. Ring a bell? Ogunjobi was the Cincinnati defensive tackle who became a punchline after failing his physical. Cynical fans and media were quick to fire from the cheap seats, then later were educated on teams bearing no financial responsibility when a player doesn't pass medicals. To his credit, Poles didn't get into a bidding war with the Steelers when they sought Ogunjobi's services. The first-year GM went elsewhere and landed Justin Jones, who was productive for two years before Arizona wooed him with a $30M, three-year deal this past spring.

The evolution of free agency has given aging pass rushers a chance to roam the league and if they chose, take short deals as a temporary fix somewhere — like Yannick Ngakoue did with the Bears in '23. After four seasons in Jacksonville, Ngakoue had stints in Minnesota, Baltimore, Las Vegas and Indianapolis. Poles then took a shot. It was a resounding miss. Ngakoue had only four sacks in 13 games. It cost the Bears $15M all tolled.

Robert Quinn, conversely, got a five-year deal from Ryan Pace in '20, and was guaranteed $30M of the $70M, five-year deal he signed. Quinn was 30 when he signed. He set the team's single-season standard with 18.5 sacks in '21, but it hardly justified a long-term deal for a 10-year veteran. Quinn made 36 starts for the Bears and had 21.5 sacks. Poles salvaged something out of Pace's gaffe and moved Quinn to Philadelphia in '22 for a fourth-round pick.

GOOD BUYS, BAD BUYS, THE BEARS HAVE HAD THEIR SHARE

Best Free Agents Since '93:

1. **Julius Peppers**, 2010

   The only "all-time best" debate easier than this one is the best running back in team history. I'll go as far as this: Peppers is on the medals stand for the best free agent acquisitions for *all* Chicago teams. Three-time Stanley Cup winner and HOFer Marian Hossa gets the gold. Cubs left-hander Jon Lester, a cog on the '16 World Series winners, gets the silver. Peppers, in his first Bears season, earned first-team All Pro honors for the third time in his career and his sixth Pro Bowl. He had eight sacks, 18 QB hits, 43 solos, three FFs, nine PDs and two INTs. The $91.5M over six years was the largest contract the Bears ever awarded a player until Khalil Mack leapfrogged it in '18. Peppers had 37.5 sacks in four seasons with the Bears. Give the man his bronze medal for this city's most impactful free agency investments.

2. ***Black & Blues Brothers II***: **Ruben Brown**, G, 2004; **John Tait**, T, 2004; **Roberto Garza**, G, 2005; **Fred Miller**, T, **2005**

The only way to hide a challenged quarterback is to assemble an O-line that can win ugly, Get 'em in the alley. In '04, Angelo augmented the line substantially, signing Brown, an eight-time Pro Bowler with Buffalo, and Tait, to a six-year, $32M deal. Brown played four good years at guard for the Bears. His three-point stance was odd looking, flirting with Randall McDaniel-funky by the end, but he was a tank on the inside run. Tait, a K.C. first-rounder in '99, was a five-year starter. Miller (yes, the guy Olin Kreutz conked on the head with a dumbbell) was regarded the top tackle on the free agent market in March of '05. The 32-year-old signed a five-year deal for $22.5M. He was a regular for three years. Garza signed a one-year deal after four years in Atlanta. Excellent in short yardage, Garza started 145 games over 10 seasons with the Bears. Both tackles were longer, leaner dudes and best in pass protection. Brown was a road grader. Garza was versatile enough to play center in a pinch. This unit was the team's second-best offensive line since the merger.

3. **Erik Kramer**, QB, 1994

The Bears let Jim Harbaugh move along in '94 and signed the former Lion to a three-year, $8M deal. The polar-opposite of a typical silver-spoon, highly-sought college recruit who ultimately get drafted in the first round. Kramer was a junior college entry (Pierce CC near his home) to North Carolina State and later went undrafted. Stops in New Orleans and Atlanta were quick ones before three years with Calgary in the CFL. The Lions had him for three years before the Bears got him in free agency's second year. Kramer's '95 season was the most productive season in team history. He passed for 3838 yards and 29 touchdowns. Both remain team standards. Kramer played five years here, passing for almost 11,000, 63 TDs and 45 INTs. His injuries — including a broken neck — necessitated the unfortunate acquisitions of Rick Mirer (via trade), the hamster-handed Dave Krieg and more.

4. **Thomas Jones**, RB, 2004

One of the toughest backs of his era, Jones was an old school plow horse whose steady performances facilitated back-to-back division titles in '05 & '06. Jones agreed to a four-year deal worth about $10M. Arizona took him seventh-overall in '00, but the Cardinals favored Michael Pittman. In '03, Jones went to the Buccaneers, who seemed to lean ... Michael Pittman again. Angelo signed Jones and T.J. made an immediate impact. Jones rushed for 1335 yards on 314 carries with 9 TDs in '05, second only to Walter Payton in team annals. A weight room animal, Jones also was an emotional, vocal leader. In Jones' three years with the Bears, he accrued 850 carries for 3493 yards (4.1 ypc) and 22 TDs. Shortly after Super Bowl 41, Angelo suggested Jones and first-rounder Cedric Benson couldn't co-exist. Jones was dealt to the Jets.

5. **Tim Jennings**, CB, 2010

A second-rounder of the Colts in '06, Jennings signed a four-year, $22.5M deal with the Bears, who guaranteed their new shut-down corner $12M. Jennings led the league in interceptions with nine in '12, when he earned second-team All Pro honors. T.J. reminded me of Donnell Woolford, the first-round pick in '89, a smallish corner who played big against the run and had excellent ball skills. Jennings made two Pro Bowls with the Bears, for whom he played five seasons. He accrued 16 picks (three returned for TDs) and five FFs for the Bears. Jennings concluded his career with one season in Tampa.

Honorable mentions: **The Grace of Pace** includes front seven signings **Akiem Hicks**, DE, 2016, and **Danny Trevathan**, LB, 2016. Hicks, aka *Mufasa*, didn't rack up Warren Sapp sack numbers, but he forced pressure consistently as a "full-figured" D-lineman. The 6-5, 325 lb. Hicks bagged a four-year, $48M contract. He carded a career-high 8.5 sacks and 3 FFs in his second year. Hicks spent six seasons as a Bear but was riddled by injuries in '19 and again in '21. Trevathan was a risky hire, given a list of injuries early in his career in Denver, for three years at $21.75M. Trevathan wasn't tasked as a pass rusher often and didn't take the ball away, but he was a smart player and an exceptionally sure-handed tackler, especially one-one-one. He played for the Bears for six seasons after four with the Broncos.

One-Hit Wonder: **Ted Washington**, DT, 2001. Former Bears linebacker and long-time radio personality Doug Buffone described the most gigantic interior D-lineman — guys who never will model underwear — as "coke machines." Think Vince Wilfork. Washington, 6-5, 375 lbs., was coke machine personified. He was old and slow with 10 NFL seasons under his 52" belt. The dude was immovable, however. Washington earned first-team All Pro in '01. He made life easier for young linebackers Brian Urlacher, Warrick Holdman and Rosevelt Colvin. Great with his hands, too, and a huge addition — for one season — to the defense that powered the '01 Central title.

Worst Free Agents Since '93:

1. **Bryan Cox**, LB, 1996

   Cox got record money from the Bears — $13.2M over four years — and understandably it sparked enthusiasm. Cox made a lot of splash plays with the Dolphins, accruing 14.5 sacks in his second season. The Dolphins moved him to the middle in his fourth year, however, and he wasn't as effective. The Bears also penciled him in at MLB and it didn't agree with him. He was an emotional player, sometimes to his own detriment, but Bears fans eat that stuff up. He flopped here, making only 25 starts and in less than two years, he was gone. When we see $13.2M today and don't flinch, it's a reminder of how quickly salaries escalated in the new millennium. Cox got on the field for the Bears and tackled people when he was healthy, which was more than some players in the flop category of Bears free agent hires did. Nonetheless, I place the Cox signing at the top because of the enormous expectations that never were actualized. It was enormously disappointing.

2. **Lovie's Loves Old Rams** - **Orlando Pace**, T, 2009, and **Adam Archuleta** (trade) S, 2007

Pace's selection to the Hall of Fame was an easy call but he was 33 and his body was breaking down in '09. Tackles have played almost 20 years but for every Jackie Slater or Lomas Brown, there are 1000 guys who struggle to get out of bed every morning by the time they're 30. Pace, the No. 1 pick in the '97 draft, signed a three-year, $15M deal, presumably to protect Jay Cutler, who had just been acquired via trade with Denver. If a tackle is dealing with chronic back issues, it's unlikely he'll have a long career.

When Lovie Smith was a Dick Vermeil assistant in St. Louis, his defenses were good, and Archuleta was a part of that. Technically, the Archuleta acquisition was a trade with the Redskins for a sixth-round pick. After agreeing to a three-year, $8.1M contract, he couldn't get on the field for the Bears. The millions blown in the deals for the former Rams didn't drain the McCaskey vault, but Pace and Archuleta serve as reminders of going to the well with *your guys* several years after the fact isn't always advisable.

3. **The 2K Hat Pack**: 2000 signings **Phillip Daniels**, DE, and **Thomas Smith**, CB

Mark Hatley's fingerprints are all over the Bears' '01 NFC Central championship squad, which won 13 games before getting drummed by the Eagles in the playoffs. These two free agent pickups in '00, however, were dreadful. The decision to make Seattle castoff Daniels the highest paid player in franchise history still shocks the system. Daniels was serviceable, hardly the return expected for a $22M deal. In three years, Daniels tallied 23 sacks, 32 TFLs, four FFs and four FRs.

Hatley called Daniels and former Buffalo cornerback Smith "the best defensive players on the market." Didn't say much for the market. Smith played one season for the Bears and didn't intercept a pass. He was demoted to fourth on the depth chart and wasn't even playing in nickel. That was one year after signing a five-year deal $20M deal, $6.5M of which was a signing bonus.

4. **Band-Aid Quarterbacks: Kordell Stewart**, 2003, **Mike Glennon**, QB, 2017

Angelo can't be spanked too harshly for Stewart because Slash wasn't expensive (two-years, $4.75M) and the Bears had to do something after Jim Miller's health betrayed him. Angelo drafted Rex Grossman late in the first round in '03 but it would have been a tall order to open the season with Grossman under center against the 49ers. The rookie couldn't have fared much worse. Stewart was picked three times and sacked five more in San Francisco's 49-7 KO of the Bears. In seven starts in '03, Stewart went 2-5, completed 50.2% of his passes for seven touchdowns and 12 interceptions with a rating of 56.8.

Glennon, on the other hand, signed a bloated deal, $18.5M guaranteed, clearly to be a stop-gap until Mitch Trubisky was ready. After four games, John Fox had seen enough and pulled the plug on Glennon after a 1-3 start. In the *look what we could have done* drawer in '17 is Case Keenum. The journeyman signed with Minnesota — for a thrifty two million — and led the Vikings to the NFC title game. Glennon proved quickly he was only the next guy to pop out of the clown car and his ineptitude led to the insertion of a wide-eyed Trubisky before he was ready.

5. **Phil Emery Drops a Deuce**: **Jared Allen** and **Lamarr Houston**, DL, 2014

The more we reflect on Emery's record as GM, the worse it looks. At the same time, ownership earns a smattering of golf applause for pulling the plug on West Point Phil after such a short tenure. Allen was an artificial surface edge rusher exclusively at this point in his career and the $15M+ he was paid broke down to about $3M per sack. Yikes.

Houston's plight is laughable, in a cruel way. He blew out his knee in Foxboro celebrating a sack. The Bears trailed New England by 25. And he didn't even get his hands on Tom Brady. In a mop-up role, Jimmy Garappolo was unable to elude the former Raider. The Pats put 51 on the board that Sunday. Houston made only 11 starts in three years and change. His contract guaranteed him $15M and included a $5M signing bonus.

Dishonorable mentions: **Pernell McPhee, Cody Parkey, Ray McDonald**
Pace curiously signed McPhee, who only had tallied six starts in his first four seasons in Baltimore, to a five-year, $38.5M deal that guaranteed the linebacker $8.5M. His three years with the Bears are described best as uneventful. He had 14 sacks and had one forced fumble every year, whether they needed it or not. Parkey scored a four-year, $15M deal in '18, but was gone after the double doink field goal miss in the playoff loss to Philadelphia. He had stops in Tennessee, Cleveland and New Orleans before retiring after the '21 season. In '15, the signing of McDonald cost the Bears only the embarrassment they suffered from hiring a player with a history of domestic abuse issues, then learn he was arrested in Santa Clara five weeks after agreeing to a one-year contract.

The Packers, on the other hand, met free agency in '93 with a bit more gusto. It played a huge role in the Pack returning to their '60s glory. Next, we spin across the Wisconsin line, zip through Milwaukee and jump on 43 North. Next stop is Green Bay. Best to take Dramamine first if you're one of those *"gotta hate the Packers"* types.

CHAPTER 6
Dairyland Drought
SINCE '92, PACKERS OWN BORDER WAR

Jordan Love concluded the 2023 regular season the way he began it — demonstrating poise under duress, making good decisions and throwing the ball crisply and accurately. Beating the Bears.

Protecting a 17-9 lead as the two-minute warning neared, Love needed one last third-down conversion, and the Packers would snatch the NFC's final playoff seed. On third-and-eight from the Green Bay 43, Love put *calm* on display again. Flushed from the pocket on his blind side by Montez Sweat, the Packers quarterback found tight end Tucker Kraft, who had released from the flat and caught the ball near mid-field. Kraft chugged forward for a few more yards into Bears' territory. Moments later, Green Bay went into victory formation and the party was on at Lambeau. Again.

The beat goes on, Chicago. The Bears could have punctuated a defensive rebound in the second half of the season by stomping on Green Bay's playoff hopes. The way Dan Campbell's Lions did in Week 18 in '22. Instead, Love owned them, as he did in Week 1 in a stunning 38-20 head stomping of the not-ready-yet Bears. Love was money, hitting on 7-of-10 third-down attempts in the finale. The "on-the-come" Matt Eberflus defense facilitated an 84% completion rate. Love went 27-of-32 for 316 yards and two touchdowns. He wasn't intercepted and posted a rating of 128.6. The Bears sacked him just once.

Love's supporting cast all were unknowns. Davante Adams was two years gone. Randall Cobb had moved on to the Jets. Christian Watson was in civilian clothes. Again. Romeo Doubs left the game with a chest injury in the second quarter. Who were these guys? Bo Melton excepted, Love's nest is stuffed with Brian Gutekunst draft picks. They're all just getting started.

Dontayvian Wicks, who caught both TDs, was a fifth-rounder, now in his second year. Jayden Reed, who had a game-high 112 receiving yards, was the Pack's second-rounder in '23. Tight end Luke Musgrave also came in the second. Doubs was a third-rounder in '22. Melton, a late-rounder in Seattle in 22, is the only Packer who isn't homegrown.

I immediately thought of the endless pardons for Jay Cutler and others.

What do you want when Earl Bennett's his best option?

Doesn't matter who's playing if Mike Tice is calling plays?

They never protect the guy!

Who's Mitch got, Adam Shaheen?

Love kept rolling and the following weeks of postseason football offered more reminders of who the Bears were not. Green Bay's offense crackled in Dallas in a 48-32 finish that was never competitive. Love again was precise with three TDs and a 157.2 rating. The following Saturday in the divisional round, the Packers had San Francisco, a 10-point favorite, on the ropes but couldn't close. Love played well but threw two picks. Rookie Anders Carlson missed a 41-yard field goal, and the 49ers prevailed, 24-21.

Make no mistake, the Packers aren't going away. It's just two games, but Love's performances against the Bears — for a first-year starter — were staggering. The money stats give you pause and wonder, *really? Again?* Almost 600 passing yards, five TDs and no picks. He was sacked once in each game. Love didn't cough it up. Coach Matt Lafleur appears to be decanting the next guy to keep the Bears, and their fans trapped in Packers purgatory. When Love was shelved in September, Malik Willis capably stepped in and played close to mistake-free in back-to-back wins.

The chasm that separates Packers quarterbacks from Bears quarterbacks is vast. The Brett Favre to Aaron Rodgers to Love succession, however, is only a symptom of the Bears' malignancies. It's undeniable the arrival of Favre in '92 was the line of demarcation in the series but Green Bay put the pedal to the floor when free agency arrived in '93.

The Dairylanders have enjoyed a decided advantage over the Bears organizationally. That's the simplest, most accurate explanation for the last 32 years of lopsidedness in the storied rivalry. Green Bay now leads the series 107-95. There have been six ties.

Love is 2-0 against the Bears. Rodgers went 24-5. Favre, 22-10. Rodgers' ownership of Chicago was 64 touchdown passes and only 10 picks. Favre was the architect of Packers' first 10-game winning streak in the series.

In three years, Justin Fields started all six games in the series and lost them all. Mitch Trubisky was 1-6. Cutler went 2-10. Eberflus is 0-4 and the three coaches who preceded him all punched out only one win. After winning seven of his first 10, Lovie Smith finished 8-11 against the Packers. The last Bears coach to have an edge on the green and gold is Mike Ditka, who went 15-5 between '82 and '92.

According to the *Merriam-Webster* dictionary, a *rivalry* means more than two entities vying for the same goal. It connotes a *competitive balance* in the opposing sides' history. Rival also can mean *peer* or *equal.* The nail may not like the hammer, but it would be silly to suggest it is the *equal.*

The nail does not have a rivalry because it never hits back. Putting the nail in its rightful place requires neither thought nor effort from the hammer.

Since Favre took the wheel in '92, the Packers have been the hammer. Young Favre needed lots of harnessing. He had the right mentor in Mike Holmgren, who also had budding assistants Andy Reid, Steve Mariucci and Jon Gruden on his staff. Coaching has been a resounding *advantage Packers.*

BLOWIN' THE WHISTLE

Packers head coaches since '92:

- 1992-98 Mike Holmgren, 12-2 vs. the Bears. 75-37-0 (.670) in regular season, 9-5 (.643) in postseason. SB 31 champs, SB 32 runner up. Three NFC Central titles in seven years.

- 1999 Ray Rhodes, 1-1 vs. Bears. 8-8 in regular season (.500).

- 2000-05 Mike Sherman, 8-4 vs. Bears. 57-39 (.594) in regular season, 2-4 (.333) in postseason. Three NFC North titles in six years.

- 2006-18 Mike McCarthy, 19-8 vs. Bears. 125-77-2 (.618) in regular season, 10-8 (.556) in postseason. SB 45 champs. Six NFC North titles in 13 years.

- 2019-present Matt Lafleur, 10-0 vs. Bears. 56-25 (.675) in regular season, 3-4 (.429) in postseason. Three NFC North titles in five years.

Impressive. Let's look at some of the memorable games in the series since '93 when Dave Wannstedt took over for Ditka. Read 'em and weep. It's Bears head coaches vs. the Packers since '92.

Matt Eberflus 0-4 2021-present

Toughest loss: Sunday, September 10, 2023 — Packers 38, Bears 20, Soldier Field

The Week 18 loss was detailed above. We rewind to the '23 opener. The Bears sputtered offensively from wire to wire. Fields: 24-37-216-1-1, four sacks, 78.2 rating, threw 37-yd Pick 6 to Quay Walker in fourth quarter, game-high 59 rushing yards. Khalil Herbert: 9-27-0. Roschon Johnson: 5-20-1. D'Onta Foreman: 5-16-0. D.J. Moore caught both of a mere two targets for 25 yards. Chase Claypool: 0 catches. Darnell Mooney: 4-53-1. What exactly Luke Getsy was aiming for is anybody's guess. Meanwhile, Love: 9-for-16 on third down; 15-27-245-3-0, one sack, 123.2 rating. Aaron Jones: 9-41-1, 2-86-1 before leaving with a hamstring injury in the third quarter. Said radio analyst Tom Thayer, a lifelong Bears fan and starter on the Bears '80s teams: "In 28 years of doing these broadcasts, I've never left a game as pissed off as I did that day."

Signature win: TBD

Matt Nagy 1-7 2018-2021

Toughest loss: Thursday, September 5, 2019 — Packers 10, Bears 3, Soldier Field

So easy to say Khalil Mack's debut when the Bears blew a 23-point lead at Lambeau on opening night. Saving that for *The Lean Teens.* Fast forward to when the curtain opened on the '19 season, Nagy's second year in Chicago. The defending NFC North champion Bears were 3.5-point favorites. Mitch Trubisky: 28-25-228-0-1, five sacks, 62.1 rating; 3-for-

15 on third down, 0-for-2 on fourth down. Bears: 10 penalties for 107 yds; 46 rushing yards. Rodgers: 18-30-203-1-0, five sacks, 91.4 rating. Green Bay was held to 213 total yards of offense and still escaped with a win. So much for "that next step."

Signature win: Sunday, December 16, 2018 — Bears 24, Packers 17, Soldier Field

Not only did the Bears clinch the North, their first division title since '10, they blew up GB's postseason hopes. The Nagy offense *erupted* for two first-half touchdowns. Trubisky: 20-28-274-2-0, one sack, 120.4 rating. Jordan Howard: 19-60-1. Rodgers: 25-42-274-0-1, five sacks, 68.9 rating; Rodgers didn't throw a TD pass and his record streak of 402 passes without an interception was snapped when Eddie Jackson came up with a deflection. Mack: 2.5 sacks, Leonard Floyd: 2 sacks. This was the last time the Bears beat the Packers. They covered the 5.5, too.

John Fox 1-5 2015-2017

Toughest loss: Sunday, November 12, 2017 — Packers 23, Bears 16, Soldier Field

GB backup Brett Hundley whipped the Bears in the game Fox won a challenge only to lose possession of the ball. Bears RB Benny Cunningham was knocked out of bounds near the pylon at the SW goal line. Fox thought it was a TD, so he challenged. Officials had ruled Cunningham out of bounds shy of the goal line. Upon review, it was learned Cunningham lost control of the ball *before* he was down. *Where* he was down was irrelevant. The ball rolled out of the end zone and the NFL's debatable possession rule awarded the ball to GB. Not all who watch football understand the rule. All 32 coaches should. Hundley: 18-25-212-1-0, three sacks, 110.7 rating. Davante Adams: 5-90-1. Trubisky: 21-35-297-1-0, five sacks, 97.0 rating. Dontrelle Inman: 6-88-0. Bears: 55 rushing yards, eight penalties.

Signature win: Thursday, November 26, 2015 — Bears 17, Packers 13, Lambeau Field

Despite 12 penalties for 95 yards, the Bears muscled out a win because they didn't turn it over. Any win in GB is a treat and the Bears did enough right to give their first-year head man a victory in the celebrated rivalry. Cutler: 19-31-200-1-0, one sack, 90.8 rating. Forte: 15-44-0. Jeremy Langford: 12-48-1. Jeffrey: 7-90-0. Zack Miller: 3-yd TD rec. Rodgers: 22-43-202-1-1, two sacks, 62.4 rating. Eddie Lacy: 17-105-0. Randall Cobb: 6-74-0. Tracy Porter: INT. Sacks: Willie Young, Lamarr Houston. The Bears, 8.5-point underdogs, improved to 5-6 while Green Bay fell to 7-4.

Marc Trestman 1-3 2013-2014

Toughest loss: Monday, November 9, 2014 — Packers 55, Bears 14, Lambeau Field

When one roots for change, there must be a willingness to endure the tortures of the damned, the proverbial bitter pill. This was it. The Patriots shelled the Bears 51-23 in Week 8, but Team Trestman had the bye to get ready for GB in Week 10 on *MNF*. Rodgers: six TD passes in first half; 18-27-315-6-0, no sacks, 145.8 rating. Cutler: 22-37-222-1-2, three sacks, 68.7 rating. Jordy Nelson: 6-152-2. Casey Hayward: 82-yd Pick 6 of Cutler in the fourth. It was the second-consecutive nationally-televised moon pounding for the Bears. Those rooting for change got it after the year when Trestman was gassed.

Signature win: Monday, November 4, 2013 — Bears 27, Packers 20, Lambeau Field

The famous *Shea McClellin Game*. The Boise bumpkin had three sacks, including one that broke Rodgers' collarbone and knocked him out for seven weeks. Josh McCown: 22-41-272-2-0, one sack, 90.7 rating. Matt Forte: 24-125-1. Brandon Marshall: 7-107-1. Alshon Jeffrey: 5-60-1. Rodgers' replacement Seneca Wallace: 11-19-114-0-1, four sacks, 53.4 rating. Lacy, 22-150-1. Julius Peppers: INT, sack. With Cutler out, the Bears were 9.5-point underdogs and improved to 5-3. Halfway through the first year of Trestman, the offense looked promising. First impressions can be deceiving.

Lovie Smith 8-11 2004-2012

Toughest loss: Sunday, January 23, 2011 — Packers 21, Bears 14. NFC Championship Game at Soldier Field

How can Smith's biggest heartbreak not be this loss. The Packers led 14-0 at halftime and the FOX broadcast crew was caught completely in the dark on Cutler's mysterious departure to the sideline in the second half. No explanation was given. Was he benched or is he hurt? Cutler was terrible in the first half, 6-of-14 with an interception and a 31.8 rating. Later, it was revealed Cutty sprained his MCL and couldn't put any weight on his leg. Caleb Hanie relieved and threw two picks, including a Pick 6 to chubby but adorable D-tackle B.J. Raji, who rumbled 18 yards for the score. The Bears went a sickly 1-for-13 on third down. Rodgers: 17-30-244-0-2, one sack, 55.4 rating, one rushing TD. Greg Jennings: 8-130-0. James Starks: 22-74-1. Sam Shields: 2 INTs. Hanie: 13-20-153-1-2, no sacks, 65.2 rating. Forte: 27 touches, 17-70-0, 10-90-0. Earl Bennett: 3-45-1. Chester Taylor: 1-yd TD run.

The nation harassed Cutler, suggesting he's soft on national shows and social media. In their haste to make an impassioned defense of Cutler's manhood, media and fans missed the bigger story. Cutler stunk. Don't worry about details, Bears enthusiasts. Just don't let anybody suggest your Messiah quarterback is fragile. Shame on Maurice Jones-Drew.

Signature win (tie): Sunday, September 19, 2004 — Bears 21, Packers 10, Lambeau Field

Lovie pandered to Meatball Nation at his introductory news conference when he stressed the importance of reestablishing the upper hand in the rivalry. And in Week 2 of his first year, Smith's Bears walked the walk and upset Favre's Packers. Thomas Jones: 23-152-1. Rex Grossman: 10-18-132-1-1, one sack, 74.3 rating. Favre: 24-52-252-1-2, no sacks, 62.8 rating. INTs: Michael Green, Bobby Gray. Mike Brown's 95-yard fumble return for TD after Brian Urlacher ripped the ball away from Ahman

Green was the prequel to the *Urlacher and Brown Game* on MNF in Arizona during the '06 Super Bowl year. Bears: only two penalties. It was a good game to take in as a fan, but I moved on the over at 41 and it made for a quiet ride home.

Signature win II: September 9, 2006 — Bears 26, Packers 0, Lambeau Field

It was opening day in Green Bay and the Bears put the nation on alert. For the first time in Favre's career, he was blanked. It was his 16th season. Favre: 15-29-170-0-2, three sacks, 40.9 rating; GB went 1-for-11 on third down. INTs: Peanut Tillman, Danieal Manning. Lance Briggs: team-high nine solos, sack. Grossman: 18-26-262-1-1, one sack, 98.6 rating. Rookie Devin Hester arrived with an 84-yard punt return for his first pro TD. Muhsin Muhammad: 6-102-0. Bernard Berrian: 49-yd TD rec. That's how the Super Bowl 41 Bears came out of the gate in the last great season for the Bears.

Dick Jauron 2-8 1999-2003

Toughest loss: Monday, October 7, 2002 — Packers 34, Bears 21, Memorial Stadium, Champaign

This one was all Favre, who got the Packers rolling right of the gate when he connected with Donald Driver on an 85-yard TD. Favre: 22-33-359-3-0, three sacks, 133.3 rating. Driver: 8-120-1. This was the game when ABC's Al Michaels bemoaned the accommodations in Champaign, the Bears' one-year home. Michaels: "I don't think they've even got a *Two* Seasons in this town." More Packers doing mean things to the Bears: Terry Glenn: 8-154-0. Ahman Green: 27-107-0. Kabeer Gbaja-Biamila: 2 sacks, 72-yd Pick 6. Jim Miller: 27-49-353-3-3, three sacks, 72.9 rating. Marty Booker: 12-141-1. John Davis: 3-33-2. These *MNF* dates against Green Bay don't have much upside.

Signature win: Sunday, November 7, 1999 — Bears 14, Packers 13, Lambeau Field

Defensive tackle Bryan Robinson blocked Ryan Longwell's 28-yard field goal as time expired to preserve a 14-13 win. It was the first game the Bears played after the death of Walter Payton. The previous day, a public service was held at Soldier Field. The Bears were awful offensively. Miller: 16-29-142-1-3, one sack, 40.4 rating. Curtis Enis: 20-88-0. Glyn Milburn: 49-yd TD run. Bobby Engram: 6-48-1. Favre: 27-40-267-1-1, three sacks, 84.1 rating. Dorsey Levins: 26-79-0. Walt Harris: team-high 11 solos, INT, sack, PD. Darren Sharper: team-high 10 solos, INT, 2 PDs.

Dave Wannstedt 1-11 1993-1998

Toughest loss: October 31, 1994 — Packers 33, Bears 6, Soldier Field

A nightmarish *MNF* loss on Halloween to Holmgren's up-and-coming Packers. It was cold and the rain came down sideways all day and night in Chicago. It was supposed to be a festive occasion as the Bears retired the jerseys of Gale Sayers (40) and Dick Butkus (51). Favre played with a badly bruised hip and threw for only 82 yards and a TD but his 36-yard TD scramble in the second quarter gave the Packers a 14-0 lead. The rout was underway. Edgar Bennett was Holmgren's "mudder." Bennett: 26-105-2, 1-13-1. Bryce Paup: 2 INTs, sack. Steve Walsh: 16-25-140-1-1, no sacks, 75.4 rating. Erik Kramer: 5-10-34-0-2, two sacks, 18.3 rating. Jeff Graham: 4-21-1. Lewis Tillman: 15-51-0.

Signature win: December 5, 1993 — Bears 30, Packers 17, Soldier Field

The Bears avenged their 17-3 loss in Green Bay in Week 9 with a defensive touchdown party in Wannstedt's first year. Favre passed for 402 yards but threw three interceptions and carded a 77.9 rating. Bobby Slowik's defense scored three TDs. Pick 6s: Jeremy Lincoln, 80 yards, and Mark Carrier, 34 yards. Dante Jones: 32-yard fumble return TD, INT. Sterling Sharpe: 10-114-1. The Bears survived a brutal offensive performance with just 210 yards total offense. Jim Harbaugh: 10-20-141-0-1, one sack, 52.1 rating. Bears: 69 yards rushing, 2-for-11 on third down. Terry Obee: 4-73-0. It was a Wanny win, for sure. Keep the *offense* off the field.

SCOUTING/DRAFTING

Packers GM Ron Wolf ('92-'99) was inducted in Canton in '15. Plausible arguments can be made Wolf is the most accomplished personnel man in NFL history. He cut his teeth in the early '60s with the Raiders and later with Tampa when the Buccaneers were born in '76. Incessant interference from owner Hugh Culverhouse caused a fast divorce but the core Wolf assembled advanced to the NFC title game in its fourth year. Wolf traded for Favre in '92 and was determined to get Reggie White when free agency was born in '93.

The Bears, meanwhile, the Bears didn't employ a true general manager between '87 and '01. Ditka and Bill Tobin collaborated on personnel until '92. In '93, Wannstedt assumed coach/GM duties and later was assisted by Rod Graves and Mark Hatley.

Ted Thompson also had an impressive record as Packers GM between '05 and '17. Thompson played a huge role in the *hammer and nail* dynamic. He drafted Rodgers when Favre still had game. Thompson provided enough depth on the roster for Green Bay to sustain myriad injuries in '10, a year in which 13 Packers went on IR, and win a Super Bowl.

Jerry Angelo, hired by Bears a month after the draft in '01, assembled most of the '06 Super Bowl roster after inheriting captains Olin Kreutz, Brian Urlacher and Mike Brown, all Hatley picks. Angelo's successors Phil Emery and Ryan Pace were disasters.

FREE AGENCY AND THE HUMAN TOUCH

Green Bay seized its opportunity to put Chicago and the NFC in the rear-view mirror when free agency began in '93. The Packers readied themselves for an open market when Plan B began to buckle and a victory for the NFLPA appeared imminent. The new free market was going to force NFL teams to play the recruiting game and upgrade facilities. The Packers broke ground on the Hutson Center before the *White vs. NFL* antitrust appeal was decided.

There was one other problem — Green Bay wasn't an easy sell. How do the Packers get players to a village of 100,000 residents in the middle of nowhere? How do they get *Black* players? Green Bay wasn't only the smallest NFL market, it was the whitest — 95% white in '93. Wolf, the savvy GM, figured that landing the big shark would quell any concerns over Green Bay's *Mayberry* image.

"Ron called me in his office and said, 'I want to get Reggie White.' I was kind of like 'What are we going to give him, a block of cheese?'" Mike Holmgren reflected in July. Holmgren and his staff were off to the races to secure the biggest prize in free agency.

White was the key figure for the players union in the antitrust case and the best defensive player in the league. He was an ordained Baptist minister who grew up in Chattanooga and his first public statement about free agency suggested God would provide his compass. Holmgren made the call to the top dog in the free market and said "This is God. Come to Green Bay." An excellent refresher course can be found in the '16 *Sports Illustrated* reflection piece written by Robert Klemko, *How Reggie White Made Green Bay Cool.* It's worth revisiting and I discovered more of the back story that never was told in a lengthy conversation with Holmgren, other Packers, and league sources.

Cleveland, not known for its sophistication either, heaped lavish gifts on White. Art Modell sent *the wings* to go get him. A limo took Reggie and Sara White straight to the Ritz-Carlton for an $800-per-night suite. Sara was welcomed by roses and a designer leather coat.

Almost *everybody* wanted White. His suitors included the Redskins, Lions, Cardinals, Jets, Falcons and Seahawks. White didn't get to all of them. He was wowed by how generous the Browns were, but Green Bay deserved his full attention. After Modell offered Reggie the key to the city, there were no guarantees anyone other than the Packers would merit a visit.

When White arrived in Wisconsin, he discovered different gestures. The generosity of spirit. Eventually the Packers offered a four-year, $17M contract but the first business agenda was talking football. No fancy gifts or trappings of a material world around every corner. Instead, the Packers served up a vat of palpable humanity.

White observed its authenticity. It wasn't a show. The Packers already had faced their unfavorable reputation years earlier and implemented informal traditions and structured programs to make their players feel comfortable. Wolf and Holmgren possessed a human touch not often regarded as requisite attributes in the violent, Darwinistic world of pro football. It was illuminated for White and brought to life by two dynamic African American Holmgren assistants.

Defensive line coach Greg Blache had been with the Pack since the late '80s. Blache later was Jauron's D-coordinator with the Bears and was an exceptional teacher with a Zen-like calm. Blache regularly visited the local penitentiary to offer free haircuts to Black inmates. Defensive coordinator Ray Rhoades, 42 at the time, was a powerful presence and connected with White immediately. Rhodes and Holmgren already had made a trip to White's 12,000-square foot home in Maryille, Tenn., replete with a gym that could accommodate a JV football team.

His castle excepted, White wasn't a worldly man, and the Packers made no attempt to be who they weren't. They steered right into their one-horse town image.

They took White to Red Lobster.

The welcoming committee, some in jeans, told the best defensive lineman of all time they wanted to talk football and let him go nuts on his favorite food at the best spot in town to get it. The only spoils of the privileged were a make-shift private room and additional kitchen staff the Packers requested in advance. The chain found a chef who could do more with lobster than Buford *Bubba* Blue did with shrimp.

Napkins were covered in magic marker streaks of Xs and Os, arrows, lines and arcs. White dropped his guard, and football was the only topic for nearly two hours. Then the Minister pivoted to questions about commitments to comfortable integration, plans for training facilities and family.

A couple years earlier, Blache the barber took his scissors and clippers to the players who weren't comfortable getting haircuts in town. Wolf noticed and made a phone call to Milwaukee. The GM recruited Black barbers, and the team hired several to make the 240-mile round trip trek. Styling products favored by Black consumers were in short supply at the local barber shops and salons, so the Milwaukee coiffeurs toted products. It might seem like a little thing but there is an ugly piece of history in some southern states that leaked into the '60s — into the lives of NFL players who were born in the '60s or earlier. Some communities passed ordinances preventing Black barbers from taking white customers. White clients were dissuaded from patronizing black establishments.

White spent the first 25 years of his life in Tennessee. If he didn't witness it, it's a certainty an uncle or a teacher told him about it. Wolf, who never was described as a people person, pounced on the opportunity to make black players' *feelings* integral to the team's behavior and actions. It was the GM's idea to start the tradition of providing diversity in cuisine for the team. Soul food from Milwaukee eatery *Bungalow* arrived on Wednesdays and it was a huge hit among Packers of all hues. Players noshed on fried catfish, hush puppies and greens. I was curious how the team presented the gesture to the rank and file, so it wasn't perceived as mocking southern or Black culture, the way Fuzzy Zoeller did several years later after Tiger Woods won the Masters in '97. Holmgren filled in the blanks.

"I had a six-player committee that would take care of getting our messages to and from the team," he said. "It worked. We brought them in to find out what the players' concerns were, and they represented their teammates. We thought it made sense to give them some food options you couldn't get in Green Bay, and they relayed the message."

Packers defensive tackle John Jurkovic ('91-'95), an ESPN radio host in Chicago since '01, suggested the presentation was matter-of-fact and authentic. Nobody batted an eye. "They told our guys 'We're aware this area doesn't offer a huge variety of food' so they asked if we'd like to have some stuff you can't get here brought in once a week. If anybody was thinking it wasn't well intended, they didn't show it," said the self-anointed Good Kid. "We all looked forward to it."

"More fried okra."

"Barbecuuuuuue!

"Cornbread, please."

Bungalow provided fuel to put more soul into the Packers mid-week routine. The bosses welcomed suggestions.

Holmgren saw a more critical need for his young players with little life experience. The often red-faced, red-ass coach was ahead of the NFL in its mid-'90s initiative of the "player programs" position. Preferably manned by a former player, the player programs director was available to offer financial guidance, facilitate counseling for personal or family issues, continuing education, etc. "I designed a program called '*Invest in Yourself*,' " Holmgren said. The Packers coach appointed a small team to meet with players on whatever issues they may need to address, be it how to manage money, problems at home, finding schools and family physicians. "One day I noticed our big tackle Earl Dotson seemed kind of down and I thought he was mad at me. A few days later, Earl was still moping around, so I asked him if I'd done something to upset him."

Dotson was 6-4 and 315. Under his breath, he confessed to Holmgren "coach, I can't read." Big No. 72 became a five-year starter in his third season in '95. Dotson survived Texas A & M-Kingsville despite his learning disability and had to summon all the courage he could to make the admission to Holmgren. Dotson utilized the *Invest in Yourself* initiative and attacked the barrier that haunted him until he was 26. He became more functional, and his self-esteem skyrocketed.

Pro sports franchises, despite the billions of dollars involved, are in the *people* business. The Packers were excelling in this capacity before the league mandated programs. Holmgren was put off by the league's request he scrap his program and warm up to theirs. His committee became more covert.

You may be wondering what the Bears did with the player programs position when the league made it a requirement in the mid-'90s.

One of the first directors was former trainer Brian McCaskey, the son of owners Ed and Virginia McCaskey. One of the owners himself, technically. How naive would a young player have to be to confide in one of the highest-ranking McCaskeys in the house? The sordid details of an alcohol problem or addiction probably wouldn't be a good thing to share with one of the guys whose name appears on the masthead. How can a guy trust that conversation won't come back to bite him?

White signed with the Packers three weeks into free agency's first spring. It tipped the balance of power in the NFC Central in their favor and continued to do so after White shook the bushes for recruits. He was a willing tour guide when players visited Green Bay. The Minister shared what the team and the town regularly practiced to make Black players feel welcomed.

Sean Jones, originally a Raider, was 34 when he signed in '94 and still could rush the passer. Tight end Keith Jackson fled Philadelphia and joined the fray. The '96 Super Bowl 29 champion defense included newcomer Eugene Robinson, an 11-year safety in Seattle, who had six picks. Linebacker George Koontz went undrafted and, after a year in Atlanta, led the Packers in tackles. Santana Dotson bolted Tampa and played the three-technique for the Super Bowl champion Packers.

Santana Dotson became the team's resident expert on the great outdoors for any brothers who desired harvesting walleye or a 100-lb doe from Wisconsin's fertile waters and woods. He inherited the mantle shortly after linebacker Tony Bennett ('90-'93) split for Indianapolis. Dotson, the '92 defensive rookie of the year with Tampa, is now 54 and still spends summers casting big baits for muskies in and around Hayward.

HOME IMPROVEMENTS: LAMBEAU FIELD vs. SOLDIER FIELD

Since I can remember, Lambeau Field has been regarded the crown jewel of football venues. And then they fixed it. Lambeau now seats 81,441 and the joint offers everything. In '99, the Packers announced a $295M renovation project. Turner Construction, regarded as the gold standard in the stadium building biz, was commissioned. It took three years until completion, but the Pack stayed in Green Bay instead of playing home games at Camp Randall in Madison. In '02, the Bears submarined Jauron and his Bears, who played at Illinois in Champaign during the Soldier Field makeover. In essence, 16 road games. The Bears went 4-12.

The new Soldier Field, which opened in '03, actually *lost* seating capacity. At 61,000, the Bears have the smallest stadium in the league. Less than 25 years later, they're vacillating over another lakefront project or committing to the Arlington Heights multi-purpose facility.

Turner kept the traditional "bowl" of intimate bleachers in the lower tank and massive interior modifications brought storied Lambeau into a new stratosphere. Private boxes emerged from their pupae and became luxury suites. A viewing deck to accommodate another 7,500 customers was erected in the south end zone. Private theater boxes arrived. Creature comforts in every direction. In the bowels of the stadium, home and visiting locker rooms were tripled in size. The Packers locker room I walked into in '89 was as stunningly cramped as the visitors' clubhouse at old Wrigley Field and Fenway Park.

As the decade rolled forward, upgrades in Wisconsin's Taj Mahal were done almost annually. High-resolution Mitsubishi jumbotrons loom in both end zones. The field *itself* won an award in '09. Who other than White Sox legendary groundskeeper Roger Bossard knew such honors exist? Bossard, coincidentally, was approached by the Bears and Chicago Park District about chronic sod problems at Soldier Field. On my ESPN 1000 afternoon show in the aughts, the *Sodfather* said the price for his wisdom was too rich for the Bears. As recently as two years ago, the NFLPA came close to postponing a Bears preseason game due to an unsafe playing surface.

A new sound system with enough wattage to reach Manitowoc arrived at Lambeau to sweeten the celebratory sound of Todd Rundgren bangin' on his drum after the Packers score. A 50-foot replica of the Lombardi trophy appeared in '14. Restrooms and concession stands were updated on both sides of the register and became much more user-friendly.

The Atrium, featuring a massive gift shop, the 1919 Kitchen & Bar and the Packers Hall of Fame, makes Lambeau a tourist trap 365 days a year. The team's HOF, which opened down the street in '70, moved inside the new Lambeau. *Is there* a Bears Hall of Fame somewhere? An enormous gift shop was added, and the attractions are available year-round. Tours for small and large groups are available with few blackout dates.

Here's one I can't believe the Bears likely missed. All profits from NFL-logoed merchandise, when sold on the team's property, go straight the team's own war chest. If you buy a Rome Odunze jersey at Dick's Sporting Goods or the like, 31 other teams and the league share the revenue. A McCaskey should have sniffed out that one.

CAMPUS LIFE

In '94, the Packers cut the ribbon on the Don Hutson Center, which features two indoor practices fields. Hutson was 81 and beamed when the Packers unveiled the first modern indoor training edifice in the division. It has two fields, both honoring Green Bay HOFers, The Ray Nitschke and Clark Hinkle fields are 70 and 60 yards long, respectively, with ceilings of 90 and 85 feet. Nitschke is field turf, the same deployed in many stadia. Hinkle is a sand-based natural grass with reinforced fibers, emulating the best natural surfaces in the game.

The Bears were the last team in the division to provide a new administrative building and indoor facilities Some may recall the Waukegan "McBubble," which collapsed in '90 after Michael McCaskey thumbed his nose at fixing its top. The top was 50' high. Not that the Bears ever needed to practice their punt teams. The Bears practiced in forest preserves and on the cement floor of the Great Lakes Naval station in Lake County. The Lake Forest College campus, which the Bears called home until '98, was a terribly dysfunctional building and practice facility for an NFL team.

The Packers have owned parcels of land around Lambeau Field since Vince Lombardi stood at a chalk board, talking about running *this play in the alley.* They've been updating and constructing new buildings on their campus since the '70s. As the Bears conclude '24 navigating another sticky stadium decision, Green Bay is adding a full-service medical building on its own property, a golf cart ride from the locker room. Packers will go there next year for all testing, imaging, physical therapy and orthopedic appointments.

The Bears own 326 acres in Arlington Heights and haven't given the impression they're anywhere close to when the first shovel goes in the ground.

Still think the disparity between the Bears and Packers is just Favre and

Rodgers?

The Bears have been outperformed by Green Bay lock, stock and cheddar block. As much as Chicago fans rolled their eyes when former Bulls GM Jerry Krause proclaimed, "organizations build dynasties," he was right on the money. A dynasty steeped in hiring *people persons* to run it has been a proven winner in a village of 100,000 people in Brown County, Wisc.

CHAPTER 7
Your Mongo
2024 HALL OF FAMER, ENTERTAINER

"Mongo only pawn... in game of life."
– Mongo (Alex Karras) in the 1974 film Blazing Saddles.

A generation of Chicago sports fans already suffered a lifetime of sour finishes to regular season thrill rides. Eric Dickerson, the third-year running back of the Los Angeles Rams, seemed a likely suspect to provide the kryptonite to quash the buzz the 1985 Bears created after they intoxicated the city for four months.

The '85 Bears defense dehumanized opponents. After waltzing through the Giants 21-0 in the divisional round, the Bears felt legitimate as a 10.5-point favorite over the Rams in the NFC Championship game at Soldier Field. Dickerson, however, was red hot. He busted the postseason rushing record the previous week with 248 yards in a 20-0 win over Dallas in Anaheim. The angular speed demon had leapfrogged O.J. Simpson's single-season rushing standard in his second year in '84 when he racked up 2105 yards.

As awe-inspiring as Buddy Ryan's 46 defense performed for two years, pianos could fall from the sky and land squarely on the heads of Bears fans. All because of Dickerson, a football version of Steve Garvey, who gutted the Cubs in the '84 National League championship series. Or Eddie Murray of the '83 World Series champion Orioles, who dumped the White Sox in the ALCS. Dickerson represented the God damned Boogeyman.

Fatalism dissipated quickly.

Steve McMichael, the Bears rough-and-tumble defensive tackle, put his signature on the game on the first series. Starting from their own 17, the Rams gave the ball to Dickerson on an inside run. McMichael, playing on the inside eye of right guard Dennis Harrah, stuffed Harrah at the point of attack, allowing safety Gary Fencik to fill the A gap and take down Dickerson for no gain.

Fencik set up in the A gap, to the left of middle linebacker Mike Singletary in a tweaked-for-Dickerson version of the 46. "Dickerson," Fencik huffed with a grin, almost 40 years later. "We talked about Dickerson all week. We knew that quarterback wasn't going to beat us. What was his name, Deiter something?"

Affirmative. Deiter Brock was a Canadian Football League castoff. He was 34 and concluding his first and only NFL season. Brock tucked the ball into Dickerson's belly again on second-and-10. Right tackle Jackie Slater provided an effective seal on defensive end Dan Hampton, but Dickerson was driven down by cornerback Mike Richardson with a solid one-on-one tackle after a six-yard gain. On third-and-four, it was more of No. 29. McMichael again whipped Harrah, shedding the block and roping down Dickerson with a wild left arm that wrapped up the 6-3, 220 lb. Dickerson at the shoulder pads, driving him to the Soldier Field astroturf for a one-yard loss.

Three and out. Trot out the punter. As he got up from the tackle, McMichael, then in his sixth NFL season, used Dickerson's chest for leverage to propel himself. *Fuck you.*

McMichael jogged off the field in a tippy-toed prance. He fancied himself as a swan sometimes, but he was a rhino first and foremost. Greeted first by the Fridge, overnight sensation William Perry, McMichael smacked Perry's hand and wrist in an errant high five by both. That might have been the only target the Bears didn't hit inside the bullseye all day.

Dickerson finished with 17 carries for 46 yards. His longest run was nine yards. John Robinson's offense muscled out nine first downs and only 130 yards of total offense. In the fourth quarter, Wilber Marshall capped the scoring with a 52-yard fumble return under falling snow. The Bears posted their second straight playoff shutout and dismissed the overmatched Rams, 24-0. The Bears were going to New Orleans for Super Bowl XX.

THE FOOTBALL PLAYER

McMichael's self-assuredness wasn't delusional. He was more than a badass with brute strength and a nasty disposition. His teammates loved to tease him for hiking up his pants too high, but they also appreciated how athletic McMichael was. As a teenager, the 100% Texan was a skilled baseball player. He was a catcher and hit .450 in his senior year of high school. A few pro teams gave him a look. McMichael was born in Houston and grew up in Freer, population 2390 in the '22 census. Laredo is only an hour drive if one yearns for a ZZ Top tribute band.

Recruited by everyone who mattered nationally, McMichael stayed loyal to the Lone Star State and took a scholarship at Texas. He was a two-time Southwest Conference first-team selection and consensus All American his senior year. He also was the Longhorn's back up kicker. When eventual first-rounder Russell Erxleben missed the A & M game, McMichael subbed. He went five-for-six on PATs and also booted a 48-yard field goal as No. 1-ranked Texas shelled the 12th-ranked Aggies 57-28.

McMichael looked good with his jersey tucked in during the first half of a 15-year Hall of Fame career. He was massive through the neck, shoulders, chest and arms, but also narrowed at the waist. A weight room monster, McMichael was thick in the thighs and powerful through the trunk. He was agile and had good bend through the waist. Additionally, he was as fundamentally sound as any Bear defender. McMichael maintained a good base and gained leverage with his powerful lower body. He had fast hands to go with power and his combination of assets made it difficult for blockers to turn his shoulders. McMichael was disciplined, engaged his man with the inside arm while keeping his play-side arm free. As a pass rusher, he was relentless and finished with 95 career sacks.

McMichael's ascent to stardom wasn't immediate, however. It took several years for him to find his way. New England drafted him in the third round, 75th overall, in '80 but McMichael didn't earn a start his rookie season. The Patriots released him before the next training camp and Bears general manager Jim Finks scooped up the reckless refuse. McMichael's first two years in Chicago, however, were uneventful. Unless he put 400 lbs. on the bar to warm up on his bench press routine. Or when the repo man put the hooks under his Cadillac and towed it from the parking lot at the old

Halas Hall.

Ryan finally trusted him in '83, McMichael's fourth year. He started 10 games and chipped in with 8.5 sacks.

"It took a little while for him to gain traction with Buddy," Hampton told me on Feb. 8, the day his former teammate and friend was voted to the Hall by the seniors committee. "He always had been such a great athlete, the devastating power and quickness, playing with good technique. All the things you want in a defensive lineman. He had such a zest to play the game. We were violent and we knew the more violent we were on the line of scrimmage, at the point of attack, the better our defense could be. And would be. He would relish that."

Ron Rivera, a linebacker and special teams ace drafted in '84, remains a McMichael disciple.

"He epitomized what it meant to be a Chicago Bear," Rivera said last fall, his fourth and final year as Washington Commanders head coach. "His impact on me was enormous. One of the things you had to prove to him was that you'll fight, that you're tough and worthy of being a teammate. There was a lot of 'proving' and once you realize that and start proving your worth, now you've become one of his guys. That really helped me early in my career in Chicago.

"He knew his way onto the football field was through the weight room. And through the classroom. He was a smart player. He saw shit some of the average players didn't see. He knew how to anticipate. He knew how to set people up. He did it to win. Steve was a very unselfish player. As a defensive tackle, you're going to get double teamed. You're going to get rolled and you're going to get trucked. But you do it because it's your job and as he would say 'let all you guys come in to sop up the gravy.' "

The '91 season was the last spark for the Bears under Mike Ditka. They went 11-5 and finished second in the Central, earning a home game in the Wild Card round, an eventual 17-13 loss to Dallas. In a Week 4 date against Bruce Coslet's New York Jets on *Monday Night Football*, McMichael willed the Bears to a 19-13 overtime win. It's best remembered as *The Cap Boso Turf Helmet* game. The win kept the Bears clean at 4-0 but it blurred the real picture of an aging team still searching for a quarterback, a team reduced to eking out wins. They opened the season with a 10-6 win over the Vikings before narrowly escaping the Buccaneers at the Big Sombrero, 21-20. The defending champion Giants came up just short, 20-17, in Week 3.

Leading 13-6 late in the fourth, the Jets needed a first down to salt away the win. New York's offensive line had its way all night with Blair Thomas carrying 27 times for 125 yards. Following the two-minute warning, McMichael viciously ripped the ball away from Thomas, then fell on the football at the Jets' 36. Soldier Field exploded, but more misadventure from a scuffling Bears offense ensued. Jim Harbaugh was sacked on first down, then eluded the dagger when James Hasty couldn't handle what should have been a game-clinching interception. The Bears survived a bumbling start to the drive, however, and Harbaugh hit Neal Anderson for a 5-yard touchdown pass to tie the game 13-13 and force overtime.

Late in overtime, it appeared the Bears had won it when Harbaugh, rolling to his right, rifled a strike to Boso, the tight end. The former Illinois star caught the ball at the 5, cradled it and plowed toward the goal line in the south end zone. Boso was wrestled down near the goal line and two officials raised both arms in the air. When Boso exploded to his feet, a huge hunk of grass came with him, covering almost half of his facemask at the eyes and a portion of his helmet. Officials huddled to discuss whether Boso had broken the plane. The party was underway in Chicago. The improbable outcome kept the Bears unbeaten.

On the field, ABC7's Tim Wiegel quickly roped Harbaugh into a live interview. Bears disappeared into the tunnel and into the locker room on the north end.

Hold the phone. The referee announced the call had been reversed. Harbaugh was ripped away from the interview and at least a dozen Bears had to be retrieved from the locker room. Al Michaels confidently and correctly predicted a Harbaugh sneak. Harbaugh scored and the Bears won, 19-13. Give the game ball to the 11-year veteran defensive tackle who flipped the outcome. This was *a Steve McMichael game*.

After the '92 season, Ditka's last on the heels of a 5-11 finish, McMichael played his 13th and final Bears season under Dave Wannstedt. The Bears went 7-9 in '93 before McMichael did the unthinkable. He took his act up to Green Bay to join forces with the evil enemy. The '94 season was his least productive year since he became a starter in '83. In a limited role, McMichael had 2.5 sacks with the Packers and called it a career after 15 seasons.

McMichael kept Bears fans in his pocket with a clever retort to any objectors to his treasonous act. "For 13 years, I helped the Bears beat the Packers every year," he twanged with a growl. "I whooped their ass, right? So, the last year, I went up there to play on my last leg and I wasn't any good anymore. So, I stole their money and whipped their ass again."

In his 13 seasons in a Bears uniform, McMichael made 157 starts and appeared in 191 consecutive games, still a team record. McMichael and Olin Kreutz are second only to 16-year long snapper Patrick Mannelly (245) for career games played for the Bears. McMichael produced. He had three seasons with double-digit sacks. He forced 13 fumbles and recovered 17. He didn't miss games. Or practices. He was one of the most imposing sons of a bitches I ever looked in the eye.

THE ENTERTAINER

The handle *Mongo*, as far as Bears nicknames born of movie characters goes, has only one rival. Jim McMahon dubbed Ditka *Sybil*, the title character played by Sally Field in a made-for-TV '76 psycho thriller. She was imprisoned by an unpredictable multi-personality disorder that led to her plight. Most of us didn't know it, and I suspect Jimmy Mac didn't, but Sybil's bad wiring was the result of sexual abuse.

I needed a refresher on *Blazing Saddles*, so I gave it a spin the off week before Super Bowl 58. The moniker's accuracy was affirmed in the first scene we meet the colorfully repugnant Mongo, portrayed playfully by former Lions defensive tackle Alex Karras. McMichael and Karras had an uncanny physical resemblance. Sporting a leather vest and misshapen Cowboy hat, Mongo spoke like he carved figures on the walls of caves. He referred to himself in the third person. Cowboys sat around a campfire and farted. Mongo punched out a horse.

That branding of Mongo McMichael loaned the pure Texan a smooth and most unobstructed entrance ramp into Bear Nation's glowing hearts. McMichael steered right into it and never looked back.

He was the resident vulgarian. In a locker room full of characters, McMichael was the most colorful. He swore incessantly and said a lot of offensive things. He was football's version of Andrew Dice Clay. He didn't care to be everybody's flavor. For those who wanted regular Mongo fixes, he was available and accessible.

Though McMichael put on the tough guy veneer for public appearances and interviews, often dismissing questions or demonstrating quiet disgust, he cherished participating in radio and television. In the pre-internet world, there were opportunities for local jockos who took to the camera like moths to a flame. The network affiliates invested resources and competed hard in the half-hour Sunday sports wrap-ups that followed the 10:00 news. All three — CBS2, NBC5 and ABC7 — swung hard for the biggest names in McCaskeyville. All posted big ratings in an era when ratings were valuable. Especially during football season. McMichael coveted a piece of the pie, and it was fortuitous Mark Giangreco at Ch. 5 got his hooks in the big fish in '90 after Dave Duerson signed with the New York Giants to create an opening.

The already-venerable Johnny Morris (you may be as fatigued by that name as you are Sid Luckman's before we're done here) was the perfect softball lob tosser for Ditka. Win or lose, Ditka typically was several glasses of Californian grape into postgame decompression mode. A Monday *Sun-Times* cover in '87 was a photo of Ditka from the previous evening's show. The image of a slumped over, eyes-half-closed Ditka said "good morning" to Chicagoans who saw the paper. Nick Nolte's mug shot was envious.

Ditka occasionally bullied his ex-teammate, and the mild-mannered Morris sometimes fumbled on the return volley. Johnny cowered occasionally. There also were some rare gold Morris moments when he'd push enough to get Ditka talking out of both sides of his mouth, shifting from an opinion of a week ago — an hour ago — and Johnny burrowed under Ditka's skin. Mike's gifts included an effective delivery system for abusive, dismissive responses. He knew how to make people feel small and knew it was an effective weapon. A patient, observant host, however, could manipulate Ditka and make him look the fool occasionally.

These were fun times in Bears history and for local media, too. It mattered more. It connected with Chicago and was a part of the city's consciousness. Today, most people couldn't tell you where to find Ch. 2 on the dial.

ABC7 hired Walter Payton to join Weigel. It was a comfortable pairing. Ditka had nothing on Walter in the Sybil department, but Payton's erratic behaviors didn't emerge prominently until after his career. In Lake Forest, most knew. And most loved him unconditionally. Walter's angelic voice was seductive enough to render his content irrelevant. On a rare off night, however, viewers wished Payton would drink some coffee.

How can any self-respecting Bears fan not try to catch at least a little of Payton or Ditka. Or McMahon when he contributed. There was no TiVo to bail you out if you couldn't peel yourself away from Ditka's big orange face or the vile Mongo once he got on the set with Giangreco. *Sports Sunday* on Ch. 5 was all some of us needed after Payton retired in '87. The Ditka cartoon had been overplayed since the '89 team unraveled. The timing was perfect for McMichael and Giangreco to produce gold.

Ratings tipped in NBC5's favor. Mongo usually brought props and an entourage to the studio. He referred to his first wife, Debra, and her friends as "the Kotex mafia." He covered Giangreco with shaving cream. Or lipstick. McMichael occasionally brought *Pepe*, his chihuahua.

"*If I didn't bring him, he'd just lie around and lick on hisself,*" he offered after a tough loss. Mongo referred to his loyalists as *Mongoloids*.

"He was one of the smartest guys I worked with," Giangreco said. "He was hammered almost every week, but he also had great ideas for content and put a lot of thought into what we were going to do. His mom came to the shows regularly. She was as foul-mouthed as he was and smoked Marlboros. Every year she had a different guy with her. We had so much fun on that show. And we out-rated the other shows. We got cocky about it. Once night, I think in '91, we were watching Ditka on a monitor, commenting on the air about how boozed up he looked."

Unsurprisingly, McMichael's crass, tough-guy persona faced

resistance. *Sun-Times* media critic Barry Cronin wrote "He's one of the least evolved members of the human species."

McMichael's penchant for the stage, coupled with his massive physique and larger-than-life presence, landed him on the professional wrestling circuit. He earned a second moniker —*Ming,* from *Ming the Merciless* of *Flash Gordon* fame. In the ring and as an announcer, Ming was a hit with WWF fans, as Mongo was with NFL enthusiasts.

In a different time, NFL alumni augmented their incomes in professional wrestling. McMichael was no stranger to the ring. He dipped his toes in that water as a player. Now, as a former player, he still had an appetite for performing. Ming dug in with the wildly popular World Wrestling Federation. Hulk Hogan was a household name in the '80s and beyond and the WWF was perfect for McMichael. He still possessed the physique to go shirtless without the audience covering their eyes. Contemporaries Reggie White, Lawrence Taylor and Kevin Greene were among the biggest stars who participated in the WWF.

McMichael wore many hats, serving not only in the ring, but as a briefcase-wielding manager and as a commentator. *WrestleMania XI* in '95 was a big thing. There was the raucous *Clash of Champions* XXXV. And who can forget *Slamboree.* Professional wrestling, once I discovered girls, disappeared from my entertainment play list. Ming didn't need my approval. It agreed with him, as it did with teammate Jimbo Covert, the left tackle who once KO'd McMichael with a wicked hook in an often-times unpredictable Bears practice.

Ming immediately dove into his second act. Opposite promoter Vince McMahon, he provided boisterous and animated commentary for '90s bouts and was a regular on *Monday Nitro.* Wife Debra also was a part of the wrestling community and *Chicago Magazine's* cover story on Chicago's power couple of the mid-'80s depicted McMichael as almost dashingly handsome. Almost. Debra was attractive, athletic and enhanced.

In the world of professional wrestling, sometimes it's difficult to determine what's real and what's scripted. There were in-the-ring bits where Ric Flair hit on Debra, to the chagrin of her jealous husband. In one bit, a wrestler stole McMichael's Super Bowl ring. So, Steve clobbered him over the head with a pipe. Art, they say, imitates life. Apparently true even in art's lowest forms. Debra, one could conclude, liked wrestlers more than ex-football players trying to become wrestlers. In '98, she filed for divorce and subsequently married *Stone Cold* Steve Austin. They divorced in '03.

Steve McMichael left *Monday Nitro* and continued to reinvent himself, taking a gig as a contributor at Chicago's ESPN 1000. He met Misty and they got married in '01. McMichael found himself again. He laughed again. And made others laugh harder.

The truth was Steve could be a jealous dude. He *did* fume over eyes that wandered over Debra's body. In the late-'80s, McMichael pulled out a switchblade and threatened Garry Meier, co-host of the popular *Steve & Garry* show on the AM Loop. It wasn't a bit. The Loop was a comfortable hangout for several '80s Bears, none more than guard Tom Thayer, a *Steve & Garry* regular. Thayer and buddy Mike Tomczak, the boyishly handsome backup quarterback, asked McMichael to tag along one night after an appearance on the air in the Loop's John Hancock building studios. Meier reflected on his harrowing encounter with McMichael, which shook out at the Limelight Club on Ontario.

"He grabbed me by my shirt collar and then started choking me," Meier said. "He'd pulled out the switchblade and set it on the table, but with one hand around my throat he shouted, 'stop fucking staring at my wife.' I'd been trying to laugh it off, thinking he was joking, but after about 15 seconds of not being able to breathe, I was pretty convinced he was serious."

Meier had another scary experience with McMichael a year or two later at a charity event. This time it was a gun brandished by the defensive lineman. "He pulled out a Derringer and said, 'this is for you if you want to stare all night.' He waved that wand at me. What was I gonna do?"

Along with Hampton and Otis Wilson, Mongo regularly sang for *The Chicago Six*, three Bears and professional rock and rollers. Ironic it is that one of his favorites to belt out was Lynryd Skynyrd's *Gimme Three Steps*, a song about a jealous husband who threatens a man with wandering eyes.

I didn't get to know McMichael well until '01 when we broadcast under the same flag at ESPN 1000. Just before that bond was forged, Mongo thrust himself into public consciousness when he was invited to be guest conductor for the *7th Inning Stretch* at Wrigley Field. The Cubs were hosting Colorado August 7 when McMichael's prelude to *Take Me Out to the Ballgame* garnered headlines.

The Cubs were on the losing end of a close call at the plate that snuffed a rally in the 6th inning. Ron Coomer was tagged out and the crowd disapproved with full-throated opposition to Angel Hernandez's call at home. Three outs later, McMichael seized the opportunity to stoke the flames when he grabbed the microphone. He promised to "have speaks" with the umpire after the game.

Hernandez wasn't having it and demonstratively began pointing at the broadcast booth where McMichael stood. He unleashed the *ejection mechanic*. Hernandez was shouting and pointing at McMichael and the Wrigley faithful were reignited. It was compelling television, culminating in a shot of McMichael being escorted by security down the ramps and out of the ballpark.

Many athletes and entertainers had produced off-the-charts "fun bad" versions of *The Stretch*. Drunk hockey players were always a crowd pleaser, be it Denis Savard or the fellow HOFer for whom he once was traded, Chris Chelios. NASCAR star Jeff Gordon elicited a cascade of boos when he said, *"Wrigley Stadium."* Ditka, drunkenly or because he had to take a leak, raced through the song in record time.

Only Steve McMichael got ejected from the park. That's the guy so many Bears fans loved. That's your Mongo.

CHAPTER 8

My Mongo
VULGARIAN FRAT BROTHER AT 40

"Oh, don't worry. Just keep your hands and feet away from his mouth." — Otter (Tim Matheson) in the 1978 film Animal House.

Platteville sits softly in Southwest Wisconsin's "driftless area" and is characterized by rolling hills, working farms and a welcoming spirit from its 12,000 occupants. Between 1984 and 2001, the Bears called Platteville their summer home. The University of Wisconsin-Platteville boasted one of the nation's most accomplished D-3 men's basketball programs in the '90s and its facilities were on par with some larger schools. UWP was extremely functional for an NFL training camp and the Bears nestled in Platteville's bosom every August. The McCaskeys stretched their legs unapologetically and paid no mind to criticism for giving tourism dollars of Illinoisans to evil Wisconsin, home of the hated Packers.

The Timbers was unequivocally the best restaurant in Platteville. Patrons realize that immediately when they're greeted by a sign in the foyer: *"No Bare Feet."* You *know* it's going to be good. The supper club even had leather-back menus. Maybe it was pleather. The fact was you could get a cold beer or a Manhattan and expect a decent steak and baked potato.

During the '89 camp, kicker Kevin Butler pulled up a chair at Timbers, accompanied by shooting star talk radio personality Kevin Matthews. Butthead was a regular contributor on Matthews' midday program on the AM Loop, the city's most popular radio station and my employer. Also seated at the loudest table were punter Maury Buford, Loop boss Larry Wert and a 28-year-old producer/weekend host called *Dangerous Dan*.

After two hours of merriment, Butler returned from the payphone with news that Steve McMichael just arrived in town and wanted company. McMichael reported to camp late after a two-week holdout, which became a tradition late in his career. Veteran teammates teased him for ducking Mike

Ditka's *fit to hit* training camps. McMichael wasn't lazy. He had nothing to prove. He never missed games. Or practices. And on a defense loaded with All Pros, Mongo consistently graded among the top three defenders by Bears coaches.

Arriving tardy was McMichael's way of flipping his middle finger at ownership and management for underpaying the boys in blue. Mongo and Jim McMahon were the most vocal critics of McCaskeyian accounting. It was part of the reason McMahon was discarded that summer when Ditka and Mike McCaskey collaborated on trading their oft-injured quarterback to the Chargers.

McMichael had an enormous thirst for the stage, always eager to put his colorful candor and foul mouth on display. Unfiltered and unhampered by sentiments of a civilized society.

Wert squared up with the server and Butler suggested we gift the remaining hunk of Chateaubriand to McMichael, who was with his wife, Debra, relaxing with a beer at a pizza joint. A welcome back gesture for the 10-year defensive tackle. Like her husband, Debra was a southerner. Butthead had the server wrap the leftover beef in a fancy aluminum foil swan.

When we arrived at Pizzeria Uno, Butler led the welcoming committee into an almost empty basement dining room, then presented the swan to Mongo. McMichael didn't speak. He clocked the room, made brief eye contract with each of us, then gazed vacantly at the foil swan. A minute or two passed awkwardly.

What's gonna happen next, we all were guessing privately. The massive Texan mulled his next act of *Blutarskyism*. He knew he the room. Then came Mongo time. He clutched the foil swan by the neck, then viciously pounded it on the table five or six times until nothing was left in his hand but the swan's head. Chunks of Chateaubriand and shreds of foil were strewn in every direction and on all who stood around or sat at the table. Debra McMichael took animal flesh shrapnel.

"*I got meat on ma faaace!*" she shrieked in an Alabama drawl.

How could I do anything but pull up a chair and take notes on a man who I thought was capable of pretty much anything. Who knows where this may go. I didn't know McMichael yet and this seemed as good an opportunity as any. Butler was the only one victimized by a Mongo hazing that night. Outside the restaurant, McMichael stuffed the kicker into thick hedges. He wouldn't let Butler escape. Every time Butthead navigated his way through the shrubs, McMichael rejected him and stuffed him back in the bushes. Butler pleaded for his freedom, but McMichael wouldn't grant it. He continued to jam Butler back into the hedges until Debra cried "uncle" on behalf of the defenseless Georgian.

I saw Butler the next afternoon in the cafeteria and asked how he made out. "Coulda been worse," he said. He set down his tray, extended both arms in front of him and rotated them to divulge the battle scars. I sympathized, saying something like "that's the price of running with McMichael, I suppose." Butthead warned me I could be next. "You never know when it's your turn to be his ragdoll. Watch your back."

The truth is, until that training camp, I did my best to avoid McMichael. As much as I admired his talent and got a kick out of him, he scared the hell out of me. My job as the executive producer of Chet Coppock's nightly talk show was to secure guests. The roster was loaded with gregarious personalities, even after Walter Payton retirement in '87 and McMahon's exiled to San Diego. McMichael had graduated from supporting player to star by the late-'80s and he was drawn to microphones and cameras. Coppock also was a professional wrestling advocate and was the ring announcer for WWF events at the Rosemont Horizon. Chet was a McMichael fan and was thrilled when I booked McMichael for a phone interview shortly before the '89 training camp opened.

McMichael dropped a few "Jesus Christs," and one "God damn it." He referred to himself as a "sarcastic son of a bitch" in the 15-minute appearance. For Mongo, it was tame. He didn't say anything that could have put the Loop in harm's way with the FCC or offend sponsors. Program director Greg Solk, however, was not a McMichael guy and instructed me to never schedule the vulgarian for Coppock's show again. The Loop was a push-the-envelope talk outlet, too, but Solk felt McMichael's lowest common denominator appeal missed the mark. To a large degree, I was relieved by the edict. It meant I didn't have to look McMichael in the eye at Halas Hall.

A month or so after Mongo beat the meat in Platteville, however, I was back in the McMichael business. As the Dangerous Dan brand was growing a little, the producers of a football show on WGBO, Ch. 66 asked me to host a one-hour, weekly TV program called *The Bear Report*. It was a low-budget, low-viewership show recorded Tuesday nights at Reilly's Daughter, 111th and Pulaski, in Oak Lawn. *TBR* aired Friday nights at 11:00. When I gleefully accepted the gig for $300 a pop, they told me we had an excellent lead-in with the *Barney Miller* Show. One of my first guests was McMichael.

Terrific. McMichael's going to kill me.

The loutish defensive tackle didn't disappoint the pull-my-finger crowd. In his opening remarks, McMichael unleashed a "bullshit" and a "god damn it." The profanity flushed the technical director out of the production truck and right onto the set. The TD waved his arms and shook his head disgustedly. "No! No! No! No! You can't *do that*. You can't use *that language*. Start it over."

So, we did. This time, Mongo interrupted me as I opened the show. McMichael did the sign of the cross and blurted "Hang on! Hang on! We want to begin this program with the *Lord's Prayer* for all you good people out there." I was a bit on edge from start to finish but I had to admit feeling exhilarated by the uncertainty of where my guest may take it. There was the suspicion of taking the same type of hazing Butler just experienced in camp, but I felt comfortable out on the ledge as a host.

McMichael gave us a good show. He dropped several angry "Jesus Christs" and proclaimed all opinions on how the Bears do business as meaningless. "It don't matter what I think. What I think is like a flea on a elephant's ass. It doesn't mean anything." But he was happy to share anyway because "the McCaskeys pay me for shit."

I didn't really get to know Steve until after his playing career. I never had a taste for pro wrestling and our paths never crossed on the appearance circuit. That changed in '01 after ESPN 1000 hired me to host afternoon drive, initially between 3 and 6. I inherited McMichael as a football contributor.

Mongo was a bit of a station mascot and made appearances with the *Miller Lite Girls* in Chicagoland establishments. A month before the season opened, McMichael was embroiled in what many termed a "classic Chicago moment." Mongo got booted from Wrigley Field for harassing umpire Angel Hernandez before leading *Take Me Out to the Ballgame*.

When McMichael joined the *Mac, Jurko & Harry* show the first time, I played up the incident, then only a month old. "So, Mongo, it's my understanding every Friday, it's going to be our pleasure to *have speaks* with you about the Bears." On August 6, McMichael said he was going to "have speaks with that umpire." Mongo ate it up. McMichael clung fiercely to his bad boy image and seized any chance he got to make "news."

I had reservations about Mongo being billed as the show's football expert. I didn't envision him putting in the homework, studying the upcoming opponents and the league. I pushed back on the meatball cry of "fire and passion" before we logged some flight miles together and I realized what I had. Mongo was ours every Friday afternoon at 5, the sweet spot of rush hour traffic. I was mindful our first football season potentially could be stained by the inaccurate perception of frat-house chuckleheads. When program director Mitch Rosen told me McMichael preferred coming to the studio instead of doing his weekly hit on the phone, it opened more possibilities. Typically, in-studio visits produce much more connective tissue.

McMichael quickly made a comfortable fit with *MJH* and we became fast friends. Mongo and I shared a fondness for the '79 satire *North Dallas Forty*, a vividly accurate depiction of NFL politics, substance abuse and tomfoolery. I asked McMichael who his favorite characters were in *NDF*. He didn't need long. "*Joe Bob's Fine Foods.... eat here or I'll kill ya.*"

He was impersonating Nick Nolte, who played receiver Phil Elliot. Team funnyman Elliot was mocking teammate *Joe Bob Purdy*, the neanderthal North Dallas offensive lineman played by Bo Svenson. Knowing the movie as well as I do, it became a regular game between us. His face always lit up when he recognized where I was going.

"*Can I show your titties to my buddy, O.W.? Can I please?*" O.W. was played by John Matuszak, the former Raiders wild man who died young.

"It always did take two of you... to hold back one of me."

"Why is he always pickin' on me, Seth?"

A month after 9/11, ESPN 1000 moved from the Hancock Building to the ABC building at 190 N. State. Following a *Mongo Happy Hour* show on a Friday in mid-October, McMichael hung around and helped us say goodbye to the *MJH* show office on the 15th floor. Co-host Harry Teinowitz, producer Adam Delevitt and I thought it was a good idea to enlist Mongo's help emptying a handle of Crown Royal. We also emptied two dugouts. For about three hours, McMichael, Del and I lined up intoxicants one after another. All three of us managed to make it home without incident. By the grace of God goes I.

Where McMichael really shined was at events. He knew how to read people and give them exactly the Mongo they coveted. Accompanied by his wife, Misty, McMichael participated in all the annual *MJH* golf outings for autism. Every time, listeners who paid $200 to play a round with a celebrity captain reported the same about McMichael. He was an excellent ambassador for the station and the show. Mongo made people laugh. He was animated and shared great behind-the-scenes stories about the glory years of the '80s. Mongo loved Mike Ditka, but the coach regularly was a punchline when McMichael held court. He also knew there were some Bears fans who quarreled with his decision to conclude his career with Green Bay and quickly dispensed his almost-famous quote about stealing from the Packers after kicking their asses for 13 years. Steve could entertain pretty much any class of people, but he gravitated to the ham and eggers.

Often willing to explore new challenges, McMichael threw his hat in the coaching ring when he took a job as head coach of the Chicago Slaughter of the Continental Indoor Football League. If you blinked, you missed it. The CIFL was operational only for a few years. The Slaughter played home games in the underrated Sears Centre in Hoffman Estates (currently Now Arena). Under McMichael's stewardship, the Slaughter were CIFL champs in '09. If you close your eyes and concentrate, I bet you can imagine Mongo boasting about his team's 58-48 win over the Ft. Wayne Freedom in the title game.

Or his .630 regular-season winning percentage. McMichael took pride in everything he tackled.

On a Friday night in January of '09, ESPN 1000 fired me. McMichael was among my first station mates who called the next day to wish me luck and suggest staying in touch. Mongo remained an ESPN 1000 personality until his health began to betray him before the '20 season. McMichael had been doing pregame or postgame shows and continued to be an asset for on-premises promotions. "He was always there early, reading the paper and getting prepared," recalls co-host Fred Huebner. "Mongo always was very generous. He always brought in Dunkin Donuts for the crew, and he'd stop by the restaurant (Mongo's in Romeoville) and bring in a big spread for the 3:00 games or night games."

In the summer of '19, a year after I'd gone back to the Score for a third run, I did an appearance with McMichael and Dan Hampton. The three of us judged a barbequed ribs contest in Griffith, Ind. When I arrived at the park, McMichael already was talking loudly, laughing and engaged by admiring fans. *Mongoloids*, in *Mongese*. Hampton was running behind, stuck in eastbound traffic on I-80. "Let's go for a walk," I said to McMichael. "Let's work up an appetite." We retreated to my truck for some Bob Marley time.

An hour or so later, and I have no idea how the topic was launched, I stepped in on a conversation McMichael was having with a chubby guy in a Walter Payton jersey. They were talking about a specific act of foreplay most men say they enjoy. Not Mongo.

"Guys say they love it, but they don't," McMichael boisterously contended. I quickly checked the area around us to make sure we weren't in mixed company. The coast was clear.

"Really?" I asked McMichael. "You gonna tell me that isn't the most precious flower on the planet? C'mon Mongo. *You*?"

"Dangerous, we all tell ourselves that, but you know god damn well that thing is nasty."

I asked Misty McMichael in July if my timing was poor to share the story. "Ha!" as she flapped the "wave-off" mechanic. "He is who is as and never apologized for it. Go for it."

There you have it. That's *my* Mongo. He wasn't everybody's flavor, but he was mine.

CHAPTER 9
1985
YOU NEVER FORGET YOUR FIRST

Mike Ditka circled the Week 6 date in San Francisco as soon as the NFL released the 1985 schedule. This wasn't going to a business trip for Ditka. It was payback. And Ditka wanted the head of Bill Walsh on a spike. The ringleader of the defending Super Bowl-winning 49ers had added insult to injury. Twice.

During San Francisco's 23-0 body slam of the Bears in the NFC Championship game the previous January, Walsh deployed guard Guy McIntrye, 6-3 and 275, as the "angus back" when the 49ers were running out the clock. It offended Ditka's football sensibilities on its own but Walsh threw down the gauntlet when he bloviated about his '84 team a few days before the Bears arrived in the Bay area.

"It wasn't a matter of them not having this guy or that guy in that game," Walsh decreed. "We were a great football team. Better than they were."

He wasn't wrong. It's unlikely Jim McMahon could have tipped the balance in Chicago's favor any more than his understudy Steve Fuller did in the 49ers' dominant win. San Francisco was a convincing champion, ultimately stoning Dan Marino's Dolphins 38-16 in the Super Bowl following Marino's record-setting second season with Miami. The 49ers head coach dripped with arrogance, and it didn't sit well with Ditka, then a fourth-year head coach.

Don't poke the big Bear.

The Bears stomped San Francisco 26-10 and remained unbeaten, 6-0. Walter Payton carried 24 times for 132 yards and two touchdowns, and the

Bears hogged the ball for 37 minutes. Joe Montana's offense mustered only 45 yards in the second half. The 49ers committed 13 penalties and couldn't protect Montana, who was sacked seven times. Ditka put his signature on the slaughter at its conclusion when he inserted William Perry, the rookie shooting-star pitchman and puffy defensive tackle, as a short-yardage fullback. Perry lined up in the backfield for the first time when the Bears were salting away the victory in the final 90 seconds. It was uneventful — two rushes for two yards — but Ditka successfully communicated *"take that"* to Walsh.

The coach remained the top story Monday morning. Ditka was arrested for DUI on his commute home to Grayslake once the boys got back in town. It was a surprise to no one, like Ditka's refusal to take a ride from a 23-year-old public relations director or an assistant coach. Persuading Ditka to do something he didn't want to do was a fool's activity.

Don Rubin, the team attorney, represented Ditka, who had refused a breathalyzer when he was pulled over on the northbound tri-state near Dempster. It was 12:14 a.m. when he was processed at the Touhy toll plaza for driving under the influence, speeding and improper lane usage. According to Rubin, Ditka didn't want a trial because he didn't want anybody on the charter to testify. Now, 39 years later, witnesses are talking.

"I had a window seat," recalled safety Gary Fencik. "Mike must have made some friends out there. The short conveyor belt that goes up to the loading area underneath kept rolling up case after case of wine. Anybody who saw it assumed it was Mike's."

Ditka and wife, Diana, always sat in the last row on team flights. More leg room, more stretch space for arthritic hips, knees and shoulders of the 46-year-old Ditka. He usually had a television, but this particular commute rendered game tapes or reruns of *Mannix* non-essential. Ditka's focus was on the nectar in the overhead bin.

"I don't think it was the same wine they usually stocked," said Bryan Harlan, the Bears former publicist. Harlan always sat in the row in front of Mike and Diana, usually with special teams coach Steve Kazor. "I think there were some bottles above. The charters always had two cold Budweisers at each seat for every guy, but Mike drank wine. I think there was more than usual that trip back."

Before the Bears left Candlestick Park, Ditka recorded an interview with CBS-2's Jeannie Morris and forecast the mid-air party that was about to commence. "I hope I remember the plane ride home," he said. It was decompression time for the fiery, lightning-rod helmsman of the undefeated and surging Chicago Bears.

Ditka refused a lift from Harlan and two assistants at O'Hare. There were any number of *drunk Ditkas* — the happy and welcoming DD or the angry and confrontational DD — but that also was true of *sober Ditka*. As McMahon said — *Sybil*. After the news broke, Ditka addressed his arrest at his Monday morning news conference. He called the incident "disappointing and unfortunate." He also said, "I have no animosity toward anyone." That's noble of him.

The arresting trooper termed Ditka "polite and courteous, very gentlemanly." Word spread fast and the state police tollway district office was peppered with calls from angry Ditkaphiles. "We've been called everything in the book you can think of," one trooper told the *Sun-Times*. "Mike Ditka is the best thing that's ever happened to Chicago," protested another livid fan. Then-secretary of state Jim Edgar was even apologetic in tone regarding Ditka's arrest and the subsequent complaint calls about it. "It's just not right to heap abuse on the police. I watched the game just like every loyal Bear fan did. Mike Ditka has done a great job as coach."

In Lake Forest, Payton and Steve McMichael flanked Ditka for support when he "faced the music." Said McMichael, "Let he who hasn't sinned cast the first stone."

How's your ride in the DeLorean going? It is '85, after all, the year *Back to the Future* was the No. 1 movie in America.

In fairness, it's important to note to Generation X and younger readers the cavalier responses from Ditka and McMichael were reflective of prevailing attitudes at the time. Views on vehicular recklessness and alcohol-related offenses hadn't shifted to reduced tolerance yet. Locally or nationally. Illinois didn't mandate seat belt safety until '85. Mothers Against Drunk

Driving (MADD) was founded in California in '80 but its migration east was much slower than that of cocaine. Illinois didn't raise the drinking age to 21 until '80 and Wisconsin didn't move to 21 until '86. Open container laws weren't even a focus of anti-drinking lobbyists and remained debated and inconsistent state-to-state.

Guys close in age to the '85 Bears recall their high school days thusly: there was always a squeaky Styrofoam cooler in the back seat of a gas-guzzling Pontiac in the gym parking lot following Friday night games. Ice cold beers were at the ready for postgame celebration and the consequences weren't severe if cops pulled over underage drinkers. Police rarely arrested offenders, typically requesting teenagers pour out their remaining Little Kings cream ale (a Cincinnati-born legend of the era). Some industrious officers simply took it home for personal consumption. The concept of "road pops" as acceptable (or even tolerated) isn't something relatable to today's teens but there was a time when it was an afterthought.

The impressive win in San Francisco meant the national arrival of Ditka's Bears. They resoundingly dumped the defending champs, who fell to 3-3, and put themselves in the driver's seat for home field advantage. Fans around the country, assisted largely by CBS analyst John Madden's enthusiasm for the Bears, were given an alternative to "San Francisco pretty." They were witnessing a defense even more jaw-dropping than Pittsburgh's *Steel Curtain* of the '70s. The NFL's all-time leading rusher, Payton, was at the apogee of his career. They were skippered by an in-your-face, '60s Bear from steel country. And a cocky quarterback in shades was the straw that stirred the drink.

America soon learned what Chicago already knew. The Bears didn't only possess a loaded roster, they were stocked in colorful personalities. From Ditka to rookie kicker Kevin Butler, the Bears were larger-than-life characters. Loud and obnoxious in some corners, cool and mysterious in others. Religious and clean-cut here, reckless and thrill-seeking there.

Every week there were new heroes to celebrate, and fresh gossip always followed to fill the downtime. It was impossible to take your eyes off the '85 Bears. Illuminating the impact the Bears had in Chicago requires a brief history lesson. For those born after 1955, there had never been a local championship experience. For those around my age (I was two when the Bears won the '63 NFL championship) there were only the memories of heartbreak. The epic late-summer collapse of the '69 Cubs was encored by a 1-13 Bears season under Jim Dooley. The Blackhawks dropped Game 7 to Montreal at Chicago Stadium in the Stanley Cup Final *twice* — in '71 and again in '73. As young adults, we saw the White Sox fold at home against Baltimore in the '83 ALCS and the Cubs fail to win one game out of three in San Diego, precluding them a ticket to the '84 World Series.

The Bulls barely had weaved their way into public consciousness yet. The franchise wasn't born until '66-'67 and there was nothing yet from Michael Jordan, only the promise of a very good rookie season on a really bad team under his belt.

It was 1985 and late Baby Boomers were thirsting for that first experience of witnessing one of *theirs* claim a world title. After the 6-0 start, it felt like the Bears were good enough to produce that. It was a bonus they operated with so much color and swagger. Beginning in Week 6, everything the Bears did made news. Whether it emanated from McMahon's statements written in marker on a headband, national endorsements or who was appearing on *Late Night with David Letterman*, the Bears were a Page 1-A item.

DITKA vs. FORREST GREGG

The Packers were up next in Week 7 and the nation pulled up a chair to see Team Ditka unleash its two most critical assets — Buddy Ryan's relentless defense and a running game that operated as if it were playing downhill. ABC's *Monday Night Football* crew rolled into Soldier Field with Frank Gifford, Joe Namath and O.J. Simpson upstairs to provide the narration of the league's most celebrated rivalry. Ditka and Green Bay coach Forrest Gregg were opponents in the series as players and both publicly expressed their contemptuous feelings for the other. The personal connection in the series upped the ante for both sides in the border war.

The first quarter was a comedy of errors. *Three Stooges* football. The Bears lost fumbles by Matt Suhey and Dennis McKinnon and trailed 7-0 after one quarter via Lynn Dickey's 27-yard TD pass to HOFer James Lofton. Dickey, who relieved Randy Wright, threw three of Green Bay's four picks. All three Packers quarterbacks scurried in a five-sack performance. An otherwise dull game turned ugly after two late hits by Packers DBs on Payton and Suhey. Mark Lee ushered Payton to the sideline and finished the tackle well out of bounds, resulting in an ejection. Ken Stills rocked Suhey well after the whistle when the veteran fullback was standing near the pile.

Ditka immediately fingered Gregg, a Hall of Fame tackle who coached "in the gray area." Ditka shifted any blame from Stills and implicated it was Gregg who encouraged dirty play. Stills drew a 15-yard penalty for unnecessary roughness and subsequently was fined $5K, which wasn't a brush-off penalty for an eighth-round pick on a first contract.

It then was *Fridge time* in prime time. Perry was deployed as the sledgehammer fullback on Payton's game-tying touchdown. Next, Perry debuted as an unstoppable goal-line ball carrier. "That's how folk heroes are made," Gifford remarked after Perry rumbled for a score. Payton got another one on the isolation out of the I-formation.

All three TDs came at the expense of poor George Cumby. The 220-lb. linebacker was Perry's A-gap victim on three second-quarter rushing scores that gave the Bears a 21-7 halftime lead. Fridge kept his pads lower than Cumby's on both isolation blocks. Perry's size, coupled with explosion from the three-point stance, made him more than a novelty act. He was a legitimate weapon. His mission statement was to run *through* any fool who obstructed Payton's path.

Otis Wilson sacked GB's third helpless QB, Jim Zorn, for a safety to cap the scoring in the fourth. Bears 23, Packers 7. The safety was a harbinger, yes. The perfect punctuation to a massacre is dropping a deuce on the junior varsity offense it just tormented. Everybody on Ryan's defense chipped in to send the Packers home 3-4. Dan Hampton and McMichael each had a sack and a half. Wilson and Richard Dent got one. Dave Duerson, Fencik, Wilber Marshall and Mike Richardson had interceptions. Seldom given equal praise was the running game. Payton again cleared 100 rushing yards (112 in 25 carries), and the Bears held the ball for 35 minutes. That was the 1985 recipe.

At 7-0, the Bears were capturing the imagination of football America. The first message was sent in Week 3 when McMahon came off the bench to spark a 33-24 comeback win over the Vikings. It was a rare Thursday night game and Ditka initially was reluctant to give the hook to an ineffective Fuller. After McMahon continued to bark at Ditka for several series, the coach finally caved. In the third quarter, McMahon collaborated with Willie Gault on a 70-yard TD pass. He fired two more to McKinnon, 25- and 43-yard scoring strikes.

There seldom was a dull moment in '85. Conflict and craziness were the norm. Oddly, the tension didn't reach divisive levels. These Bears fed off abnormality. Typically, a team whose in-house dysfunction flirts with insanity oozes into the gutter. This group seemed to welcome it. Make it a game *within* the game.

"Who says 'fuck you' to the other first today, Ditka or Buddy?"

"Did you hear the basement flooded again?"

"We walkin' to South Park for practice or bussin' to Park Ridge?

"Who pissed hot?"

There was drama around every corner, but it impaired nothing. It was a luxury facilitated by a roster that was one of the deepest collections of elite players ever. It didn't hurt that most of them could endure all that goes with life in McCaskeyville.

BUILDING THE '85 BEARS

General manager Jim Finks began stacking blue chip, first-round picks — including three Hall of Famers — in '75 when he took Payton with the fourth pick. Almost every first-rounder was a tape-measure home run: Hampton in '79, Wilson in '80, right tackle Keith Van Horne in '81, McMahon in '82 and Jimbo Covert in '83. Finks believed a championship roster is built on the offensive and defensive lines and his vision provided Ditka with an embarrassment of riches.

In the fall of '82, Finks and scout Bill Tobin collaborated on the intel that would lead them to the most impactful draft in team history. Finks wasn't the GM of record when the draft arrived in the spring, but it was under his watchful eye when Tobin was tracking the class of '83. It produced two HOFers and *seven* core players.

The Bears '83 draft:

1. (6)   Jimbo Covert, tackle, Pittsburgh
1. (18)   Willie Gault, wide receiver, Tennessee
2. (33)   Mike Richardson, cornerback, Arizona State
3. (64)   Dave Duerson, safety, Notre Dame
4. (91)   Tom Thayer, center/guard, Notre Dame
5. (107)   Pat Dunsmore, tight end, Drake
8. (203)   Richard Dent, defensive end, Tennessee State
8. (219)   Mark Bortz, guard, Iowa

The Bears drafted five more players between 230rd and 313rd, but none stuck.

Here's what the '83 class did for the offensive line:
LT Covert: GP: 111; GS: 110; 2x first-team All Pro; 2 PBs; 8 yrs; HOF class of '20. RG Thayer: GP: 123; GS: 120; 8 yrs. LG Bortz: GP: 171; GS: 155; 12 yrs.

Here's what the '83 draft provided for the defense:
DE Dent: GP: 170; GS: 147; first-team All Pro; 3x second-team All Pro; 4 PBs; Super Bowl XX MVP; Sacks: 124.5; FFs: 34; FRs: 13; INTs: 8; 12 yrs; HOF class of '11. CB Richardson: GP: 88; GS: 80; INTs: 20; 6 yrs. S Duerson: GP: 102; GS: 76; 2x second-team All Pro; 4 PBs; INTs: 18; Sacks: 16; FRs: 4; 7 yrs.

Seven difference makers, including two HOFers, in one draft. Gault, the second of the first-rounders, also was valuable as a deep threat and occasional home run hitter. WR Gault: GP: 76; GS: 72; Rec: 184; Rec yds: 3650; Rec TDs: 27; 5 yrs.

The three O-linemen, coupled with '81 first-rounder Van Horne and center Jay Hilgenberg, an undrafted free agent in '81, comprised one of the best run-blocking offensive lines in NFL history. Hilgenberg was one of the most decorated centers of the era. The vitals, as they appear above, are with the Bears only. The big boys: C Hilgenberg: GP: 163; GS: 130; 2x first-team

All Pro; 2x second-team All Pro; 7 PBs; 11 yrs. RT Van Horne: GP: 186; GS: 169; 13 yrs. The Bears O-line was comprised of not only excellent players — but several were gregarious enough to share the limelight with offensive catalysts McMahon and Payton. Taped to the bedroom walls of teenage boys all over Chicagoland was the *Black & Blues Brothers* poster. The freakin' offensive line had a poster, sponsored by Chevy. In an era when few players were making six-figure salaries, the $2K each player pocketed for the photo shoot was meaningful.

Payton remained a great player in '85, but his success was facilitated by a front wall that took enormous pride in dominating in time of possession each week. The Bears were the No. 1 rushing team in the league between '84 and '86 and were third in '88 in the first year of Payton's retirement. Here are the vitals for Payton and skilled position regulars.

Payton: GP: 190; GS: 184; 5x first-team All Pro; 3x second-team All Pro; 9 PBs; ATT: 3838, 16,276 yds (4.4 ypc) 110 rush TDs; REC: 492, 4548 yds (9.2 ypr) 15 rec TDs; 13 yrs; HOF Class of '93. Suhey: GP: 148; GS: 100; ATT: 828, 2946 yds (3.6 ypc); REC: 260, 2113 yds (8.1 ypr) 5 rec TDs; 10 yrs. McMahon: GP: 66; GS: 61; PC-PA-YDs: 874-1513-11,203 (7.4 ypa); 67 TDs, 56 INTs; 1 PB; 15 rush TDs; 7 yrs. WR McKinnon: GP: 85; GS: 54; REC: 180, 2840 yds (15.8 ypr) 21 rec TDs; 129 punt returns, 3 ret TDs; 5 yrs. TE Emery Moorehead: GP: 106; GS: 79; REC: 200, 2730 yds (13.7 ypr) 14 rec TDs; 8 yrs.

Of course, the big, bad defense had its own poster, the *Junkyard Dogs*. The concept of the "46 defense" was this: The "46" referred initially to the jersey number of safety Doug Plank ('76-'83). Plank was physical enough to play close to the line of scrimmage, essentially an additional linebacker. The 46 defense covers every gap. Defensive backs, typically the safeties, were expected to play in the gaps and on the edge. DBs had to be trustworthy in man-coverage. Aggressive blitz packages had as many as eight rushing the passer, leaving coverage guys on an island with a receiver. Fencik and Duerson also played big for smallish safeties and were excellent in the high-risk, high-reward concepts of the 46.

Woof, woof, woof! The Bears bit as hard as they barked and put together consecutive seasons of tormenting quarterbacks. Two seasons that *still* dazzle historically. One year after setting the NFL record (still stands) with 72 sacks, the Bears collected 64 sacks, second only to the Giants (68). The '85 Bears allowed the fewest points per game, 12.4. San Francisco was a distant second (16.4 ppg). The Bears led the NFL with 54 takeaways. The Cowboys were second (48).

Hampton, a '02 Hall of Fame inductee, was the lynch pin but had capable co-conspirators all over the field. Like three fellow Cantonites — Singletary ('99), Dent ('11) and McMichael. *Mongo* was a New England scrap-heap pick up in '81. In that same year, Finks moved up two spots in the second round to take Singletary. Fencik, drafted as a wide receiver by Miami in the 10th-round in '76, was the most tenured member of the defense. Singletary won the defensive player of the year award, but most observers suggest '84 first-round pick Wilber Marshall was the most impactful member of the '85 defense. Perry, the first-rounder in '85, was immovable and a very effective player early in his career.

The vitals for all the defensive regulars who aren't listed above:
DE Hampton: GP: 157; GS: 151; first-team All Pro; 4x second-team All Pro; 4 PBs; Sacks: 82; 12 yrs; HOF Class of '02. DT McMichael: GP: 191; GS: 157; 2x first-team All Pro; 2x second-team All Pro; 2 PBs; Sacks: 92.5; FFs: 12; FRs: 16; 13 yrs; HOF Class of '24. Perry: GP: 114; GS: 94; Sacks: 28.5; 9 yrs. MLB Singletary: GP: 179; GS: 172; 7x first-team All Pro; second-team All Pro; 10 PBs; 2x DPOY; 12 yrs; HOF Class of '98. OLB Wilson: GP: 109; GS: 90; second-team All Pro; 1 PB; Sacks: 38; INTs: 10; 8 yrs. OLB Marshall: GP: 59; GS: 43; first-team All Pro; 2 PBs; Sacks: 16.5; INTs: 9; FFs: 8; FRs: 5; 4 yrs. S Fencik: GP: 164; GS: 140; first-team All Pro; second-team All Pro; 2 PBs; 38 INTs (team record); FRs: 13; 12 yrs. CB Frazier: GP: 64; GS: 49; INTs: 20; 5 yrs.

The ESPN *30 for 30* on the Super Bears erroneously painted the defense as the only weapon in the arsenal. As dominant as the 46 performed, the praise it received was disproportionate. The Bears were second in the league in scoring, averaging 28.4 points per game in '85. The Bears hammered out sustained drives that led to points while the 46 defense kicked up its heels on the sideline. The *Black and Blues Brothers* extracted the will to resist from opposing defenders. The offense was slighted in the documentary, which also went way too heavy on Ryan, who was losing to cancer and stroke complications when the *30 for 30* was produced. Buddy's players revered the man, but he was a mumbling curmudgeon to those on the outside.

The Bears also excelled on special teams in '85. Rookie kicker Kevin Butler was money and set the team's single-season scoring record with 144 points. Gault's 26.2 yards per kickoff return was second best in the league to the Rams' Ron Brown (32.8 ypr).

There wasn't much the '85 Bears didn't do better than anybody else in the league. They were the Rolling Stones in shoulder pads and their concerts intoxicated Chicago for five months.

In a world devoid of social media, the Bears didn't hide. McMahon's Thursday night tradition of taking the big boys out for dinner and drinks didn't go down in private rooms. The Bears were front and center at establishments in the northern suburbs. They walked tall, talked loud and weren't too cool for the room. The players recognized their doting public and willingly were a part of the city's fabric. At auto dealerships, grocery stores and sports bars. Bears were everywhere. It was a different time with a different team, one that believed reciprocity is the key to every meaningful relationship.

CRUISING THROUGH THE BRUISINGS

"It didn't just happen overnight. There's a ramp up. Nobody was calling Chicago the Monsters of the Midway in the '70s. We wanted to change that. We wanted to be known as something bigger." – Dan Hampton

After the Bears beat the Packers, they used the same recipe of playing keep-away and tormenting the quarterback to reel off three more NFC Central wins in Weeks 8, 9 and 10. They intercepted Vikings quarterbacks five times, including a 23-yard Pick 6 by Wilson, in a 27-9 waltz at Soldier Field. Payton rushed for 119 yards and caught a 20-yard TD pass from McMahon. The Bears kept the ball for almost 35 minutes. At Lambeau in Week 9, the Bears wobbled into the fourth quarter and trailed 10-7 before

McMichael sacked Zorn in the end zone for another "get 'em up" to make it 10-9. Payton delivered the knockout punch with a 27-yard touchdown sprint for a TD and the Bears won, 16-10. Payton ran for 192 yards. In the second quarter, the Bears got more out of their cuddly new toy when Perry caught a four-yard TD pass from McMahon to even the score 7-7. The Fridge made his national talk show debut with Letterman after the Green Bay win. The Bears clobbered helpless Detroit, 24-3. With Fuller at the wheel, Payton and Suhey both cleared 100 yards rushing and the Bears kept the ball for 41 minutes. The Lions turned it over four times and muscled out only eight first downs and 106 total yards.

America was on full alert. On the road to Irving to trade haymakers with the Cowboys in the CBS national game of the week. For the network's "Next Week on CBS" tease, the freeze frame was a close up of Singletary's bug eyes peering from behind the face mask. Dallas was 7-3 and the game went off as a pick 'em.

"It was meaningful to me because I'd never beaten them. I mean for 10 years; they kicked our ass. I remember thinking if we win this game. we've got a good chance to go to the Super Bowl. Everybody knew it was a big game. After two series, the defensive line is saying 'these guys can't block us.' " – Gary Fencik

It wasn't a fair fight. The Bears cruised in a 44-0 laugher and the most unsuspecting members of the ensemble cast did touchdown dances. Dent opened the scoring with a one-yard interception return. After Butthead's 44-yard field goal, Richardson returned a Gary Hogeboom pick 36 yards for a score. Fuller plunged in from a yard out and the Bears led 24-0 at halftime. The second half followed suit. Butler banged two more field goals and Calvin Thomas and Dennis Gentry ripped off 17- and 16-yard TD jaunts, respectively. *"Pinkeeeee!"*

Hogeboom threw three of Dallas' four picks. Danny White tossed the other and was victimized on four of the six sacks. The Bears earned the cover of *Sports Illustrated* for the second time in the season and were 11-0. The cover was an image of Duerson, sitting upright on the artificial turf with White entangled in his web. Singletary flew wildly over the pile. White's name plate was legible as he lied face down across the legs of Duerson. A clever *SI* staffer would have written *Whitewash in Dallas*. Instead, the cover headline was merely block numerals of the final score *44-0*. I've waited 39 years to share that one.

The only loser in Dallas was receiver James Maness, a third-rounder out of TCU in '85. Maness was back home in Texas and the word was he and some former teammates did dawn patrol. Maybe it never stopped. Maness, who dressed for the first eight games, was overheard with an incurable case of the sniffles in a bathroom stall. He was released immediately after and never played another NFL down.

Bears popped up everywhere in national ad campaigns. In the center of it were Ditka, McMahon, Payton and Perry, selling everything from chunky soup to shoes to automobiles. In Chicago, a dozen or so of the biggest names on the roster made weekly radio and television appearances. They were playful and connective with hosts and the target audiences each station reached. Hampton appeared regularly on the flagship, WGN. Fencik was a staple on Jonathan Brandmeier's hipper popular morning show on the Loop AM & FM. Thayer was a regular on the AM Loop's *Steve & Garry* show and he often had teammates in tow. Payton, McMahon and Ditka did Sunday night wrap-up shows on the network TV affiliates. The marketing department was bombed by requests for player appearances and the soon-to-be *shufflin' crew* shuffled all over Chicagoland.

"There were no petty jealousies. We were all getting a bite of the apple." –Keith Van Horne

There was no let down in Week 12 in Atlanta. The Bears smothered the Falcons, 36-0. Payton rushed 20 times for 102 yards, including a 40-yard TD run in the second that gave the Bears a 13-0 lead. Perry bulldozed in from the one to make it 20-0 before the half. Thomas and Thomas Sanders also had short TD runs. Henry Waechter had 2.5 of the five sacks and the defense collected three more takeaways.

Every week, new players took bows, but two forces remained constant — the dominant ground attack and the relentless pressure from Ryan's 46. Players up and down the roster contributed. There were new names in the box score each week. All's well in Lake Forest, right?

"Close the drape. There's never going to be any sun in here anyway. Kenny Margerum walks in and looks around the room at all the long faces and said, 'this has to be the most unhappy fucking 12-0 team of all-time.' There was no room for celebration, always room for improvement." – Tom Thayer

SHUFFLIN' PAST MAYHEIM IN MIAMI

The Bears were the biggest bad asses in football. They took a three-week cumulative advantage of 104-3 into Miami for a Monday night date with the Dolphins. What possibly could stand in their way.

Marino. A wet field. Unlucky Week 13. The unbeaten '72 Dolphins lurking in the Orange Bowl.

Miami's third-year quarterback, Covert's teammate at Pitt, was the hottest quarterback in the AFC and looking to build on his unprecedented 5,084 yards passing and 48-TD season of '84. He lit up the Bears in stunning fashion. Marino's 'Phins put 31 on the board in the first half and Ditka's 12-0 Bears trailed 31-10 when they went to the locker room.

Don Shula later referred to his team's performance "the best first half of football I've ever been around." Ditka demanded coverage changes from Ryan. Specifically, he wanted Ryan to take Marshall off receiver Nat Moore. Moore had five catches for 74 yards and two TDs in the first half. Bears corners had their hands full with "the Marks," Clayton and Duper. Typically, pressure applied by Ryan's attacking defense was a luxury for Bears corners, who were isolated in man-to-man coverage. The Dolphins were a challenging assignment with three lightning-fast, water bug receivers. And Marino was on the move more than what Miami had shown on tape. Ryan never had been deferential to Ditka, and he wasn't going to start then.

Some players said they heard the much-ballyhooed shouting match and others didn't. Some probably heard it but it didn't register. Coaches and players shout obscenities at each other on sidelines, in meetings and in practice. Sometimes media make it sound like disagreements should escalate to the human resources department. The NFL world is an atypical work environment. Temper tantrums and shouting matches go with the territory. This dust up was magnified because Ditka and Ryan's deteriorating partnership had become more public.

Fuller pulled the Bears within two touchdowns, capping a signature time-of-possession drive for the Bears with a one-yard touchdown run. On the ensuing possession, unlucky Week 13 reared its ugly head. Marino rifled a pass off the crown of Hampton's helmet. The ball ricocheted to Clayton, who took it 42 yards for a touchdown and the Dolphins again led by 21. Margerum hauled in a 19-yard TD pass from Fuller in the fourth, but the Bears went down, 38-24.

It was a quiet flight home. Aspirations for a wire-to-wire perfect season evaporated.

The Bears went right back to work Tuesday morning, but at their side job. The '85 Bears made a cottage industry out of being the '85 Bears. Have moves, will travel. Can't sing, will try. *The Super Bowl Shuffle* was recorded on Tuesday, Dec. 3 at Park West. No surprise here — there was conflict.

There was disagreement over the timing of the *Shuffle's* production. Payton and McMahon initially took a pass, both thinking it was too chesty too soon. Other shufflers felt otherwise and proceeded without the two nationally-known cogs in the offense. After further review, Payton and McMahon recorded their parts at Halas Hall and the producers inserted their parts during post-production. Hampton was a hard pass on the *Shuffle* at any point.

In 10 days, the *Shuffle* was pressed and released on Chicago-based Red Label Records and distributed by Capitol Records. It didn't fly off shelves faster than Springsteen's *Born in the USA* had in '84, but the *Shuffle* sold a half million copies and made it to No. 41 on *Billboard's* Hot 100. It received a Grammy nomination for best R&B from a duo or group with vocals in '87. The networks picked up on it as well and the wild and crazy Bears were penetrating the country with their bravado as much as their ferocious play.

"They call me Sweetness, and I like to dance.
Runnin' the ball's like makin' romance."
"I'm Mama Boy Otis, one of a kind.
The ladies all love me for my body and my mind."

"I'm Samurai Mike, I stop 'em cold.
Heart of the defense, big and bold."
"So, bring on Atlanta, bring on Dallas.
This is for Mike and Papa Bear Halas."

With their feet back on planet earth, the Bears tuned up for the playoffs with three more scrimmages against doormats. Payton rushed for 111 yards and the Bears had the ball for 39 minutes in a 17-10 win over Indianapolis. The Jets slowed Payton in Week 15, but a now-healthy McMahon spread the ball around to seven receivers and the Bears almost hit 40 minutes possession time in a 19-6 sleeper. Marshall's impactful season was punctuated by a vicious hit in the curtain closer against Detroit. The second-year linebacker ducked his shoulder under the shoulder pads of quarterback Joe Ferguson, who had just released the football. Ferguson's head snapped back and both feet were whisked skyward.

"The only time in my career I saw a guy get knocked out before his head hit the ground," Lions then-rookie left tackle Lomas Brown reflected last fall. "I looked at Joe, whose body almost completely flattened out after the hit, and he was out before he fell. It was a devastating collision."

The defense punctuated the season with seven takeaways and six sacks. Bears 37, Detroit 17. Merry Christmas, Chicago. The Bears were 15-1 with home field secured for the playoffs.

The Giants were first up in the Wild Card round and were nine-point underdogs. Dent backed up the bark and racked up 3.5 of six sacks of a sluggish Phil Simms. Most memorable perhaps is Shaun Gayle walking into the end zone for an easy six when Giants punter Sean Landetta practically whiffed inside his own 10. It gave the hosts a 7-0 first quarter lead. Payton had a long run of only 12 yards, but the Bears bogarted the ball for 37 minutes and McMahon was sharp, going 11-of-21 for 216 yards and two TDs, both to McKinnon.

The Rams were no match in the NFC Championship game the next week. The Bears corralled Eric Dickerson, who'd busted up Dallas in the divisional round the previous weekend in Anaheim (Chapter 7 detailed the Bears' 24-0 victory). Snowflakes fell from charcoal-bitten skies on the lakefront in the final minutes. The Bears punched their ticket to the Crescent City for the organization's maiden voyage to a Super Bowl. The best was yet to come.

NEW ORLEANS WEEK

From the moment McMahon stepped off the plane, he was the cock of the walk. Behind the signature sunglasses, he chewed tobacco and spat in a cup. In the French Quarter, McMahon rifled fruit at by-passers from a second-floor balcony with Jim Kelly. He whizzed outside a restaurant after being asked about his meal. Everywhere he went, Jimmy Mac verbalized disdain for the conventional and his distrust of authority. He called out Michael McCaskey for refusing to fly an acupuncturist to NOLA for treatment of a sore butt cheek. When a local television crew flew over practice in a helicopter looking for a peek, McMahon flashed his tender cheek.

McMahon's *headband de jour* was a side dish he served after public battles with commissioner Pete Rozelle, who fined the Bears quarterback for promoting *Adidas* on his headband. *The Punky QB* was the pied piper of Chicago. He marched this colorful collection of NFL bad boys into the Big Easy for a few days of debauchery and misadventure before they sharpened the blades for the next victim. The hijinks were chronicled vividly in *Tribune* columnist Bob Verdi's book *McMahon*, published by Warner in '87. It easily ranks near the top of the most informative, honest and enjoyable books I've read about the games people play in Chicago.

Jimmy Mac was *NFL Jim Morrison*, the enigmatic front man of late-'60s American rockers, the Doors. Saluting authority with a middle finger is among the duo's common traits. Both elevated the boys in their bands to new levels of excellence and extracted maximum effort from all players. Nobody could take their eyes off them when they performed. Or when they weren't performing. McMahon could be the quarterback you loved to hate, just as many said of Morrison's iconic L.A.-based band.

Buddy Diliberto was a television reporter for New Orleans' NBC affiliate who reported McMahon commented "the women of New Orleans are all whores" and "the men are all stupid." The Bears brass had a fit and marketing director Ken Valdisseri tore apart the credibility of the report. By Wednesday, they were so nervous about their quarterback's next move, they softened and popped for his acupuncturist's air fare. Diliberto was suspended but McMahon didn't feel better as the phone incessantly rang in his hotel room. Women called and screamed at him for the alleged remark. The Bears' hotel received a bomb threat and NFL security was on high alert.

Only the '85 Bears.

When Saturday night's final meetings neared, Ryan addressed his 46ers for the last time under the Bears' umbrella. He was visibly shaken and simply said to his disciples "Whatever happens tomorrow, I want you guys to know you'll always be my heroes." Ryan exited the room and confusion reigned. A story appeared in the papers earlier in the week about Ryan possibly taking another job, but the Bears seemed oblivious. It didn't take long before they connected the dots, although Singletary was in disbelief.

"No way," I thought. "He didn't say anything to me about it and I would have known." Ryan and Singletary had a relationship that went beyond the typical player-coach friendship. It remained that way until Ryan's death in '16.

Ron Rivera takes it from here.

"Fencik was the first guy who got up and spoke. Of course, it was intellectual. Singletary was next and Mike was emotional. He couldn't believe it was even possible Buddy would be leaving and he was upset. Then McMichael got up. 'What the fuck is wrong with you sissies? What is this? You're about to play the biggest game of your lives tomorrow and look at you.' He and Hamp destroyed the projector, then Steve picked up a chair and hurled it toward a chalkboard where it impaled it with all four legs."

The Bears filed out of their meeting and went off to their rooms quietly. They'd had a big week. Time to rest up for the formality that was Raymond Berry's AFC champion Patriots. No more words.

SUPER SUNDAY

It was January 26, 1986, and it was the first Bears game of the year when I got to kick up my feet and be a fan. My last day as an intern producer at flagship station WGN (720-AM) was the NFC Championship game. After five months of shagging coffee, editing highlights and hustling behind the scenes to facilitate station hosts Chuck Swirsky and Dave Eanet, I got together with friends to watch Super Bowl XX. It was the event that marked the day Chicago finally got to experience the view from the top of a sports mountain.

Butler's third field goal just before halftime gave the Bears what seemed to be an insurmountable advantage. On NBC, which broadcast the game with Dick Enberg and Merlin Olsen describing the action, studio host Pete Axthelm said it best: "If it were a fight, they'd stop it."

It was a thorough ass kicking. New England rushed for only seven yards and turned it over six times. Other than slowing Payton, who carried 22 times for 61 yards, Berry's team didn't do anything well. The Patriots mustered only 123 yards of total offense. Only Minnesota, in its 16-6 loss to Pittsburgh in SB 9, recorded fewer yards, 119. Rookie second-teamers Reggie Phillips and Jim Morrissey had long interception returns. Phillips went 36 yards for a touchdown while Morrissey's return covered 47 yards before receiver Stanley Morgan knocked him down near the pylon just shy of the goal line.

New England couldn't protect quarterbacks Tony Eason and Steve Grogan, and the Bears collected seven sacks. Dent, who won the game's MVP, had 1.5 of them, collaborating with Marshall on the half-bird. Wilson had two sacks. Hampton and McMichael got one and "Old Haystacks" Henry Waechter got into the mix, too. Waechter dumped Grogan in the end zone in the final minutes to conclude the scoring with a safety. *Supermen* was the *Sports Illustrated* cover headline, adjacent to a photo of Marshall, Wilson and Hampton, index finger in the air, mauling Eason, who's lying on his left side. The image encapsulated two years of performances by Buddy's boys.

Bears 46, Patriots 10.

With so much youth on the roster, it was easy to daydream about how many parades were ahead before the one on Tuesday, January 28 even concluded. Ticker-tape in downtown Chicago. *There's* a tradition worth keeping. *"They should win it again next year!"* was the prevailing narrative.

Not even a skeptic would have believed it if you said the Bears still would be searching for the encore 39 years later.

The punky QB and the best offensive lineman in team history, getting loose for Camp Ditka in Platteville. (courtesy of Jimbo Covert)

Only Payton tops Matt Forte in Bears annals. Matt's durability and versatility shined. For one season, however, both at their peaks, gimme Neal Anderson. (courtesy of Patrick Mannelly)

141

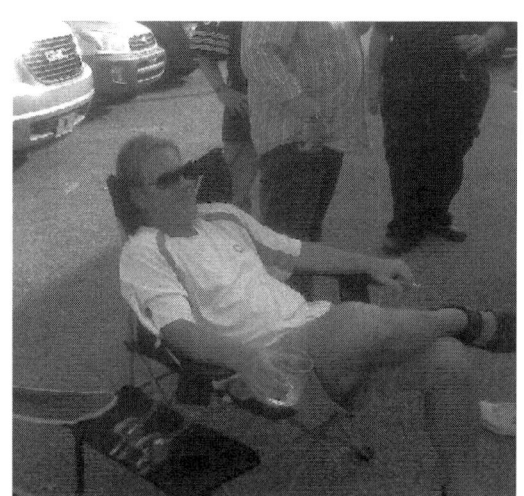

A scotch and a smoke jump start the tailgate at Lambeau in '09. Jay Cutler's debut was sullied by four picks that night. (courtesy of Matt Spiegel)

Walter, chillin' on his Harley, with Thayer, whose family in Joliet always enjoyed Payton's unannounced visits. (courtesy of Tom Thayer)

142

Mongo belts it out for the Chicago Six, with Hamp laying down the riffs (rear left). That's young Daniel Hampton whipping the Ribfest crowd to a frenzy in '20. (courtesy of Dan Hampton)

Mongo, bronzed and buffed, working the room on my Wayne's World version of a Bears show in '89 in Oak Lawn. Skinny ties were a thing in the '80s.

143

Jay Cutler was upright for the coin toss in the NFC title game against the Packers. Julius Peppers' first year as a Bear was a damn good one. (courtesy of Patrick Mannelly)

Dave Wannstedt in '22, on WJOB, the The Voice of the Region. Dave brings the 'A game' for the general in Wanny's Army, which surrendered after the 4-12 finish in '97. (courtesy of Greg Spata)

144

Dave Wannstedt's game face, November, 1994.
(courtesy Harlan Sports Management)

Special friends. Robbie Gould leapfrogged Butthead as the best kicker in team history. Super snapper Patrick Mannelly played in more games than any Bear ever. (courtesy of Patrick Mannelly)

145

*New Year's Eve '88
with the mentor,
Chet Coppock,
after the fog
cleared. Hey, all
the cool kids had
teal Starter jackets.
(courtesy of Jim
Modelski)*

*Brian Urlacher:
fierce competitor,
revered teammate,
unrivaled athlete.
Greatest Bears
defender ever? I
kind of lean that
way. (courtesy of
Greg Zahn)*

Backups always are popular Bears. Tyson Bagent is a colorful insurance policy. He spent '24 "grindin' my face off" if Caleb couldn't go. (courtesy BetRivers podcast network)

Bears of a feather. Dick Butkus took to Dan Hampton in the King's rookie year in '79. Hampton is football Benjamin Button, better looking at 50 than at 22. (courtesy of Dan Hampton)

147

Brian Urlacher popped by the Drive one morning in '16 to hustle hair replacement and be annoyed. I told the new PD, not from Chicago, Lack could pick any AC/DC song he wanted to intro. Options list? "He's f__in' Urlacher, interloper." (courtesy of Kathy Voltmer)

Old guys at a reunion. Ron Rivera, me, Jim Morrissey and Glen Kozlowski shortly after Riverboat Ron took Carolina to Super Bowl 50, at Mo's domicile in the 'burbs. (courtesy of Amy Morrissey)

Super Bowl 41 coin toss, February 4, 2007, in Miami. The Colts won the toss, then foolishly kicked to Devin Hester. (courtesy of Patrick Mannelly)

Charles Martin had a "hit list" and made good one on one threat – ending the season for Jim McMahon, and effectively, the Bears. Martin was tossed; the Bears fizzled with Doug Flutie in the playoffs a month later. (courtesy of Bob Baer).

9 December, 1981

Dear Mr. Halas,

We the undersigned members of the Bears defensive football team are concerned about the future of our team. We recognize that with the disappointing season the Bears have had this year that there may be changes in the coaching staff and/or the administration of the team. Our main concern is over the fate of Buddy Ryan and the other defensive coaches.

Buddy and his staff have done an excellent job improving the defensive teams performance. You need only look at our defensive statistics over the years to see the improvements that have been made. Even this year after our poor start he was able to pull us out of our slump and turn us into what is now a good solid defensive team.

Buddy has maintained the discipline, moral, pride and effort that we need in order to play well defensively, in spite of the fact that we haven't had much help from the offensive team. It would have been easy for us to fold our tent and play out the season but Buddy and his staff wouldn't let that happen.

Our concern centers on the fact that if Buddy and his staff are replaced it will set our defensive team back a minimum of two years and possibly more by the time we learn a new system and adjust to new coaches.

We feel that if there is to be a change in the coaching staff Buddy Ryan and his staff should be retained in order to avoid a setback for our defense. We feel that we are a good defensive team and that with their help we can be a great defensive team in the near future.

Thank you for considering our request.

Sincerely,

The Chicago Bears Defensive Team

The gentlemanly Hit Man, Gary Fencik, implored Papa Bear Halas to retain Buddy Ryan after Mike Ditka's arrival in '82.

Every member of the defense affirmed his affection for the architect of the "46." (documents courtesy of Gary Fencik)

CHICAGO BEARS FOOTBALL CLUB
55 EAST JACKSON BOULEVARD
CHICAGO, ILLINOIS 60604

GEORGE S. HALAS
PRESIDENT AND
CHIEF EXECUTIVE OFFICER
312/663-5100

December 22, 1981

Dear Gary,

My thanks to you for sending me the letter asking me
to retain Buddy Ryan and his staff and giving me your
reasons why.

This is a magnificent letter! It is a beautifully
written letter! It is the highest tribute a coach
could receive!

I can tell you without fear of contradiction that
this is the first time in the 61-year history of the
Chicago Bears that such a letter was written about a
Bear Coach. I think I can also say that this is the
first time any owner in the NFL has received such a
letter.

I am so fortunate to have you boys on my team.

It was my pleasure meeting with you last Friday and
I am most grateful for your genuine concern for the
future of the Chicago Bears. God bless,

Sincerely yours,

George Halas

Geo. S. Halas

Mr. Gary Fencik
3120 North Sheridan Road
Apt. 2A
Chicago, Illinois 60657

*Papa Bear's response to the '82 team's plea for Buddy Ryan's return.
I've wondered how different the team's history would be if Halas
dismissed the request.*

Mike Ditka stopped making public appearances about two years ago. In a happier time, with fellow Bears Hall of Famers Dan Hampton, Gale Sayers (seated) and Richard Dent, at the centennial celebration. (courtesy Rosemont Chamber of Commerce).

Frick and Frack. Doug Buffone and Ed O'Bradovich. A must-have postgame therapy session during the Marc Trestman experience, and the first year of John Fox's retirement fund tour. (courtesy of the Score)

The Walter Payton statue on the south end of Soldier Field, visited by an admirer since the truck with Mississippi plates pulled into Lake Forest. (courtesy of Timothy J. Vanzo)

CHAPTER 10
Foggy Memories
NFL *FORCE MAJEURE*
MEETS IMPLODING BEARS

"I think now, looking back, we did not fight the enemy. We fought ourselves. And the enemy was in us." Chris Taylor (Charlie Sheen) in the 1986 film Platoon.

It's necessary to unpack history because so much of it — written and spoken — has been a revisionist's version. History, of course, being the refuse of *cowards and losers* (from the Book of Ditka). It's probable Mike Ditka first fired that salvo while defending his manhood after others' accounts of Bears activities didn't jibe with his own.

The truth is Ditka's fingerprints are all over both the successes and failures of the Bears before and after 1985. Heavy is the head. The bigger the head, the weightier. Da Coach's noggin became colossal.

The '85 Bears never climbed back into the ring for another title bout. *Why* they didn't has been debated in bars and at church socials for decades. At Thanksgiving dinners, wedding receptions and funerals.

"At least Uncle Frank got to see 'em win that one Super Bowl."

"If McMahon could have stayed healthy..."

"Cheap ass McCaskey."

It appeared ordained this dominant, young, fear-inducing squad would collect Lombardi trophies in route to immortality. *Just* one? Perish the thought.

Super Bowl XX MVP Richard Dent pointed the finger at Ditka when Dent was nearing his enshrinement in Canton 13 years ago and the Colonel freshened the script when I talked to him in late August. "We would have been the first team ever to win Super Bowls in row if Ditka knew how to handle the quarterback position," Dent said on the Score in '11. "Bringing Doug Flutie in and thinking that he's going to be on a team for three weeks and start him in a playoff game? Hell, I mean you're trying to change the name on the Super Bowl trophy to Mike Ditka instead of Vince Lombardi when you do something like that. We had won with (Mike) Tomczak and (Steve) Fuller. That's all we needed to do is stay with that plan. Then you bring a guy off the street."

Revisionist history alarm. The truth was Fuller was a pedestrian quarterback whose job was to tuck the ball in the belly of the running back. Jesus, this was a backup who threw six TD passes and nine interceptions during three years in a Bears' uniform and he would have made the Super Bowl a lock? Tomczak, who went 21-10 as the starter and 2-1 in the postseason, threw 33 touchdowns against 47 interceptions in his six years with the Bears. He had three playoff starts and went 2-1 with wins over the Eagles in '88 and the Saints in '90 and a bad loss to the Giants in January of '91. None of his playoff performances received a high grade. He fared no better than Flutie in '86 loss to Washington to which Dent referred.

Secondly, Flutie was acquired in a deal with the Rams in mid-October of '86, not "three weeks" before the postseason. The Boston College folk hero appeared in four games and was the starter in a 16-13 win in Detroit in Week 15. Dent still points the finger at Ditka's bad judgment. "If it would have been Ditka who would have left and Buddy Ryan stayed, we'd have won two or three more Super Bowls," he said.

Otis Wilson was selling the same narrative in August when I ran into him at a summer music festival in Northwest Indiana. "We won with Tomczak before, but Ditka didn't know what he was doing. We had everything going on defense with Buddy, man. Should have been Buddy runnin' it." Fiction. Man, I wanted Tomczak to succeed. Our history dated to our teens, and he favored appearing on the Loop with me to the host for whom I booked guests, the late Chet Coppock. The truth is T-zak's performances didn't merit the endorsements.

Dan Hampton still sacks McMahon if pressed. In the '80s, Hampton called McMahon "the monkey driving the limo" and he still was firing at McMahon 10 years ago. "We had a quarterback who didn't always feel like playing," Hamp said in a documentary on *The Fog Bowl* produced in '14. In

2014, McMahon tosses off the insult with a shrug.

Dennis McKinnon, an underrated asset on the '85 Bears, distributes the blame in whichever direction the wind is blowing. Typically, it's Ditka and Hamp who catch the shrapnel from the edgy receiver. McKinnon accused Ditka of plunking down on a propositional bet for William Perry to score a Super Bowl touchdown. Silky D still hammers Ditka for icing out Walter Payton, the heartbeat of the franchise since '75. McKinnon impugned Hampton's character after he passed on the White House trip when Barack Obama was in office. The Bears finally went to meet the President in '11 — 25 years after the space shuttle Challenger tragedy postponed the customary visit shortly after being crowned during the Ronald Reagan years.

Did prop wagers on Super Bowls exist in '86? Does McKinnon have anything nice to say about any ex-teammates other than Payton or Wilber Marshall? He blasted Mike Singletary, too, calling the '98 HOF enshrinee "a politician." The now-63-year-old McKinnon unloaded his contemptuous feelings in a book he collaborated on with Coppock in '19.

Everybody, of course, blamed, and still blames Bears ownership for the absence of a second trophy. In Chicago, ownership sadly also means management. Let's dig deeper and sharpen the focus, beginning with distorted memories of a foggy day that concluded with a happy outcome. The win over Philadelphia in '88 was the first playoff win since the Super Bowl romp over New England.

THE FOG BOWL
December 31, 1988
Bears 20, Eagles 12

The Bears and Eagles divisional-round game made for a compelling documentary and NFL network's "lists collections," like the "Top 10 Name Games" or "Top 10 Weather Games." The game should have been paused at halftime. The head coaches — Ditka and Ryan — were responsible for the continuance. The NFL offered no resolution in New York and referee Jim Tunney left it in the hands of Ditka and Ryan, who was in his third year with Philadelphia.

Ditka and Buddy were there to settle a personal score and ability to reason went out the window. In saloons, the dynamic is referred to as a big dick contest. It was a terrible football game. Big plays were the results of confusion, the kind that leads to seven turnovers collectively. It felt like a first preseason game.

Also needing a defogger is the significance of the Bears surviving in a 20-12 finish. Millennials and younger football fans perceive the '80s Bears as the *one-hit wonder* Cubs of '16 but that's untrue. The '85 Bears never got back to a Super Bowl, but they continued to win well the party in New Orleans. They didn't disband within three years. It was a much slower burn. Ditka's Bears went playoffin' five of the six years that followed the Super Bowl win. The Fog Bowl was the first of only two postseason wins after the Super Bowl. Some of the most integral '85ers pressed on in Chicago into the '90s. Dent, William Perry, Steve McMichael, Keith Van Horne, Mark Bortz, Shaun Gayle and Kevin Butler were still on the roster when Dave Wannstedt succeeded Ditka in '93. One-hit wonders don't sustain success. The Bears did.

Ditka's marriage to Ryan, arranged by George Halas, survived four years. There's no consensus on when exactly the relationship soured but the legends of a turbulent '85 season are confirmed universally. They *needed* dissolution after SB XX and their disdain for each other only escalated after the breakup. It's not unreasonable to suspect Ditka ever could have warmed up to Ryan, who was retained by Halas after the '81 defense signed a letter pleading for Halas to retain Ryan. Gary Fencik wrote the letter, which he located in May, after much excavation, and forwarded to me for publication.

Ditka and Ryan squared off in '86 in Ryan's first season in Philly. The Bears claimed a 13-10 overtime win at Veterans Stadium. This game was a different animal. As time passed, Ditka and Ryan kept firing at each other from a distance. Ditka mandated a terminology change to cleanse the team of Ryan's memory. Ryan's 46 defense became "the Bear defense." This also was a playoff game, and the Bears hadn't won one since the title.

In back-to-back divisional round games after Ryan's defection, the Bears were stuffed by Washington. Both losses were at Soldier Field. What appeared to be a clear path to a dynasty had been detoured by injuries, the '87 players' strike and McMahon not playing as well as he did in '84 and '85. Damned if Ditka was going to be thwarted by a former assistant who usurped his authority. Ditka's last memory of Ryan as a co-worker was *both* coaches being hoisted on broad shoulders for a victory lap in the Superdome. With McMichael under Ditka's right butt cheek and Perry under the left, King Michael Keller Ditka waved to his court and admiring public. Wilson, Dent and Dave Duerson lifted King James David Ryan for his *Hail to the Chief* moment.

How dare anybody deny Ditka a monopoly on *his* championship.

Ditka wasn't a regular in defensive meetings but when he did offer a comment, Ryan dismissed them summarily after Ditka exited. "Don't listen to a fuckin' word that asshole ever says," Fencik recalled of a Ryan response that followed a Ditka fly-by. Linebacker Jim Morrissey and others recalled hearing that Buddy sentiment.

The fog radically altered the scripts for both teams and contracted offenses. Players said they never felt unsafe, just terribly limited and confused.

It was a Chamber of Commerce Saturday morning on the final day of '88. The air was chilly, but it was early winter in Chicago and a sun-splashed lakefront glistened under cloudless skies. The grudge match kicked off at 12:30 on CBS, then the NFC's network partner. Verne Lundquist and Terry Bradshaw called the game. When the Eagles arrived at 14th and McFetridge Drive, Ryan pulled a stunt typically reserved for high school rivalries. He instructed drivers of the team busses to circle Soldier Field three times and honk their horns intermittently. His team's presence was announced "with authority."

Late in the second quarter, thick fog descended on the south end of Soldier Field. Most of the haze entered the stadium just above the upper tank seats, then swirled in large masses down toward the field, behind the Bears' bench and into the stands on the west side. Eagles owner Norman Braman was furious they didn't stop play. Tunney asked both coaches for input at halftime when the Bears held a 17-9 advantage. Ryan only wanted to discuss the Eagles not getting any calls. Ditka said he had no objection to the second half starting as scheduled. So be it.

Ditka and Ryan wanted a pound of flesh *now*. Limited visibility wasn't going to postpone their own private war.

CBS drew huge ratings, but viewers weren't parked in front of a 27" Magnavox because it was a great game. The images in the second half were provided almost exclusively from field-level cameras. They were unique and magnetic. Lundquist and Bradshaw couldn't see the field and described the action off the same monitor viewers were watching. America was getting the pilot of *NFL Twilight Zone*. CBS showed the tandem several times, accentuating the compromised visibility from the press box level and how Lundquist and Bradshaw had been reduced to one small monitor to see *anything*.

In the press box, public relations director Bryan Harlan escorted working media to the north end zone on both sidelines for the second half. The field was engulfed in fog and visibility beyond 20 yards was only an occasional respite as clouds of fog swirled. Philadelphia media watched from the Philly sideline to the east while Chicago's credentialed crews worked on the west sideline, stretching from the end zone to about the 15-yard-line.

I set up shop next to the pylon at the goal line, not far from where the Bears tunnel to and from the locker room. My eyes met Neal Anderson's from a few feet away after he scooted around left end before getting shoved down near the goal line. Television viewers saw breath emanating from players' face masks. I *heard* it. The huffing. Coughing up phlegm. Conversations after huddle breaks. Grunts and groans. Feet trampling on the first-year natural grass sounded like thunder when a play neared our vantage point in the northwest end zone.

It's impossible to deny getting swept up in the magic of the moment. A working press credential dangling in a lanyard at training camp and on the Big Ten beat for the *Hammond Times* in '86 afforded me field-level views before, but this was different. This was a bizarre weather system wreaking havoc on a playoff game and media were within a ref's underhanded spiral distance of the game's most fearsome warrior, Reggie White. He was right there in front of me, hands on hips, panting, waiting for the Bears to break the huddle. Everyone I talked to was mindful of our ringside view of what surely would become a mythical playoff game.

The Bears were terrible. That's part of the myth. Nobody remembers it. The Bears survived and advanced to the NFC title game only because the Eagles made even more mistakes. Randall Cunningham threw for 407 yards, at the time second only to Bernie Kosar in an NFL playoff game but had little support. One of Cunningham's three interceptions was gifted to the Bears when fullback Anthony Toney's bobble was swiped by *Cool Mo D*, Maurice Douglass. Usually reliable tight end Keith Jackson dropped an easy touchdown pass early. The Eagles had two TDs negated by penalty. Luis Zendajas missed a 43-yard field goal. Philly had to re-kick after being ruled off-sides on a kickoff and the Bears gained 34 yards on their second chance with Glen Kozlowski's return to midfield. Eagles punter John Teltschik stunk. Four punts with a long of 36 yards.

Tomczak, who started for the dinged-up McMahon, was intercepted three times before White knocked him out of the game and into '89 a bit early. The Calumet City native went 10-of-20 for 172 with one touchdown, a 64-yard strike to McKinnon that gave the Bears an early lead. McMahon mopped up. The typically reliably running game was sparked by two big plays — a 58-yard jaunt by Thomas Sanders and Anderson's long run of 23 — but was bottled up most of the day.

The Bears dodged disaster. Afterward, players in both locker rooms reported similarly. The sideline markers that served as route distance guides weren't visible, useless. Coverages literally were disguised to the offense. Offensive shifts and motions were undetectable in the secondary. Nobody told me they felt it was dangerous to play with such limited visibility but players confessed unfamiliar uncertainty.

The following day was New Years of '89, and most were dialed into the 49ers' dismantling of Minnesota 34-9 in the nightcap. I debated weather's influence on meaningful football games with colleagues and friends for the first time. Over the years, my conviction has grown stronger. The NFL needs to serve its participants first, then consider its thirsty-for-more viewing public. When the stakes are raised, the integrity of the game never should be compromised. Get 'em indoors if it's a blizzard or in wind-blown, hard rain.

If it's foggy, wait until is passes.

"C'mon dude. Aren't some of your best memories of backyard football when you and your buddies bundled up and trudged through the snow?"

That was where it belonged — in the field behind my dad's house. The sport's most elite players shouldn't be reduced to perform under such debilitating conditions. Arrowhead Stadium in Kansas City, which hosted the ugliest weather game in January, is not a backyard in your neighborhood. Patrick Mahomes and the Chiefs are a tick more skilled than pals who lived on our blocks.

The Fog Bowl was made legend for its uniqueness and for the churlish grudge match between Ditka and Ryan. What many don't know is how their egos precluded good judgment and how uninvolved the NFL actually was. It also brought the Bears one step closer to the end of the era. After blitzing New England in the Super Bowl, the Bears went 2-5 in the playoffs under Ditka. A 16-6 win over New Orleans in the wild card round in '90 was the last feather in their playoff caps.

Eight days after the Fog Bowl cleared, Bill Walsh's 49ers zoomed into Soldier Field and *The Genius* took care of unfinished business with Ditka. The Bears were pulseless, and the 49ers smoked 'em 28-3 in the NFC Championship game. The '9ers went in to win it all with a 20-16 win over MVP Boomer Esiason's Bengals in SB 23.

Bear weather. Sure, it is.

PERSPECTIVE IS ELUSIVE

The more we experience, if we're paying attention, the sharper our focus. It's hard to win a Super Bowl. *This just in*. In the spring, I asked Jay Hilgenberg if his perspective changed on the '85 Bears never getting a second parade. Years ago, Hilgenberg told me he never wore his Super Bowl ring. The seven-time Pro Bowl center saw the ring as a symbol of a one-hit wonder.

"We should have had more. I can't remember the last time I wore it. It's in a box in a drawer," he said in '07.

Time heals wounds, yes. I asked if he still feels a bit low over winning that lone championship.

"No, I don't," Hilgy said, a hint of relief detectable in tone. "One of the things I've thought about is how my uncle got there four times and never won once so that puts in perspective better."

Uncle Wally Hilgenberg was a linebacker on all four of the Vikings' Super Bowl teams in the '70s. Minnesota lost all four and hasn't been back to a Super Bowl since SB 11, a 32-14 loss to the Raiders in '77. Winning a championship is hard, I offered. So often that's overlooked when expectations aren't actualized and sports hearts break. So many stars must be aligned. Timing is among them.

One of the greatest defenses in the NFL's first 75 years was the '70s Vikings, the *Purple People Eaters*. Their ascent to greatness coincided with a sluggish, pedestrian Minnesota offense. No Warren Moon, Randy Moss, Adrian Peterson, or Justin Jefferson. In fact, the Vikings' offense was so impotent, it didn't score a first-half touchdown in *any* of their four Super Bowl appearances.

In their loss to the Steelers at Tulane Stadium — which Jay Hilgenberg attended with brother, Joel, and father, Jerry — the Vikings' offense not only failed to score, it *gave up* the only points of the first half. A confused Fran Tarkenton stumbled and fell on a bobbling ball in the end zone. Dwight White jumped on him for the deuce. Pittsburgh 2, Minnesota 0 at halftime. The Steelers won 16-6. The Vikings' only score came on a block punt recovered in the end zone. Then they botched the PAT. Minnesota rushed for 17 yards.

Timing was not on the side of Minnesota's great defense. Wally Hilgenberg played 12 years with the Vikings and four more with Detroit but never won a Super Bowl. Minnesota never gets mentioned with the *Steel Curtain*, Seattle's *Legion of Boom*, Ray Lewis' *Purple Reign* Ravens, or the *Shufflin' Crew* Bears.

Joel Hilgenberg played center for the Saints for 10 years, but his circle never intersected with Drew Brees. Joel snapped to the Billy Joes and Bobby Sues. Timing.

THE TWO MIKES — *McDITKA*

The Bears had timing issues, too. More soon, but the one-hit wonder narrative is fueled primarily on the Bears self-destructing. External factors have been obscured by all the finger pointing. Teammates at teammates. Or at coaches. Or coach on coach crime. Contempt toward ownership. Interestingly, McMahon isn't among those still casting blame. The sassiest, brassiest Bear of all has mellowed. Right now, he just wants his foot to feel well enough to walk comfortably again.

Ditka once galvanized the Bears before losing his way. Meanwhile, management stuck its nose in personnel decisions and sometimes predicated them exclusively on the exhaustion of resources or a personal dislike for a player. Ditka's Bears didn't win more for a lot of reasons. A look at the periphery will follow these pockets full of implosions.

The Bears head coach began morphing to a cartoon version of himself after the '85 season. He warned players about falling for the trappings of success and the spoils that go to the victors. He demanded his team remained focused and not pounce on every endorsement or appearance. Then he showed up in television commercials hustling everything. Ditka's benefactors included a rustproofing outfit that plopped him on a horse, clad in a Knight's shining armor.

Remember *The Grabowski Shuffle*? Dancin' Ditka snatched 10 grand a day for the ridiculous video that spoke of the Bears being a family of blue-collar ham-and-eggers, not quiche eaters. Then he lit a $30 Cuban and uncorked a high-end Napa cabernet.

Ditka grasped for every check he could get in his clutches. He began charging huge fees — and getting them — for speaking engagements. He collaborated with *Tribune* football writer Don Pierson on his biography —*Ditka*. In the biography, the coach besmirched Halas for reneging on a $5K bonus he promised to each player on the '63 championship team. The average player salary was $20,000 in '63 while the elite players earned up to $35K with bonuses. Perhaps McCaskey grinded over Grand Papa Bear getting taken down a notch right after the Super Bowl. Stiffing the worker bees was among the traditions Halas passed along to his grandson

Michael. How McCaskey screwed the Bears on their championship rewards and other petty expenses follow in *Team McCaskey*.

The owner and Ditka clashed more, and McCaskey flipped a middle finger at his coach when he fired GM Jerry Vainisi in '87. Ditka and Vainisi were tight. Vainisi's role was more as "the money guy" while Bill Tobin spearheaded player personnel but Jerry was a Ditka confidante. His dismissal bruised Ditka. The Bears didn't hire a successor to Vainisi and Tobin and Ditka shared the GM's responsibilities.

Ditka stayed busy in the off seasons with endorsements, speaking engagements, golf and drinking. After several years of Da Coach not leading by Da example, McCaskey called him out in '89. The owner publicly stated he sought "equal commitment" from the guy who warned his players of taking their eyes off the prize.

The Bears coach stayed boozy for most of the 20th century. Ditka exhibited alcohol-induced irritability, which once led to feuds with Halas and the eventual trade to Philadelphia after six years in '66. The '88 HOF inductee regularly was hammered on his Sunday night wrap-up show with Johnny Morris on CBS-2. Ditka always was unloading on somebody and often punched down.

"Get'cher mouth shut... Jerk." (to a fan)

"Here's your IQ, buddy." (also to a fan)

"Ditkith." (imitates an inarticulate, heckling fan)

"Talk to the trainer. Next?" (to media)

"We like our people. Those of you who don't like our people, there's 27 other teams you can root for." (also, to media)

It was a tired record and almost everybody was fatigued by the same predictable choruses. Except for the ardent Ditkaphiles — guys in Coogie sweaters that draped over their sausage-filled bellies.

The players strike in '87 fractured the Bears. After getting a reasonable effort from the union-busting replacement players, Ditka referred to the *Spare Bears* as "the real Chicago Bears." That went over well. Steel country Mike. Got it. Ditka grew more cartoonish with each obstacle.

Ron Rivera said the 24-day work stoppage divided the tenured Bears even further. Their daily intake of mutinous behavior and verbal barbs went far enough with Ditka and Ryan pitting offense against the defense. The strike brought internal friction and fueled heated disagreements over "work or not work." It splintered the units within the unit. Deep-rooted grudges didn't dissipate quickly for some.

Ditka's reactions to Buddy's cheap shots from afar were the replies of a petulant teenager and offensive to the defense.

"Hell, our defense should have been great. They only had to play 20 minutes a game. We had the ball the other 40 minutes."

"I'm not happy he's gone. I'm *elated*."

"Never again in history will an assistant coach get so much credit as Buddy did. I handled it well."

Wow. Keep telling yourself that.

When Ditka was available and present, he was good with his players. He didn't tell them only what they wanted to hear. Mike was erratic, however. Approachable and amenable one day, then completely oblivious to a vow he made two days later. Ditka would agree to sign an item for charity or say a quick hello to a small group visiting the building, then thumb his nose and walk away from the promise on the back end. "Not today" or "I don't have time right now" he'd bark curtly, detached and annoyed by the exchange.

McCaskey ignored upgrades necessary for the team's decaying and cramped Lake Forest College headquarters. The weight room and meeting rooms were undersized for an NFL team. The field behind Halas Hall flooded regularly and players grew tired of shlepping all over Chicagoland to practice. The basement also flooded occasionally and stunk up the building. Players walked several blocks in their gear to practice at South Park. They worked out in a forest preserve off Route 176, Maine South high school, the Great Lakes Naval Station (with a dry cement floor), the *McBubble* in Waukegan — until it collapsed in '90. McCaskey didn't want to drop $5M on fixing the roof. Its replacement was near $20M.

The Bears didn't upgrade much of anything until they moved to a brand-new campus before the '98 season. When they trained for the playoffs, they hit Champaign, South Bend or Madison. Or the Falcons' dumpy summer camp site in Suwanee, Georgia, which was where they prepared for Philadelphia in '88. *They've been everywhere, man. Yeah, they've been everywhere.*

Players had to fight for every dollar, and it's believed only two Bears — Payton and Hilgenberg — ever got to $1M a year in annual salary. Hampton would have joined the two-comma club in '90 but missed two games and narrowly missed the whole whack. Dent was incentivized and got close. Covert flirted with it.

"They said after the Super Bowl they were going to reward their own and then they turned around and did the exact opposite," Keith Van Horne said. Twice near the end of the Ditka era, Van Horne was a training camp holdout, trying to milk another $25-50K out of accountant Ted Phillips. As Phillips' role expanded, so did his self-assuredness. At the Super Bowl in '86, a more deferential and feet-on-the-ground Phillips was tasked with making sure all the rental cars and accommodations for assistant coaches were buttoned down. Fast forward a couple years and the accountant's voice was on the radio, giving his opinions of football games, critiquing players and reminding them of their place on the food chain.

Van Horne fired back in an interview with me on the AM Loop in August of '91 and again in March when we sipped tequila and noshed on prime beef for three hours at Alexander's in Northbrook. "Ted Phillips, that son of a bitch. He's one of those guys you look at for the first time and his face just tells you not to trust him."

PLAYER SHORTAGE

Plan B free agency first drew blood in '88 when Washington swooped in and made an attractive bid for Marshall. The Bears had no interest in matching and Marshall became a star for the Redskins. Washington beat Buffalo in SB 26, and the Florida Gator earned another ring. The Bears denounced Plan B publicly and were one of only two NFL teams (Cincinnati) that didn't sign a Plan B free agent in '89.

Magnifying the absence of outside help was the lack of top-tier reinforcements plucked from the draft. As the '80s met the '90s, draft prosperity waned and progressively worsened. Tobin was a terrific scout under Jim Finks, but Toby and Ditka whiffed on most collaborations in the second half of their 11-year partnership. Other than running back Neal Anderson, the 27th-overall pick in '86, the Bears didn't add elite players. At the same positions where Finks' former first-rounders flourished, first-rounders Trace Armstrong ('89), Stan Thomas ('90) and Jim Harbaugh ('87) weren't as impactful. The *JAG corps* (*just-a-guy* level talent) can't elevate a team to playoff contention. The depth chart took hits from underwhelming draftees in the second rounds and beyond as well.

When Hampton played his last game in the 31-3 playoff loss to the Giants in mid-January of '91, there was way too much Brad Muster and not enough Matt Suhey on the roster. Too much Ron Cox and not enough Singletary. By Ditka's last year in '92, a 5-11 finish, the Bears had excessive tread wear on their tires and in too many positional groups. And they still hadn't found a leader like McMahon to run the show.

It was Ditka and McCaskey who engineered McMahon's exile to San Diego during the '89 camp. "The two Mikes didn't want him anymore," Van Horne said. Ditka grew annoyed by McMahon's recurring medical malfunctions and attributed it to the quarterback's lifestyle. That's rich on so many levels.

"Ditka wanted a weight room guy," Thayer recalled. "Jim was a golfer. Mike was a purist. We wanted and needed Jim around."

"Mike called me the morning of the trade and said, 'we're going in another direction.' At that point, I didn't care," McMahon reflected in July. "I would have loved to have played with Mike. Number one, he was a great player, but I also could have shown him and explained to him what I saw and what I was dealing with out there."

In an interview with FOX in '20, Singletary fell on his sword over the endless soap operas that veered the Bears off course. "We were so exhausted from all of the drama we were going through. 'This guy is mad at him' and 'this guy is making more money' and 'this guy is getting more endorsements.' When I look back at it, it was fair that we only won one Super Bowl. I wish I had done a much better job as a leader. I wish I came to camp with a bat one day and started whaling on people because we had something really special."

Stark candor and rare introspection. Singletary's transparency is refreshingly authentic. His conclusion, however, is pure nonsense. Pretzel logic. Singletary couldn't have ball-batted the Bears back to their '85 standard. Corporal punishment wouldn't have healed McMahon or make anybody's aging legs feel spry. Going to the whip wasn't going to make Vestee Jackson a better corner or turn Stan Thomas into Stan Jones. Perhaps John Roper, a linebacker out of Texas A & M the Bears took 36th-overall in '89, would have made more plays if Singletary's wrath contused Roper's arms and legs. Yeah, that's it.

The Two Mikes were going to do as they pleased. They proved it repeatedly and over a long period of time. Whatever bulldog Singletary had in him wasn't going to deter a narcissist and a lucky sperm club heir from their own self-accommodating journeys. Singletary is spot-on acknowledging the gravity of the messes they made for themselves but the most injurious realities they faced weren't fixable by a trip to the woodshed. Verbally or literally.

The accounts and reflections on the slow demise under Ditka have omitted one essential component to complete the picture. People so often see only what's sitting in front of them and pay no mind to the periphery. This is shameful for all of us who've been flapping our gums and tapping keys for the last 30-some years.

MT. BEARSNOMORE

The laments of joylessness rarely are paused to credit the evil enemies who crashed the Bears' extended party. There were legends of their own out there who swung the wrecking ball at the cracking walls in Lake Forest and this is ignored. Selective memory or ignorance. There were huge impediments over which the Bears had no control. Great players, some the best of all time, and at key positions. The boys of Ditka also opposed A-list coaches, headmasters and first lieutenants. Some of the most effective and respected owners and general managers in history also had a hand in the perceived choke job by the Bears.

I've selected four outsiders who best represent one-hit

wonders imprisonment. The men whose busts appear on the Mt. Rushmore of "Bears oppressors" are Charles Martin, Lawrence Taylor, Joe Gibbs and Joe Montana. *Mt. Bearsnomore,* if you will.

CHARLES MARTIN

The '86 season undeniably was the Bears' best shot at a return to the biggest stage in sports. Payton still had some gas in the tank in his 12th year and Anderson was capable of a fast passing of the torch. Ryan was gone, but Vince Tobin's "Bear" defense allowed fewer points (11.7 ppg) than Ryan's in '86 (12.4 ppg). The Bears went 14-2. Unfortunately, McMahon went down in Week 12 after Green Bay defensive tackle Charles Martin bear-hugged McMahon around the waist, then slammed him to the astroturf on his right shoulder.

Martin wore a towel with a "hit list" under his belt and over his crotch. It included the numbers 9, 34, 63, 83 and 29. That's McMahon, Payton, Hilgenberg, Willie Gault and Dennis Gentry (why the last two, I have no idea). McMahon already had released the ball by 10 seconds and was watching his third-down interception by Mark Lee unfold downfield when Martin assaulted him. Green Bay's DT was flagged and ejected by Jerry Markbreit, but it hardly was equitable sanction for McMahon's separated passing shoulder. He already was playing with a torn labrum.

McMahon was done for the year and the Bears defended their title with Flutie at the wheel. Whether Ditka chose Flutie or Tomczak is irrelevant. Neither had the intrinsic qualities of McMahon.

Markbreit picked up a flag on Covert, who went after Martin. The Martin ejection market the first "match penalty" for an action away from the play and it set a precedent. Any violent act that's not considered part of the game can merit an ejection. Martin also was suspended for two games. The consequences for McMahon, meanwhile, didn't end with his being scratched for the duration of '86. It cast further shadow on the Bears quarterback, who already had been a regular in trainer Fred Caito's treatment room.

JOE GIBBS

The Redskins knocked the Bears from their bully pulpit after the '86 season with a 27-13 win at Soldier Field. They came back to the lakefront and repeated the TKO the next year, a 21-17 heartbreaker. This time, McMahon was healthy, just ineffective. Gibbs was the face of the franchise in Washington and the three-time Super Bowl winning coach was enshrined in Canton in '96. Best known for innovations with the passing game, Gibbs was on Don Coryell's staff with the Chargers and instrumental in the development of Dan Fouts. He was 40 when owner Jack Kent Cooke hired him, and Gibbs quickly resurrected the 'Skins and won the coach of the year award in '82 and '83. Washington punched out Miami's *Killer Bs* in Super Bowl 17 in '83, largely because of a dominant offensive line.

That's right, admirers of the *Black & Blues Brothers*. Washington had a poster-worthy O-line, too. *The Hogs* became a national brand and guard Russ Grimm was an HOF inductee in '10. Mark May was the other guard, Jeff Bostic the center, Joe Jacoby and George Starke were the tackles. The second iteration of Hogs included guards Raleigh McKenzie and Mark Schlereth and tackle Jim Lachey. That's some high-quality pork right there, *gang*.

The Redskins won three Lombardi trophies Bowls in 10 years under Gibbs, who deployed a different quarterback for each championship. That never had happened before and hasn't since. Joe Theismann was the man in SB 17, followed by Doug Williams in SB 22 and Mark Rypien in SB 26. Cooke wasn't driven by the bottom line exclusively and Washington was active in Plan B. They stole Marshall from the Bears in '88 and won the Super Bowl that year. GM Bobby Beathard, the architect of the 10-year run, also had a keen eye for talent and built the old "Bear way" under Finks — on the line of scrimmage. The defensive line featured Dexter Manley and Charles Mann, both great players who wreaked havoc on the Bears in the two playoff losses. Darryl Green is one of the most accomplished corners in NFL history. Green had an interception in Wash's 27-13 win and his 52-yard punt return for a score was the dagger in the 21-17 game. Green was one of the fastest players in league history (4.09 40 time in '86) and is a class of '08 HOFer.

LAWRENCE TAYLOR

L.T. is arguably the most impactful defender in NFL history. Taylor's penchant for collapsing the pocket and running down quarterbacks revolutionized the linebacker position. No. 56 in blue was a hybrid, lining up where defensive ends typically did, but not with his hand on the ground. He was a game changer of the highest order and is the last defensive player to win the MVP, which he claimed in '86 when the Giants won the Super Bowl. Bill Parcells quickly became a household name, and he transplanted a beating heart into a long-moribund franchise.

The '86 Giants' defense flirted with the same level of potency as the '85 Bears. DC Bill Belichick's 3-4 wasn't as hell-bent-for-leather as Buddy Ryan's 46, but it was the second stingiest D in the NFL, allowing just 14.8 ppg. Nobody defended the run better than New York, which allowed only 80 rushing yards per game. Even if Martin's body slam hadn't ended McMahon's season, these Giants would have been an extremely huge challenge for the Bears.

Taylor was the catalyst, and he was the biggest reason the Giants enjoyed sustained success. They won Super Bowl 21 with Phil Simms at quarterback, but when Simms but suffered a broken foot in Week 15 of the '90 season, Parcells' offense was directed by game manager Jeff Hostetler. The Giants annihilated the Bears 31-3 in the divisional round that January, due largely to an O-line that manhandled the Bears aging front seven and Armstrong, a second-year DE. Ottis Anderson had 21 of the Giants' 48 rushes for 194 yards. In the NFC title game in San Francisco, New York kept the ball for 39 minutes, keeping Montana off the field, in a 15-13 win. Parcells and Belichick went on the win the Super Bowl in a 20-19 win over Buffalo. Anderson was the SB 25 MVP after he rushed 21 times for 102 yards and a touchdown. New York's GM was '20 HOF inductee George Young, whose stewardship began in '79.

JOE MONTANA

San Francisco's Hall of Fame quarterback was the consensus GOAT until Brett Favre changed the conversation in the late-'90s. Montana had been in the winner's circle twice already before he beat the Bears 28-3 in the '88 NFC title game, in route to his third ring. The third-round pick in '79 finished among the top six MVP vote getters four times before winning consecutive MVPs in '89 and '90. His *magnum opus* is the 93-yard drive he engineered to win SB 23 with a comeback against Cincinnati in *The John Candy Game.*

As excellent as Montana was, the 49ers' success story is the textbook example of "organizations build dynasties." Owner Eddie DeBartolo and GM Carmen Policy had a comfortable partnership, and the duo met free agency in '93 with vigor. The Niners didn't fear overspending. Their stress was keeping the bar at "championship or bust" in a free market with a cap. And when they did win big, players were rewarded. DeBartolo also was quick to upgrade facilities. He believed in Walsh and gave him total space command of the football product. Walsh and Policy worked in concert together and the roster was stacked with some of the most accomplished players ever. Montana. Wide receiver Jerry Rice. Safety Ronnie Lott. A bevy of disruptive pass rushers. Rice still holds all the money stats records for receivers. In '10, NFL Films did a documentary on the *100 Greatest Players of All Time.* Rice was No. 1. Almost 23,000 receiving yards are more than 5,500 yards more than Larry Fitzgerald, who's second. His 197 receiving TDs dwarf silver medalist Randy Moss, who accrued 156.

While most think *West Coast Offense* when they consider the San Francisco dynasty, the 49ers boasted the No. 1 scoring defense in the league in '84 when they won their second championship. SF trashed the Bears 23-0 in the NFC title game that postseason, then went on to thrash Dan Marino in the Super Bowl. The 49ers' title was on the heels of Marino's record-setting sophomore season with the Dolphins, 5,084 passing yards and 48 TD passes.

Ronnie Lott's arrival in '81 produced one of the most eye-popping debut seasons by any defensive player ever. The eighth-overall pick out of USC in '81, Lott was bested only by L.T. in defensive rookie of the year voting. Taylor also won the DPOY. Lott was voted first-team All Pro as a rookie, the first of six first-team recognitions, and took three of his seven interceptions back for touchdowns. He finished sixth in MVP voting *as a first-year safety.* In his 14-year career, Lott accrued 63 picks, 51 of which came in his 10 years in San Francisco. In addition to his ball skills, Lott was a ferocious tackler. He played like a linebacker and his contemporaries regard him one of the most fearless, game-changing defenders of all time.

Fred Dean was pretty good, too. San Francisco got the defensive end in a trade with the Chargers in '81, the second of Dean's four-straight first-team All Pro seasons. Dean was inducted in the Hall in '08. His last year was '85, but the acquisition speaks to the brilliance of the chess game the 49ers played in the front office. For the late-'80s, they reloaded with the disruptive (and disturbed) Charles Haley. Policy took Haley in the fourth-round in '86 and immediately the James Madison product turned up the heat on quarterbacks. Listed as a linebacker, Haley turned in double-digit sack seasons in four of his first five seasons and also forced 12 fumbles.

As integral as Haley was, the 49ers moved him to Dallas after the '91 season due to chronic behavioral hiccups. San Francisco already had traded for Green Bay holdout pass rusher Tim *Six Shooter* Harris five games into the season. Accounts differ as to how Haley welcomed his new teammate. Legend had it Haley cut a hole in the top of Harris' convertible, then urinated on the interior. Haley said they were buddies, just out boozing before relieving himself between the players' cars.

When the Bears won Super Bowl XX, it was the second straight title for the NFC, which was amidst a 13-year run of Lombardi trophies. Of the 13, 11 were blowouts of 10 points or more. The only two competitive games were SB 23, San Francisco 20, Cincinnati 16 and SB 25, Giants over Buffalo, 20-19 (wide right). The 13-game streak is the longest for either conference since the Super Bowl was born after the '66 season (although it wasn't given the *super* title yet). The second-longest streak is the AFC's five-year reign between SB 7 and SB 11, two wins for Miami and Pittsburgh and one for Oakland.

That 13-year stretch isn't accidental. The NFC was markedly better, a real thresher.

The Bears undeniably were self-destructive, but they weren't gifting title shots to above-average teams. Washington, San Francisco and the Giants possessed some of the greatest players in history and it was during the zeniths of their careers. Those three organizations were model franchises, administratively crisp and staffed by qualified employees with people skills. Better GMs, scouts and coaches. Vision. A willingness to grow and to spend money.

The Bears were, well, they remained the Bears. Still reliant on *fire and passion*. Run the ball. Stop the run. Harass their quarterback. Lather, rinse, repeat. That recipe never earned the Shufflin' Crew a second bite at the championship apple. The post-'85 Bears won a lot of battles, but too many were against one another unfortunately. The in-fighting drained the battery for seven more Ditka-led years of long races against legendary high-octane vehicles. The Redskins, Giants and 49ers were special teams, well-oiled machines that beat the Bears to the finish line every year since *that one Super Bowl*.

No worries. Dave Wannstedt is on the way. *"We'll be fine."*

CHAPTER 11

He's Got a Knee
THE WANNSTEDT YEARS

"We're a running team. Remember what I told you. Now, go fetch me a championship." – fictional coach Bud Kilmer (Jon Voight) in the 1999 film Varsity Blues (speaking to West Canaan (Texas) Coyotes backup quarterback Jonathon Moxon (James Van Der Beek).

If the Bears hadn't pulled the trigger on Dave Wannstedt in January of 1993, chairman Michael McCaskey would have been crushed for it. Under Wannstedt's direction, the Dallas defense was No. 1 in the NFL during their first of three Super Bowl seasons over a four-year stretch. The Cowboys didn't have a defensive Pro Bowler in '91. *Wanny* was the hottest coaching candidate on the market.

The Giants also coveted Wannstedt, who had an amiable relationship with New York general manager George Young. At the 11th hour, when Wannstedt was first-and-goal on a contract with the Bears, Denver and New England zoomed in late to make a play for him. With a Super Bowl date against the Bills looming, however, the detail-oriented Wannstedt felt he'd expended enough energy on a future employer. There was a Super Bowl to win, and Young wanted a decision the Monday before the Super Bowl. It was too late to entertain a third or fourth suitor.

The Bears — and Chicago — were a sensible fit for the mustachioed Pittsburgher. There was tradition, especially on his side of the ball. Wannstedt heard Chicago described as "a big Pittsburgh." Since childhood, through college at Pitt and to this day, there's way more of the stockyards in Wannstedt than there is Madison Avenue.

Presented at a Soldier Field news conference on Dallas' off day, Wannstedt impressed and was received warmly by most fans and media. Even some of Mike Ditka's most ardent fans had grown exhausted from the tantrums and postseason disappointments. Wannstedt was cut from the same cloth. He was a younger, still-hungry Ditka and it made the transition seamless for the coach and most Bears enthusiasts. In some ways, the new head man was *Ditka Light.*

Wannstedt was a meat and potatoes football guy. Like Ditka, he believed in winning the line of scrimmage, the running game and a physical, disciplined defense. His two-a-day practices at training camps in Platteville, Wisc. were like Ditka's — physical and demanding. "Old school" football men believed practicing football makes one better at *playing* it. Novel.

Unlike his predecessor, Wannstedt was approachable, amenable and accessible. I met him the day he was introduced in '93, and we've remained connected since. In recent years, Wanny has settled into a comfortable second Chicago act as a media darling.

What Wannstedt inherited was an aging roster in most spots and not good enough in others. The harsh realities of life with Team McCaskey smacked him in the face before the staff's first draft. The 41-year-old coach wanted to assemble his team for workouts and the get-to-know-ya stuff before April, but there was no venue to assemble the troops.

"I said to Michael McCaskey, I've gotta get these guys together to see what they can do," Wannstedt reflected. "We've gotta have a practice or two before the draft. Michael said, 'we don't have a facility.' The snow caved it in, the bubble or whatever. So, I said we've got to go someplace warm so we went out to Mesa, Arizona. And I remember that first practice like it was yesterday. There were 14 players on that team who were on the Super Bowl team, so we were an *oooold* team that needed to be turned around."

After the customary stretch, Wannstedt requested a lap around the track before players broke off into positional group meetings and a walk-thru. Everybody accommodated, except William Perry, the veteran defensive tackle who captivated football America with a gap-toothed grin, a 54" waist and occasional offensive heroics in the '80s. "I looked over at the Fridge and saw he was walking toward the stationary bicycle. I said 'Fridge, what are we doin' here, man. We all gotta take a lap.' He looked at me, as only he could, and said 'coach, I can't run anymore.' I thought to myself, 'God, this is just a great start.' "

A harbinger. More obstacles lie ahead, and they lurked around every corner. What unveiled itself quickly was a six-year personnel slump from the previous regime. The Bears were old, slow and had no difference makers at the skilled positions. Wannstedt remembers being floored by Bears fans who booed incumbent starting quarterback Jim Harbaugh in the preseason opener on the lakefront.

Also stacked against Wannstedt was ownership. The Bears were the property of Ed and Virginia McCaskey, as penny-wise and pound-foolish as Ginny's father, George Halas. And '93 marked the arrival of free agency, making Wannstedt's plunge into the NFC Central even more daunting. One year after Green Bay traded for Brett Favre, they signed Reggie White. Nobody saw it then, but it was the genesis of the enormous gap that still separates the Packers and Bears.

Michael McCaskey's ego and involvement with the team soon mushroomed. So did that of lead bean counter Ted Phillips, who came to believe his football savvy qualified him to determine compensation in trades. Bill Tobin, the temperamental player personnel veteran, was readying for his departure when Wannstedt pulled into town.

In June, before Wannstedt and Tobin got a look at their first draft class in pads, Tobin bailed. Toby was an old-timer and put off by the Jimmy Johnson's Dallas model that Wannstedt intended to follow. Dave wanted a strong voice in player personnel decisions.

Tobin, most-aptly described as easily-agitated, wasn't having it. He took his projector and went home.

It was easily discernible Tobin was sour about younger brother, former defensive coordinator Vince Tobin, being passed over to succeed Ditka. Bill Tobin was inflexible on some of his strongest convictions. He believed *"players play, coaches coach, scouts scout"* and abhorred the new trend. Coaches flexing their muscles in the war room and with veteran acquisitions was foreign to Tobin, so he resigned and later landed in Indianapolis.

"I think you've seen it — I can get along with anybody," Wannstedt says of the relationship never forged. "He, uh (pauses to weigh his words) … That was disappointing. It just wasn't gonna work."

The Tobin irritability I experienced in the late-'80s soon became a punchline around the country in the '90s. Tobin unloaded on lowly media types, specifically ESPN draft expert Mel Kiper, and comedic actor Jay Mohr, who was taking a whack at sports talk. Sound bytes of edgy Tobin were played on sports yak outlets across the country.

Hard miles and an absence of simply ambulatory veterans weren't just a Fridge Perry problem. Among the veteran players with compromised mobility were the running backs. All of them. Wannstedt wasn't expecting Emmitt Smith but what he didn't see coming was a backs contingent of injury-riddled, past-their-prime, plodders. They were hardly capable of supporting Harbaugh, who still was struggling to find his way after six seasons.

BEAR CUPBOARDS, BEAR BONES

I was relaxing with a beer in one of my favorite August destinations — Dainisi's bar in Platteville, Wisc. — with eventual play-by-play man Jeff Joniak, then a twice-an-hour update guy on WBBM News Radio 780. We swapped thoughts on the first practices under Wannstedt before I commented on an overweight black guy who was sitting alone at the bar's entrance. He was holding a pool cue but wasn't playing and it was easy to assume he was security. I cracked something judgmental, like "man, that bouncer could use a few salads and a walking regimen."

"You're kidding me," Joniak grinned. "Bouncer? You don't recognize him?" Another look didn't get me closer to the puffy man's identity. "That's Ironhead Heyward," he said.

Craig Heyward spent five unimpressive years in New Orleans and signed with the Bears to help comprise the island of misfit toys that was the Bears' running backs room. Neal Anderson was 29 and suffered from debilitating, chronic hamstring issues. The No. 1 pick in '86 was at the end and '93 was the least productive (just 3.2 ypc) and final year of his career.

Darren Lewis, a sixth-round pick in '91, was the opening day starter at tailback. It was the last start of his three-year career. Heyward's longest run of the '93 season was 11 yards. He survived the year as the starting fullback but averaged a meager 3.0 yards per carry. Bobby Christian also was on the roster. Christian concluded his Northwestern career as the school's all-time leading rusher but wasn't NFL timber. He didn't pack enough punch or attitude to play fullback, either.

Tim Worley, a Pittsburgh castoff, also had a roster spot. Like his peers, Worley had little to offer. He made headlines only for speeding with weed possession. The diminutive Robert Green, an undrafted free agent of Washington in '92, was on the team for the first of four seasons with the Bears. He started seven games in a six-year career.

Here's a peek at the receivers room. There was Tom Waddle, a gritty but limited veteran nearing the end. Terry Obee was a regular. A third-year little guy out of Oregon, Obee made five starts and caught 26 passes and three touchdowns. Curtis Conway was a rookie in '93, the first pick in the Wannstedt era. Conway wasn't NFL-ready and caught only 19 passes. Wendell Davis, an undersized but fearless late first-rounder in 88, was a serviceable player. Davis suffered a season-ending injury in a 17-6 win in Week 6 against the Eagles. Harbaugh overthrew Davis, who freakishly got his feet tangled in the infamous seam of Astroturf at Veterans Stadium. Davis blew out both patella tendons and never played again.

The tight ends were Keith Jennings (aka *Godzookie*), Ryan Wetnight and rookie Chris Gedney. None were ever compared to Ditka. Or Emery Moorehead. Or Greg Latta.

The '93 Bears' offense was their worst since '74, the year before they drafted Walter Payton. Ron Turner's unit finished 24th of 28 teams in scoring, averaging 14.6 points per game.

Wannstedt's first year was a four-month roller coaster, a season of streaks. The Bears opened with losses to the Giants and Vikings before winning three in a row against the Bucs, Falcons and Eagles. They then lost three straight again, to the Vikings, Packers and Raiders.

What made me a Wannstedt supporter in '93 was the manner in which he kept his team unified and prepared after a 3-5 first half of the season. Defensively, the Bears were well prepared, and it was *only* on that side of the ball where the Bears sparkled in three straight road wins. If an NFL team ever reeled off three consecutive road victories with less offensive talent than those Bears, I didn't see it or hear about it.

The Bears survived two turnovers and only 224 yards of total offense in a 16-13 taffy pull in San Diego to start the streak. The following week at Arrowhead Stadium, Harbaugh threw two picks and carded a 37.1 rating in a 19-17 sleeper that pulled the Bears to .500. Four days later, the Bears punched out a mere 11 first downs in a 10-6 Thanksgiving victory over the Lions at the Silverdome.

Three weeks, three wins. All on the road. With an offense that scored all of four touchdowns. That just doesn't happen in the NFL. Aesthetically blemished as it was, the streak pulled the Bears to 6-5 and kept postseason aspirations alive. The Packers were next up for a Week 14 homecoming.

In the NFL's most-heralded rivalry, the Bears unearthed a new recipe for success. The best way to hide a bad offense is to keep it parked on the sideline. Kevin Butler kicked three field goals, and the rookie head coach's defense scored *three* touchdowns. The Bears beat the Packers 30-17 for a fourth straight win.

Turner's offense again struggled to move the chains with 10 first downs and less than 22 minutes of possession time. Detailed more in Chapter 6, it was "a Wannstedt win." Defensive scores came from Jeremy Lincoln, Dante Jones and Mark Carrier. Favre threw for more than 400 yards in his second season with the Packers, but the mistakes undid Mike Holmgren's Packers.

After two meetings, it was Holmgren 1, Wannstedt 1. That would change.

The limp Chicago offense ultimately smothered postseason hopes. In their final four tilts, the Bears squeezed out only 33 points. Four consecutive losses — Bucs, Broncos, Lions and Rams — and '93 vanished with a 7-9 start to the Wannstedt regime. Squeezing seven wins out of the roster was an accomplishment.

Defensively, Wannstedt's first Bears were battlers, relinquishing 14.4 points per game, third best in the league. Jones led the team in tackles and Richard Dent, in his 12th season, and Trace Armstrong consistently provided pressure. Dent had 12.5 sacks, Armstrong 11.5 and 36-year-old Steve McMichael chipped in with eight. McMichael was in his 14th NFL season, his last as a Bear.

It was time to move on from Harbaugh, who bolted for Indianapolis in '94. Turner's offense soon became the Erik Kramer and Steve Walsh Show. It was enough to suspend, albeit temporarily, the clown car of bad quarterbacks.

HAPPY NEW YEAR, 1995!

Optimism was in short supply when the Bears eked into the playoffs for a New Year's Day of '95 date with the Vikings at the Metrodome. The Bears again were pedestrian offensively in '94 and concluded the year in a listless 13-3 loss to New England. That was after getting kicked by the Packers two weeks prior, 40-3. The 9-7 Bears backdoored their way into the postseason when the Giants spit the bit in Week 17.

Dan Reeves, who was New York's consolation prize after the Bears hooked Wannstedt, started the dreadful Kent Graham at quarterback against Dallas. A win and Graham and the Giants were in while the Bears watched the playoffs on the couch for a third straight year. The Cowboys prevailed 16-13 to eliminate Reeves' Cowboys and the Bears got a date in Minnesota.

Kramer made five starts in '94 before a separated right shoulder ended his season. Walsh, who was a game manager, took the wheel. Meanwhile, the Vikings had Hall of Famers Warren Moon and Cris Carter, Chicago's offense had receiver Jeff Graham and a spunky rookie back in Raymont Harris. The Bears hadn't fared well in the *Baggy Dome*, either. They dropped five of their first 13 games there and many weren't contested. Surprisingly, the Vikings, who put 75 on Wanny's defense in the regular season, were only six-point favorites.

The Bears made fewer mistakes and erupted for a 35-18 upset victory fueled by the defense. The Bears harassed a gimpy Moon enough to make his 292 yards irrelevant. Barry Minter, who Wanny brought in from Dallas, and Lincoln intercepted Moon. Trace Armstrong sacked him twice. Meanwhile, the offensive line kept Walsh vertical. John Randall, one of the fiercest defensive linemen in his era, went sackless. Walsh, a Johnson-Wannstedt favorite at the University of Miami and briefly with the Cowboys, posted a sturdy 107.1 rating, throwing touchdown passes to Graham and Jennings. He was picked once and sacked once.

No better way to punctuate a win than a defensive touchdown. Kevin Miniefield, a Detroit castoff, scooped up an Amp Lee fumble and raced 48 years to conclude the scoring. Okay, it wasn't Wilbur Marshall as the snow fell on Soldier Field in the '85 NFC title game, but it was satisfying for anybody who loves defense. With the Bears, that's been the team's calling card since inception.

Wannstedt, who was sick the night before the game and needed IVs and a bit of rest before kickoff, recalled the essence of a *team* win.

"Our assistants did a great job," he recalled. "Everybody contributed. Defensively, we forced them to kick field goals. Got a few turnovers. Offensively, we did a lot of movement passing with Steve Walsh (he lights up saying the name), who we had just signed. Steve wasn't the greatest athlete, but we did a lot of play action and rolled him out. Special teams, Danny Abramowicz did a great job. We blocked a punt. So, it was a game where everybody had a piece of it. Everybody contributed. Football games like that just don't happen often."

Indeed. The Bears haven't won a playoff game on the road since. On New Years' Day of 2025, it will be 30 years since that win over the Vikings. They've copped only three postseason wins anywhere in the last 33 years. Bear Down.

KRAMER SETS THE STANDARD

In the second year of free agency, Kramer signed a three-year deal for $8.1M. He'd played a huge part in Detroit's only postseason triumph since the Eisenhower administration when the Lions rocked the Cowboys 38-6 in divisional round two years earlier. Kramer looked, walked and talked the part of a veteran NFL quarterback with leadership skills. When he strode onto the practice field in Platteville in the red *"Don't Tackle Me"* vest, a yapper aptly described the new QB's entry as "regal."

The Bears went 9-7 for the second straight year in '95 but Kramer's record-setting year was sullied by the absence of a playoff berth. He threw for franchise highs of 3838 yards and 29 touchdowns with 10 interceptions. As impressive as that was for a Chicago quarterback— in team history — it barely scratched the surface in else parts. Kramer wasn't even best in *the division* in his '95 — fourth, as a matter of fact. Favre, Moon and Mitchell, all topped it.

The refurbished offensive line kept Kramer upright and allowed only 15 sacks, a franchise best. Wannstedt and Graves did a nice job piece-mealing a credible O-line. Guard Todd Perry, the elusive fourth-round hit, was the best of the bunch. Free agent tackle Andy Heck still was productive. Jay Leeuwenburg, who played center and guard, was a good player and Chris Villareal and Todd Burger compensated for a lack of natural ability via their grinder's mentality, the weight room and a penchant for playing to the echo of the whistle. Still surviving '80s Bears Keith Van Horne, Mark Bortz and James "Big Cat" Williams were veterans who were willing teachers. The trio aided in building a bridge to the newbies who arrived early in Wannstedt's tenure.

One of Wannstedt's fondest memories remains the '96 season opener when the Bears pasted Dallas 22-6 on *Monday Night Football*. The Cowboys were missing Michael Irvin and Jay Novacek, but they weren't even competitive. The Bears created four takeaways from Wannstedt's former team, which also was penalized nine times. Late in the fourth, Smith was carted off on the spine/neck immobilizer board. Soldier Field got quiet, but only for a few minutes.

The offense needed a little razzle dazzle, a little trickeration, to dump the defending champs. They milked a touchdown out of a 33-yard reverse pass from Conway to the *ultra back* Harris. The Bears also executed a successful fake punt to set up a Carlos Huerta field goal. Troy Aikman and Barry Switzer hammered their team's effort and execution after game. It was a terrific way to open the curtain for the season after back-to-back 9-7 years. It was the third consecutive opening day victory for Team Wannstedt.

OVERMATCHED

The timing for Wannstedt's arrival (or that of any Bear's arrival in the

'90s for that matter) was unfortunate. The NFC Central was stacked and the Bears took beatings of Biblical proportion. A handful were nationally televised games. Even the great Ditka teams of the '80s wobbled on *Monday Night Football* and the *MNF* crew was in Chicago on Halloween in '94 for the Bears and Packers. The Bears were 4-3 and came in as slight favorites. Holmgren's Packers were 3-4 and had not yet achieved the stratosphere they reached after Favre logged a few more flight miles.

I was doing my show from a saloon on Michigan Avenue when news broke an American Eagle twin-engine flight out of Indianapolis, bound for Chicago, crashed in Indiana farmland about 110 miles southeast of Chicago. There was a de-icing issue, and all 68 passengers and crew perished, many of them Chicagoans. A cast of pall hovered over Chicagoland. Cold rain never stopped. Neither did the Packers once they got going.

Green Bay's 33-6 blowout win was detailed in *Dairyland Drought*. Running back Edgar Bennett had a career night for the Packers and the virtual unknown's success spawned a bit on my afternoon show on the Score. The "Edgar Bennett award" was bestowed upon any mere-mortal running back of little renown when he torched the Bears for 100 or more rushing yards. Future Bennett award recipients included Ray Zellars of New Orleans, (20-174-1) on 10/13/96 and Packer De'Mond Parker (19-113-2) on 12/05/99. Zellars' effort represented 25% of his yards for the season and easily was the best game in his four-year career. Parker appeared in only 19 games in his career and rushed for only 269 career yards.

It wasn't only the Bears who couldn't solve the Packers. Green Bay cut the hearts out of the Vikings until Randy Moss arrived in '98 and the Packers were rough on the Lions and Bucs, too. The Central was top heavy, and the Bears weren't helping themselves in the draft or via free agency. Draft gaffes under Wannstedt and scout Rod Graves were presented in *Cold Draft Bears*. John Thierry, Rashaan Salaam and Curtis Enis all were first-round bust outs. Conway, at best, was serviceable.

Meet some of the worst misses *after* the first round. Carl Simpson, a defensive tackle from Florida State, was the 35th overall pick in '93. Simpson only looked the part. He became a regular late in his second year but was just a guy (*jag*, in some circles). Simp didn't blow up guards to get penetration or clog gaps so linebackers could fill and disrupt the run game. He seldom got to the quarterback with just 7.5 sacks in five years, and didn't create turnovers, forcing only two fumbles in 48 starts and 74 games.

Gedney, a '93 third-rounder (61st overall) was *not* the "Novacek type" the Bears thought they were getting. The Bears burned a second-rounder (56th overall) on punter Todd Sauerbrun in '95. Not that the Bears couldn't use for a thunder-footed punter every year, and in this case, one who also kicked off, but in the second round? There was Stanford tight end John Alred. Northwestern running back Darnell Autry (I was wrong, too). Notre Dame defensive tackle Paul Grasmanis. Washington O-lineman Bob Sapp (yes, the MMA monster). Sapp's biggest obstacle was not being able to distinguish left from right. The Huskies staff took to writing an "L" atop his left shoe and an "R" on the right. As a result, the muscular Sapp couldn't acquire a driver's license. That omission from his college coaches incensed the brass at Halas Hall. Lots of misses.

Among the few draft successes was cornerback Walt Harris, the top pick in '96. Harris was a much more skilled player than fans and media acknowledged. The Mississippi State alum took bad advice from an agent and wore a ridiculously boastful t-shirt before he busted his first NFL grape: "Water covers two-thirds of the earth. Walt Harris covers the rest." Whoa. Actually, water covers more than that but who's splitting hairs. Harris set himself up for verbal thrashings.

The otherwise bashful Harris made 13 starts in his first year. He had good closing speed and was lanky, with a solid vertical jump to get up and contest the catch. Heavy is the lifting when playing corner on a team with a limp pass rush. Harris defended Herman Moore, the 6-4 Lion, who had his way with the Bears. The Vikings went from Carter to Moss. It didn't really matter who the Packers had because they had Favre. In his first three seasons, Harris collected 11 INTs and also forced seven fumbles. Take that, Jaylon Johnson. Walt had a 13-year pro career, man, the first six in Chicago. Finally, in '06, Harris went to the Pro Bowl after an eight-pick season with San Francisco. He finished with 35 picks and an impressive 17 forced fumbles.

Most of the Wannstedt-Graves picks, in and after the first round, were misses. In '97, Mark Hatley was brought in as the club's VP of player personnel and de facto general manager. Hatley had been a Kansas City scout in Kansas City for 10 years. The Bears started drafting better players. Hat busted a drive 350 yards and in the fairway in '98 when he identified Washington center Olin Kreutz in the third round, 64th overall.

The affable Hawaiian made six straight Pro Bowl appearances between '01 and '06 and was first-team All Pro in the Super Bowl season of '06. Kreutz started an amazing 183 games, one of the top iron men in franchise history. It was unfortunate for Wannstedt the center's arrival was in his Dave's sixth year. Had there been three or four more selections like Kreutz in preceding years, the Bears would have competed more capably.

Wannstedt was right when he told others "Jim Flanagan isn't too small to play in this defense" before taking Flanagan in the second-round selection in '94 (74th overall). He was a productive tackle in six of his seven years. Harris, who Wannstedt nicknamed the *ultra back* because Raymont resented the term "fullback," was a solid fourth-round pick in '94.

ALL BARK, NO BITE

Wannstedt brimmed with pride when he described the qualities free agent linebacker Bryan Cox was bringing to the Bears in '96. "An emotional player," Wannstedt beamed. He lauded Cox for earning Miami's captaincy under Don Shula and boldly forecast "a new direction" for the Bears, who were bringing in the kind of players "who take you that next level." The former Dolphin signed a four-year, $13.2M deal with the Bears in February of '96. At the time, it was the richest contract in Bears' history.

The Western Illinois product returned a fumble for a score in his first season in Chicago but only had three sacks and played in nine games. He forced one fumble. Three of the team's top four tacklers were from the secondary in '96 (safety Marty Carter was tops, followed by Harris, the corner, Minter, the strong-side linebacker, and Donnell Woolford, a corner). Cox's second year was a little better, but the Bears didn't get the player they thought. He started 15 games in '97 and again forced only one fumble. He had 19 FFs in his last four years with Miami. The tackles numbers weren't awe-inspiring, either. An every-down "mike" backer should rack up more than 68 solos in a season, especially on a team that doesn't win many time-of-possession battles.

Big plays weren't all Cox was missing. He struck some of us a guy who was great to have during prosperity but not so much when skies darkened. In the '97 opener in Green Bay, Cox lost his composure in a sideline explosion directed at Wannstedt, gesticulating and power pointing. It's the kind of give and take that happen regularly in the NFL and usually they're way over-discussed but I was among those who thought Bryan crossed the line. Without the bump, it was similar to Travis Kelce unloading on Andy Reid in Kansas City's Super Bowl 58 victory. Green Bay smacked the Bears 38-24 on *MNF*, hardly the tonic the Bears needed to rid themselves of the '96 stink.

Though Cox enjoyed only one great year as a pass rusher in Miami — 14 sacks in his second season in '92 — he made splash plays and was regarded a high-end defender. In '94, however, moving to middle linebacker diminished his impact. When the Bears got him, his production dipped more.

It was disappointing to me because I had been beating the drums loudly for the Bears to sign him (make no mistake, all of us want to be right). And, as a high-ranking officer in *Wanny's Army*, volunteered to join the recruiting team when the situation presented itself. Cliff Brady, Cox's agent, called me at home on a weeknight in the dead of winter and asked "you wanna meet Bryan? He's in town for a visit." Brady said.

Brady heard me imploring the Bears to sign his client and he lived five minutes from me in Northwest Indiana. I asked Brady what spirits Cox enjoys and 10 minutes later I was ringing the doorbell with a half-gallon of Captain Morgan in tow. Once Cox and his wife appeared comfortable with me, I gave them a sales pitch. It was more about Bryan's future after football, and it was genuine. In Chicago, former Bears find work. If they're stars, keep their names off the police blotter and make themselves accessible to fans and media, the world is theirs. The '85 Shufflers still are prospering from a season almost 40 years gone.

We sucked down a few Captain and Cokes and he asked a few questions about personnel. I didn't oversell anything. It was an enthusiastic but honest assessment. I *did* consider Flanagan and linebacker Joe Cain good football players. I told him Wannstedt and his assistants were good teachers. "Demonstrative" was an adjective that appealed to him. I stayed an hour, wished him well and told him once the signature is on the document, he must make his first radio appearance with me. Cox smiled, thanked me for the rum and promised to call the show once the deal is done.

And he did, two days later. Bryan was engaged, playful even, and signs pointed to the Score's *Heavy Fuel Crew* scoring an A-list regular. Cox was a badass who spoke his mind and went to Pro Bowls, and I was eager to get him in the mix on my show.

Or not. Overreacting to criticism from Mike North, the Score's midday host, Cox boycotted the station. After two unimpressive seasons, he was gone.

MIRED AGAIN IN McCASKEYVILLE

Kramer started all 16 games in his standard-setting season of '95. He wasn't old yet at 32 but his injuries were stacking up and Wannstedt wanted the security blanket of Walsh as the backup. It was an effective parachute in '94 when Walsh took over and went 8-3 before directing the playoff win at Minnesota.

But Walsh was too rich for the Bears' blood. He split for St. Louis over a lousy 250 grand the Bears refused to cough up to keep him. Sure enough, Kramer got hurt again in '96. A broken neck ended his season after a 1-3 start and a 38-year-old Dave Krieg assumed control. Wannstedt laughed when reflecting on the quandary in May but there was nothing humorous about the low budget and juggling quarterbacks in the mid-'90s. When I asked him if there was one personnel move he couldn't make that distressed him most, he said it was the accounting team not ponying up for Walsh.

"That's when I knew we were never gonna go over for anybody," he said. "When I put Krieg in the first time, he had to burn a timeout to dry off his hands and pants from what I thought was blood. He had tobacco spit and stuff all over him."

The veteran from now-defunct Milton College in Wisconsin barely managed to tread water. The Bears won six of his 12 starts but they were 26th out of 30 teams in points scored (17.7 ppg) and finished 7-9. It was another playoff miss and time to go hunting for a younger quarterback. What the offense desperately needed was somebody who could compete with Kramer. At the minimum, they needed a better player to be the understudy. Preferably, one not needing to be rinsed of tobacco juice before his first snap.

Rick Mirer was the staff's solution. In four years with the Seahawks, the No. 2 pick in the '93 draft had regressed instead of improving.

The Bears parted with their upcoming first-round pick for Mirer and Chicago was stunned. To his credit, Wannstedt never sought absolution for wanting Mirer. "I didn't need him to do that much in our offense," he said. "Just don't give it away." Former Seattle coach Tom Flores, a Wannstedt ally, had given Mirer a favorable projection to accomplish the minimum and manage a game.

The decision to part with a first-rounder, however, apparently was above Wannstedt's pay grade. Accountant turned-GM Phillips and Michael McCaskey made the decision *without* conferring with Wannstedt or Graves. The fifth-year head coach was informed by one of the suits "We got Rick Mirer." After taking a breath, Wannstedt asked "what did *we* give up for him?" He wanted Mirer, but never would have dealt a No. 1 for him.

Mirer never threw a touchdown pass for the Bears. In three starts, he went 0-3 and was intercepted six times. The former Notre Dame star completed only 51.5 % of his passes and posted a sobering 37.7 rating in his one season in a Bear uniform.

The day after the trade, Wannstedt had an appearance for Ford at the Chicago auto show. Good timing for my show, which was broadcasting from the Blue Oval exhibit that Friday afternoon. Wannstedt arrived early enough to do a 20-minute interview on my afternoon show with Terry Boers. He was aware the trade quickly was overwhelmingly unpopular among Bears fans and media and steered right into it.

With a smile on his face and jump in his presentation, Wannstedt joked about how the Mirer deal was a make-it-or-break-it scenario. Paraphrasing

Dave: "This is it. I know that. If we didn't get this one right, that'll be it." It was an atypical response from a pro coach. Historically, it's seldom when they offer admissions of failure. And instead of dishing the standard defensive reply, an emotionally bankrupt reply or intellectualizing the trade, Wannstedt flashed a self-deprecating humor. He walked into the lion's den and pulled up a chair.

After the show rolled closing credits, we went to the dealer's green room for a few beers. Wannstedt peeled off the layers of filters and let a few things off his chest. Not about the Mirer trade, but about some of his critics' demands for a more *in-your-face* taskmaster on the sideline.

Again, I'm paraphrasing Wannstedt: "Some of these fans and some of you guys want me to criticize these players like Mike did when guys didn't produce," he said. The expression on Wannstedt's face revealed frustration. Helplessness, maybe. "It wouldn't be hard if I wanted to but that's not me. That was Ditka. What am I gonna do, stand up there and hammer Michael Timpson? You tell me how a wide receiver catches 68 balls for 800-some yards and can't find the end zone once? How can a receiver catch that many balls and not find the end zone at least once, by accident? But I'm not gonna cream him in front of everybody. That's counterproductive. That's never been how I do it."

He was as animated as I'd ever seen him and it was easy to see the collar tightening after back-to-back seasons without a playoff appearance. Frustrations about which I was unaware then also had to be on his mind. The Bears still hadn't moved into appropriate facilities or employ a pro personnel scouting department. Cox was the only "big money" free agent they signed in four years and the McCaskey-Phillips duo was flexing its muscles more each year.

The '97 Bears dropped their first seven games and finished 4-12. The defense was second from the bottom in points allowed (26.3 ppg) and the offense continue to wallow in the mire. Somehow, Wannstedt survived and returned for a sixth year. Unfortunately, '98 produced more of the same. Kramer went 3-5 as the starter and got hurt again. Enter Steve Stenstrom, a fourth-rounder in Kansas City in '95. In seven starts, Stenstrom won once.

Seventh-round pick Moses Moreno also got a start, a loss in Tampa. The Bears couldn't run the ball, either and No. 1 pick Curtis Enis failed to impress in his rookie year. Bennett, the former Packer, was the No. 1 tailback. He was 29 and the Bears again were among the bottom feeders in both points scored and points allowed.

After a second straight 4-12 finish, Wannstedt was canned. In six years, his Bears teams went 40-56 (.417) in the regular season and 1-1 in the playoffs.

In 2024, Wannstedt holds no grudges or lament obstacles over which he and his staff and players had to leap. I believe it's genuine when he says he forever will be grateful to the Bears for affording him that first head coaching opportunity. He gained redemption after his dismissal.

Wannstedt was successful with the Dolphins, going 42-31 (.575) and 1-2 in the postseason in five years. Miami went 11-5 in '00 and again in '01 and also won 10 games '03. Wanny was fired after a 1-8 start in '04, but his tenure with the Dolphins is categorized most accurately as a rebound from expectations unfulfilled in Chicago.

He returned to his roots at Pitt for a six-year run as Panthers head coach. Wannstedt's teams went 42-31 before his return to the NFL. Wanny settled into assistant roles with his former underlings — Chan Gailey with Buffalo and Greg Schiano in Tampa.

Wannstedt slayed more dragons than higher profile previous head coaches the Bears fired. Or Bears assistants who went elsewhere to be a headmaster. In Philadelphia, Buddy Ryan went 43-35-1 (.551) in five seasons but never won a playoff game in three tries. Buddy later flopped conclusively with the Cardinals. Arizona went 8-8 under his tutelage in '94 before a 4-12 season spelled the end after two years.

Ditka was a disaster in New Orleans, posting a record of 15-33 (.313) and no playoff appearances in three seasons. Iron Mike's Saints went 3-13 in '99, which was enough for owner Tom Benson. Ditka never blew the whistle again.

Lovie Smith was axed after just two years in Tampa. The Bucs went 8-24 (.250) under Smith. Texans owner Cal McNair popped Lovie after only one year, the infamous 3-13 finish in '22 that gifted the Bears the first pick in the draft.

Vince Tobin was an abject failure in the desert, going 28-43 (.384) and 1-1 in the postseason in four years and change.

Ron Rivera is the only former Bear assistant or head man who put more skins on the wall than Wannstedt *after* leaving Chicago. Rivera got his first crack as an assistant with Wannstedt in '97 and later earned two Coach of the Year awards with Carolina. His Panthers made it Super Bowl 50 and narrowly lost to Peyton Manning's Broncos. Carolina went 76-63-1 (.546) and 3-4 in the playoffs in almost nine years under Chico. In Washington, Rivera's teams went 26-40-1 (.396) and 0-1 in the postseason.

When Wannstedt hung up the whistle in the early teens, he quickly morphed into a media star, locally and nationally with FOX studio shows for college and pro football. He remains a regular on the Score and on *Pro Football Weekly's* television show.

It took 25 years for most of Chicago to get to know the Wannstedt some of us discovered shortly after arrived. Wannstedt not only was a terrific defensive coach, he's personable, likeable and unassuming. Dave's a great storyteller and has been as entertaining as any former coach or manager who's worked in Chicago media.

In the *city that works*, Dave Wannstedt is as real as working a double at Inland Steel.

CHAPTER 12
Payton's Place
CHICAGO'S FAVORITE SON

> *"Some birds just can't be caged. Their feathers are too bright. And when they fly away, a part of you... does rejoice. But still, the place you live in is that much more drab, empty, when they're gone."*
> *– Red (Morgan Freeman) in the 1994 film Shawshank Redemption.*

Friday, November 1, 2024, marked the 25th anniversary of Walter Payton's death. He was 46 when a rare liver disease led to the bile duct cancer that claimed his life. I cannot remember a sadder day at work in my work. It felt like all the oxygen had been extracted from the city's lungs.

More than Mike Ditka, Michael Jordan or any other superstar, Payton belonged to Chicago. I prefer to begin this chapter with how he lived.

If you watched Payton for his entire career as I did, you too will learn things left unsaid or unpublished. If you weren't here to experience the magic of Payton, you'll get much deeper on Payton than from what can be gleaned from highlight reels or documentaries that chronicle the greatest player in football history. Arguably, the most interesting, too.

DON'T POKE THE BEAR

You'll pardon a Bears fan if he groans when the schedule reveals a Thanksgiving date in Detroit or Dallas. Another turkey day sullied by bad Bears quarterbacks. Millions of Americans nod off in the *La-Z-Boy* before pie because Chicago's offenses have been *football Ambien* for most of my 63 years. Positive outcomes have been elusive on Thanksgiving.

In November of 1977, the Bears had playoff aspirations as they arrived in the Motor City for a Week 11 date against a lousy Detroit roster. Like the Bears, however, the Lions were 5-5 and chasing Minnesota in the NFC Central. Detroit had nothing offensively in '77. So, by what game plan would Bears head coach Jack Pardee be best served? Just punch out grumpy. Win ugly and wear them down with heavy doses of their third-year running back — Payton.

It would have been indefensible organizational malpractice. Payton was overtaxed from his Superman act in the 10-7 win over the Vikings just four days earlier. He carried 40 times for an NFL-record 275 yards. While battling a fever that peaked at 104 a few hours before kickoff.

That volume of work on Soldier Field's artificial playing surface was abusive on everybody, especially somebody whose position requires running hard on it almost every snap. The knees took high-impact blows from what basically was a concrete surface underneath a thin carpet. The Bears finally switched to natural grass in '88, the year after Payton retired. Astroturf was a reprehensible product that never should have been deployed by NFL teams or gone unchallenged by the players association. Trauma to the muscles, tendons and bones with a side order of strips of skin that have been harshly scraped from the hands, arms and knees. Even Payton's chiseled body needed downtime.

With Payton running on fumes, the Bears couldn't get out of first gear. Detroit was about to take a 7-0 lead into the locker room at halftime when a Lions staffer made a galactically foolish mistake. The clever employee tasked with programming the jumbotron in the Pontiac Silverdome (replays, updated game stats) mocked the wrong man. In large letters on one of the NFL's first mammoth in-stadium monitors, a message read *"Walter Who?"*

Bad idea.

"Walt made sure everybody saw it," recalls Dan Jiggetts, then a second-year tackle out of Harvard and Payton confidant. "He ran up and down the sideline, chirping and pointing to the scoreboard so we all saw it." Jiggetts said Payton's yap was incessant. *"Who the hell do they think they are? Walter Who? Are you kidding? You guys see that? What the f____. Look at that! What's wrong with these people? Stick around, you'll find out."*

Payton would have favored skipping the halftime skull session and jump right back into the ring, I suspect. If you didn't see Payton play, think "the Jordan of football." His game had no weaknesses. Think of Payton on the same plane as M.J. when debating the fiercest competitors. And as athletes who remained capable of *willing* their team to victories even when their bodies betrayed them.

In the second half, Payton jumped out of the phone booth and returned volley. *This* is *Walter Who?* He led all rushers with 137 yards and a touchdown on 20 attempts. Payton also led all receivers with 107 yards on four catches, including a 75-yard TD that gave the Bears a 14-7 lead in the middle of the third quarter.

The Bears won 31-17 behind Payton's heroics. Four days after his record-setting performance against Minnesota *with a fever*.

The *Walter Who?* salvo, coupled by Payton's reaction to it, sparked everybody in the white-on-white uniforms. Quarterback Bob Avellini even dialed in, posting a robust 101.4 rating on 14-of-21 passing attempts for 260 yards and two TDs with two picks and a sack. On most charters returning from Detroit, Avellini's face resembled that of the heavyweight steppingstone of the era, Chuck Wepner, aka the *Bayonne Bleeder*. This was a pleasant short flight home.

Pardee's Bears subsequently ran the table, winning at Tampa, at home against Green Bay and at the Giants and finished 9-5. For the first time since the '63 NFL Championship game, the Bears went to the playoffs. Payton was the NFL's MVP after leading the league in rushing (1852 yards), attempts (339) and touchdowns (14). Dallas drummed the Bears 37-7 in the wild card round but there was a renewed sense of hope. Five years after the expiration of the great careers of Gale Sayers and Dick Butkus, first-round picks in '65, Chicago again could claim possession of the best player in the league.

Payton had arrived and finally the Bears landed in the playoffs. And with Payton, the face of the franchise was likeable. Sayers was aloof as a younger man and Butkus was as amenable as a freshly-neutered Doberman.

SUPERHUMAN

Every season, until his 13th and final year in '87, Walter Payton was *the truth*. He not only was the greatest *pure* football player in the history of a charter franchise, but he was also the most dedicated. Payton just didn't miss games. Ever. And he averaged 335 carries a year in the 11-year stretch between '76 and '86.

Payton was 5-10, 205 lbs. and built similarly to Emmitt Smith, who eventually took down Walter's all-time rushing yards record in '04. W.P. was the fourth-overall pick in '75, the only season he didn't go to the post every week. The '82 season was truncated to nine games because of 57-day players' strike. Other than the nine games lost due as players fought for a new CBA, he was always there. Payton started 184 games and appeared in 190 games.

Walter credited his unrivaled durability to relentless training, which included the famous hill runs in South Barrington and tireless hours in the weight room. He ran sprints until he couldn't in hot and humid weather. In an era when there were newspaper stands, he'd have raced anybody to one and broken their jaw if he needed to get there first. Payton couldn't stomach losing to anybody. In any contest. Anywhere.

At Jackson State, he picked up the nickname *Sweetness*. Payton had a sweet and soft tenor voice but physically, he was stout and powerful. Thick through the thighs and narrow at the waist, he possessed unworldly grace and body control. The jump cuts. The hurdles and the way he timed each leap. In short-and-goal from inside the two-yard line, he seemingly defied gravity, pausing a millisecond before going airborne as a defender overran the tackle. Payton's calling card was the up-and-over at the goal line. His quick-twitch muscles, combined with uncanny shiftiness in the open field, afforded him an incredible advantage. He was difficult to target and had counters to whichever body part a tackler chose to strike.

There was one other club in Payton's bag, and he loved to swing it. The stiff arm. Sweetness, my ass. Payton was one of the most violent football players of his era. His stiff arm was explosive and a potent weapon. If a defender had the angle on Payton in space, the tackler was best-served going low. Payton did a clever, effective toe-drag hesitation to keep tacklers guessing. And then he uncorked rage via the heel of his hand, typically at the chest. Or under the armpit. Under the chin strap. He had a knack for spotting a tackler's vulnerable zone based on the position at which the two combatants were angled. The objective was to get the sonofabitch off his feet. At full speed, Payton had the mental acuity to find the trouble area where a tackler is susceptible to a de-cleating. At the minimum, Payton was a good bet — and I'd have risked big odds — to get the tackler off his base.

Payton had soft hands as a receiver. On the occasions he was asked to throw the halfback option pass, he was good at it. He also could kick and did it regularly at Jackson State. Payton could walk on his hands for damn-near 100 yards. As a teenager, a bell-bottom pants wearing Payton flashed his dancing chops on the popular Motown show *Soul Train*.

Those are just details. Payton's gifts exceeded athletics. He had an aura, a presence that was magnetic. As ruthlessly as he played, there was a gentle, sensitive soul beneath the veneer of muscles and punishing playing style. At radio station events, I saw him play peek-a-boo with infants until they smiled or laughed. So many layers to Payton.

"I guarantee you this," proclaims guard Tom Thayer, a Payton loyalist on and off the field, "if 10 strangers are on an elevator and Walter is one of them, everybody walks out with a smile. Can you imagine saying that about some of the more modern superstars? If it was Jay Cutler, nine people walk out looking at the floor."

On occasion, Payton would jump on his Harley and ride to Thayer's house — unannounced — to hang out in Joliet with Tom's parents and siblings. He'd stay for several hours, and impromptu barbecues lightened everybody's spirits. Walter, at his best, was a man of the people.

"He called me one time in a woman's voice," reflected left tackle Jimbo Covert. "I couldn't tell it was him. 'Oh, hi this is Debbie. I met you one time up in Platteville.' I don't know you. Don't call here anymore."

Covert hung up, but the phone rang again and wife, Penny, was set to get it. "Penny goes to pick up the phone and I jumped up 'don't answer that!' He was a character."

Payton was 32 when the Bears went to the Super Bowl. In his first nine seasons, the Bears finished above the .500 mark only twice, both resulting in first-round playoff exits. The '77 team was drilled by Dallas and Neill Armstrong's 10-6 Bears were 27-17 losers in the wild card round in Philadelphia two playoff seasons later.

For years, all we had was Payton.

Payton was in his 10th season when the Bears finally won a playoff game, a 23-19 thriller at Washington's RFK Stadium in late-December of '84. Running all over the Redskins, however, wasn't enough. Payton had to *throw* for his supper, too. With Steve Fuller in at quarterback for the injured Jim McMahon, Payton threw a 19-yard touchdown pass to Pat Dunsmore to give the Bears a 10-3 lead going to halftime. Payton carried 24 times for 104 yards in the divisional-round victory.

It was the team's first postseason win in 21 years. Mike Ditka was a third-year tight end when the '63 team won trimmed the Giants 14-10 in the NFL championship. In '84, he was a third-year head coach.

Even at 32, in the year of *Our Trophy,* Payton still was a blue-chip bell cow. He carried 324 times for 1551 yads (4.8 ypc) and nine TDs. Beginning with the Week 6 blowout win in San Francisco, Payton reeled off nine straight games with 100+ rushing yards. He also caught 49 passes (tops on the Bears) for 483 yards (9.9 ypr) and two TDs. In the last 10 years, Derrick Henry is the only player to exceed 324 attempts more than once (three times). Since '14, Josh Jacobs, Jonathan Taylor, Adrian Peterson and Demarco Murray are the only other backs with more totes than 324. Payton was in his 11th season, and he remained the Alpha. There was no such thing as *load management.*

Before I interviewed Payton's former teammates and Jarrett Payton, I wondered *What's left to be said about Walter Payton?* My eventual answer had little to do with his accomplishments as a gridiron God.

Some sports fans just desire the Xs and Os, the amazing stories about perseverance overcoming adversity. I like those tales, too and I trust you're finding this diary replete with compelling anecdotes and events, but it's also my conviction to explore the human condition when appropriate. The psychological scars on Walter Payton made for thoughtful conversations with many of his closest allies. When I asked Bears of the early- to late-'80s to describe Payton in one word, their replies ran the gambit. The organic exchanges we had afterward were authentic, honest and heart-felt.

"Magnificent."

"Sweetness." (original, I cracked).

"I can't in one word. As awesome as he was as a player, he was consistently unpredictable personally. You had to read his mood before talking to him."

"Relentless."

"Willful."

"Perfect."

"I'd rather not say what I'm thinking."

"Greatness."

"Complicated."

None of the responses were surprising but what resonated with me most was the last — "complicated," offered by right tackle Keith Van Horne, the '81 first-round pick out of USC and Payton's teammate for seven years. We talked at length about Payton's detectable wounds. My read was Payton possessed an insatiable thirst for affection. Not just adulation. Walter wanted *to be loved*. Keith agreed.

And it wasn't the world that mattered to Payton. He was content to be property of the City of Chicago. It became his home. Jordan, conversely, sought global affirmation from the minute he set foot in a pair of Phil Knight's shoes. Perhaps it was driven by the money-grubbing super-agent David Falk, but the fact was, Chicago was merely the location of M.J.'s employer. Jordan had no interest in being *among the people*.

The irony is the greatest Bear of them all didn't take a public misstep until immediately after the Super Bowl XX thrashing of the Patriots. He was bottled up all day, gaining only 61 yards and 22 carries. Payton's longest run was seven yards. In the first quarter, a Payton fumble led to New England taking a 3-0 lead on a 36-yard Tony Franklin field goal. The Bears then scored 44 unanswered points. None of them came from Payton.

McMahon and fullback Matt Suhey scored on short rushing touchdowns, but every time Walter touched the ball, Payton had tacklers draped all over him. McMahon scored on a two-yard TD run in the second quarter and on a one-yard sneak in the third. When the Bears led 37-3, William Perry, the rookie defensive tackle, barreled in from the one.

Payton sulked. Agent Bud Holmes and Bears marketing director Ken Valdiserri had to drag him from a closet to get him to talk to media after the blowout win. Holmes talked tough to his client, insisting it wouldn't be

Ditka who took the most heat for the snub, but Payton for pouting selfishly. Eventually, Payton emerged and spoke to NBC's Bob Costas. He kept a stiff upper lip and didn't allude to his bruised feelings about being passed over for the Fridge.

"It still hasn't sunk in yet," was among Walter's detached replies.

Years later, Ditka said he regretted not being cognizant of Payton not scoring a touchdown before he called Perry's number. It seemed genuine. I was in the room when he said it in a *Waddle & Silvy* show appearance on ESPN 1000 in the aughts. Opinions of Payton's saltiness ran the gambit among his teammates. Over the years, some takes have evolved. A change of heart is something to which I relate. As a Payton fan at 25, I was disappointed in his behavior. Years later, I accepted the notion I don't have to understand everything. Feelings are neither right nor wrong. They're *real*.

TORTURED ARTIST

Payton wrestled terribly with civilian life after his football career. His addictions included perfection and nothing he ever could accomplish would flirt with what he did on a football field.

More than any superstar I encountered, Walter Payton was *human*.

Payton wanted Chicago to wrap it arms around him and never let go. When the cheers faded, Jordan immediately and almost seamlessly assumed the spotlight. Walter felt irrelevant. I don't think it was envy. Payton and Jordan were buds. In fact, the greatest Bear of all time rushed to the defense of the greatest Bull of all time when Jordan was taking abuse from fans and media in the early-'90s on my radio show on the Score, then Sports Radio 820.

It was one of the first *"wow!"* moments in my work life. Like tens of thousands of teenagers who played high school football in the late-'70s, Payton was a hero to me. I mean, I wore people out flapping my gums about the things Payton did and what I admired about him. Even into my 30s, I displayed a framed action shot of Payton getting to the edge on a prominent wall position in the man cave. When Payton — unsolicited — called my show, it really meant something to me.

"Pick up line 3! PAYTON wants to defend MJ!" was punched into the computer by a producer.

The Score hadn't reached the tipping point yet and still felt like a niche radio station. Nobody in the early years of the station imagined *the little engine that could* ever packing the same wallop of the Loop in the '80s or WGN in the '70s. On that day, none of us cared. Walter freaking Payton had been listening and the conversation stirred enough in him to pick up the phone and call on the listener line to participate.

It wasn't often when Jordan took heat so I should remember the specifics, but I can't recall what led to criticisms of His Airness. I was on a cloud because Payton called on his own accord. Walter warmly greeted me and co-host Terry Boers and suggested everybody "cool down and give Michael a little break once in a while." It was a telling comment. If anybody knew what it felt like to do all the heavy lifting and subsequently take blame when expectations aren't met, it was Payton.

In the fall of '95, I was doing a Bears pregame show on the Score with Doug Buffone, a 14-year Bears linebacker ('66-'79). Prior to a noon game at Soldier Field one Sunday, Buffone and I did a show at the nearby Congress Hotel. As I was in the middle of a question for Uncle Doug, somebody snuck up behind me and startled me on stage. Who in the hell would slither on stage, sneak behind a host, and then wrap their hands around what used to be pectoral muscles for a squeeze and feel? Frightened, I looked down and saw two black hands firmly gripping my chest, then turned my head to find Payton almost cheek to cheek with me. He flashed a gaping grin.

"Shit, Mac, you're solid!" he said loudly before slipping on the headphones. Payton was being nice, or he really found a taught chest because I tensed up so much as a reflex. I was 34 and had fallen terribly out of shape. I couldn't have my role model discover the truth about the man boobs under a navy velour long sleeve.

Walter powered us in a terrific half-hour segment about that day's game, the state of the Bears and a few "back when you played" questions from the audience. He was in a playful mood and engaged in every piece of the conversation. That, I later learned, wasn't always the case. It's my belief almost all of us are moody. Some, however, are those whose moods are so heavily weighted in one direction, they need to be read before one deciphers how to address them in that moment. Walt was one of those guys. Not proud of it but I am, too.

Shortly after his retirement, Payton began looking for that next challenge in a variety of business ventures. He struggled to find esteem in any of them, from his auto racing teams to restaurants. Walter wanted, in the worst way, to become part of an NFL ownership group but he didn't have the capital independently. To Payton's chagrin, Bears president Michael McCaskey was uninterested in providing any insight to him that would facilitate achieving his dream.

In '96 or '97, Payton joined the Score as a part-time regular contributor. He agreed to be available for any breaking news that required an A-list guest for reaction, but his main role was appearing in a Tuesday lunch series with the midday team of Jiggetts and Mike North — *The Monsters of the Midday*. Occasionally, I needed to scratch a Payton itch, and my producer would book him for 10- or 15-minute guest shots when convenient. He usually accommodated.

It was a great fit for the Score and seemingly for Payton, who usually played nice with media when he was a Bear. There were shows that emanated from Payton's Roundhouse restaurant in Elgin and some at four-star establishments in Rosemont and Schaumburg. *Jiggetts & North* were the station's biggest stars in the first decade and I was grateful they were the ones who handed us the baton at 2:00 every weekday. They were particularly good with big name guests, Jiggetts playing the good cop and North the relentlessly pressing but playful irritant.

The trio meshed. In the first year, from the moment the show open rolled — *Low Rider* by War — Bears fans nestled in their vehicles or at the venue got the warm and fuzzies. I was among them. After a season and change, however, the vibe on the show became inconsistent. Walter often was disengaged. He admitted to it at least twice. There were Payton shows when 90 minutes passed, and he hadn't expressed an interesting thought or strong emotion on anything. He was furniture.

"He gets like that sometimes," was a response I got from several ex-teammates when I grew curious about his inconsistent moods. A couple times a year, I went to a lunch or two to support my midday brethren, sales staff and mingle with listeners and sponsors. At the core of the Score's mission statement from the day it was plugged in, January 2, '92, was to be visible and interactive with the customers. It was grass roots-level marketing, and everybody agreed it was a requisite element to our potential.

I never forged a friendship with Payton but for a couple years we were cordial co-workers. *Pinch me*, is something I said to myself regularly in the '90s and beyond. Long before Payton became terminally ill, he suffered. Happiness was elusive. I'm not sure what hole Walter couldn't fill in his heart and soul, but he was never going to find peace without being able to compete like he once did. Even then, I learned after his career concluded in '87, Payton wasn't a peaceful man. Whatever he chased, it fell way short. After each triumph, a new mountain needed climbing.

He sunk low. Unearthed in Jeff Pearlman's 2011 book *Sweetness - The Enigmatic Life of Walter Payton* were the battles Payton fought with pain meds and other intoxicants. He was unfaithful. Manipulative. His moods were more extreme. Brooding, sad and feeling his relevance diminishing, Payton retreated and isolated. He contemplated suicide.

None among us haven't had or still have somebody to whom we're close who doesn't check some of the same boxes. Those habits and emotions are what make the people in our lives human beings. All have flaws. All have needs. And some of the strongest people we know are fragile. Vulnerability is not a weakness. Even for superstars with international fame. Their tragedies — cancer, loss, disharmony at home — hurt as much as they do for people who live in anonymity.

Many sports fans don't want to hear it. There are some who expect their heroes to be perfect at every turn. *That's* what makes them heroes. Those simple minds don't understand that mental illness does not discriminate. Clinical depression — the brain's inability to produce serotonin, the neurotransmitter that creates a stable, content mood and calm behavior — doesn't care how many touchdowns one scored. Addiction doesn't consider one's net worth, level of education or sex appeal. Mental illness isn't *imagined*. It's as real as a tumor.

MORE THAN ANYTHING, HE WAS HUMAN

Perhaps at the root of Payton's psychological plight was his deeply-rooted need for perfection. He expected perfection from himself with every challenge he tackled. Payton wanted to deliver. He never was going to find contentment with anything else he endeavored. What could he possibly do as well as he played football?

Payton has been on my mind a lot since I began this project in earnest in January. How he played. How he laughed. His hypersensitivity to pranks at his expense. I thought about Pearlman's book and how most called the biography dark and unflattering. People accused Pearlman, an A-list sportswriter with nine *New York Times best sellers* of profiteering, taking advantage of knowing a few blemishes of a famous person who's been gone for years and crushing his reputation. I don't agree with that at all. What Pearlman's book did, more than anything, was illuminate Payton's *reality*. He was a real person with real problems. He was a human being.

This past Father's Day, as I was anticipating the arrival of my sons, I thought about Jarrett Payton and what his challenges were, growing up with such a famous father and later accepting and digesting his father's illness and death. Jarrett, the now-44-year-old son of Walter and Connie Payton, was not among Pearlman's critics. His reaction, even initially when the publication was released, was one of acceptance. Of truth. Of reality.

"Human is totally the word," Jarrett said in June when I asked him for the best one-word description of his father. "When you looked at him and what he did throughout his career, it's almost like a comic book hero. People looked at him as this mythical creature that people talk about like he wasn't even real. Like he was indestructible.

"Then I think about his last appearance at the Cubs game when he threw out the first pitch to Sammy (Sosa). To see the smile on his face that day... people didn't know the pain he was in that day... and to make that happen and to get him to Wrigley with the pain he was in that day, then you see that smile on his face... that's who my dad was."

Two months before Payton publicly announced his health problems on the Score with *Jiggetts & North*, Payton and I had a disagreement over signing autographs at station events. Walter didn't want to sign anything at the lunches. He'd been taken advantage of by merchandise hawkers and refused unless he completely trusted it wasn't going up for auction.

Payton reluctantly signed a Riddell authentic Bears helmet for me. I donated it to a charity golf outing's silent auction, with the written description "donor will attempt getting item signed by the Bears player or coach of the highest bidder's choice, if accessible." On a cocktail napkin, I wrote down how Walter could inscribe the helmet "To Trojan Boy Mark" should ease concerns about it being resold for profit. He was unconvinced so I continued and said I knew the highest bidder, which was truthful. "The guy who made the high bid said 'Payton,' so I said no problem because you work at the station," said. He was visibly annoyed but signed the helmet.

I respected his concerns over being used and expressed that to him. When I asked others who were regulars at the Payton show about his history, however, I learned how inflexible he was — even for show sponsors. It didn't agree with me. At the minimum, the businesses that shelled out tens of thousands for advertising time and tables for eight at the appearances should get an autograph and a chance to pose for a picture with Payton. He wouldn't do it.

Had I been a more mature host, I would have had entertained an off-the-air conversation with a contributor like Payton. I was young and relished the "edgy" reputation. Giving station management a rough ride was a more common practice in the '80s Chicago talk radio North and I once consumed, and we both flexed those same muscles when the Score began gaining momentum. So, I yakked about it for a couple minutes on a show a few days after learning of his obstinance.

The bullseye was on station management for not policing Payton, not mandating Sweetness learns to be one of the guys. The criticism was aimed directly at program director Ron Gleason, who I said enabled unacceptable behavior. Gleason was a good guy, but he wasn't a strong-willed leader, and this was evidence of it.

I was a founding father of the radio station and there was a lot riding on the station's continued success and solid reputation. Walter breached the spirit of our fraternity. We were "of the people" and Payton wasn't playing by our ethos. My commentary wasn't a verbal crucifixion of him. It was an inter-office memo to *all* our contributors. The full-time air staff expected all those who wore the '90s orange and black station colors to respect and honor the Score's customs. That included signing a few autographs.

As was the case when Jordan was taking a trimming on the show in '93, Payton was listening in his car. Matt Fishman, my producer told me to pick up the hot line after I threw to a five-minute break. "Payton wants to talk to you," Fish said.

"You're making me look an asshole," Payton alleged.

"*I'm* the reason you look like an asshole. Got'cha," I returned.

"You have no idea what's in my contract because if you did, you'd know I don't have to sign anything."

I told Walter he was right, that I didn't know but I really didn't care, either. I suggested to him some things are obviously the right things to do. He didn't agree and we went back and forth on it. It was uncomfortable and contentious, I suppose, but never escalated to shouting. When Fish told me we were back on in 30 seconds, I interrupted Payton and told him we had to get back on the air. I said I appreciated him remaining relatively calm and we should continue the discussion down the road.

It could have gone differently with either or both of us. Don't be fooled by his nickname. Walter could be a stubborn and sometimes volatile dude. Me, too. I proved it the next day when decibel levels rose considerably higher in Gleason's office when it was just the suit and me.

The autograph issue never resurfaced on the show, and I let it go. It was my intention to get with him before the next station golf outing or on the phone to finish the conversation long before the next football season, shake hands and move forward. There was an abundance of testosterone at the Score, and we all argued like teenagers on occasion. Resolution and harmony, however, were important to the key players and my strongest want was to remain allies with Payton.

I never loved watching an athlete more than Walter. I enjoyed him as a radio contributor, and we played for the same team. I appreciated the man. Sometimes, unfortunately, waiting for things to cool down doesn't pay dividends. The next season of Payton shows never arrived. Walter announced his liver disease on February 2, '99. Specifically, bile duct cancer. *Jiggetts & North* knew Payton was ill, evidenced by radical weight loss and change in skin color to a jaundiced yellow. He wore shades during the last month of shows in '98.

"He fell into my arms, and I'll never forget it," Jarrett Payton said. "I was always falling into his arms and now I'm holding him. I was a high school kid. I didn't know what was coming. I knew he was going to fight and do whatever he could, and we were all there for him and we were going to come up with a game plan. But that moment was like everything that was lifted off him. He didn't have those pressures anymore. He could be himself again."

Walter removed his sunglasses. His eyes were sunken, bloodshot and distant. Jarrett was only 18 and a budding star of his own at Miami. After his father broke down and sobbed hard during his announcement, the Paytons embraced, squeezing and not letting go. It's an image indelibly etched in my mind. As Boers and I watched the surreal public statements on television, the feeling of Chicago's hearts collectively sinking was palpable.

In August of '99, the station paired me with Jiggetts in the first of the Score's many radical lineup shakeups. Dan and I did the 4-7 p.m. shift and North flew solo between noon and 4. Boers was paired with Dan Bernstein in a mid-morning show position between 8 and noon. In the two months that followed, Jiggetts kept in contact with Suhey and Connie Payton for updates on the rapidly deteriorating health of his friend of more than 20 years. During commercial breaks, Dan shared them with me and when I could tell he was suffering, I'd ask for a happy story about Walter. As I watched Jiggs go through his own grief and struggle to accept the inevitable, he also was mindful of my misgivings about the disagreement Payton and I had in the winter. It remained unresolved but now was a blip on the radar. Inconsequential, given the terminal liver cancer that quickly was emaciating and emasculating Payton.

At around 3:30, on Monday, November 1, the Score's marketing director Jeff Schwartz walked Jiggetts and me into his office and closed the door behind us. Schwartz was a bubbly guy almost invariably. On this day, he was oddly quiet and business-like when he picked up the phone and dialed. "Francine, they're here with me. It's just me and Dan and Dan," he said. It was Francine Portrey, a long-time Bears fan club officer and loyal Score supporter. Francine was an extremely energetic woman with a tremendous passion for things she loved, like the Bears and our little radio station in a low-slung bunker on Chicago's heavily-Polish northwest side.

She could barely get it out. "He's gone."

Nobody spoke. Jeff looked at the floor. Sucking for a deep breath, I slumped in my chair and put my left hand over my eyes. Dan was seated to my right and he also was lost for words. And breath. I put a consoling hand on Dan's leg, and he gently squeezed for support. We sat for a few minutes without a word being spoken. All of us were rocked.

Schwartz finally broke the silence. "I have to go tell George (Ofman, the twice-hourly update reporter) to go in and go on with it," he whispered. Schwartz wanted us to know before Ofman went on the air with the news. Dan and I had to pull it together. The show we were hosting started in less than a half-hour.

It was a little more than three months after his 46th birthday when Walter succumbed to bile duct cancer. It was the most bitter pill I ever swallowed regarding a celebrity death. It would be difficult to recall a day when news made in Chicago dealt such a more emotionally debilitating blow to the city. For three hours, the *Dan & Dan* show processed the passing of the city's favorite son. We talked to several of Payton's teammates, took phone calls and shared our own emotions. By the time our show's *Closing Time* theme rolled, Jiggs and I were on empty. There were four more days of it ahead, as well as previewing Sunday's date between the Bears and Packers at Lambeau Field.

The Saturday after Walter died, a public service was held at Soldier Field. My intention early in the week was to attend but by Saturday morning, I was too spent emotionally to leave the house. I stayed home and watched the service with a friend who also worshiped at the *Roos* on Payton's feet. Jiggetts emceed the event, which featured many '85 Bears and other alumni.

As ex-Bears walked to their seats in front of the lectern and makeshift VIP seating area on the field, I asked my former teammate if something looked amiss to him. "Yes," he quickly snapped. Some of the most notable former Bears were smiling as they walked to their designated seats close to the podium. Some waved to the crowd as if they were strolling in a parade. I understand grief is processed differently and it's presumptuous to assume somebody is unaffected by death by a smile. Still, my buddy and I wanted better form from Payton's closest allies on this day. It was a bad optic.

On Monday, before we went on the air, I thanked Dan for having the appropriate tone and expressions as he introduced the speakers. *"Tight face"* I called it, noting not all alums exhibited a funeral dirge. Jiggs' face again revealed his heart and head. Dan wasn't a judgmental guy but under his breath, he whispered a similar emotion. "Just another victory lap." Jiggetts and I took phone calls on the service and the Bears' surprising win 14-13 win at Lambeau. It was the *Bryan Robinson Game*, when the defensive tackle blocked a 28-yard Ryan Longwell field goal as time expired, preserving a 14-13 win for rookie head coach Dick Jauron and the Bears.

During a break, D.J. shared something Connie told him at the private service in Barrington. Walter's widow said one of the few things that helped Walter gain a respite from his sinking health was listening to the Score. Specifically, our show. Withered and weak, the greatest player in football history limped to one of his antique cars, sat down and listened to the radio to forget about, albeit briefly, his dire health. Near the end, Suhey, Walter's bodyguard on and off the field, assisted him and the two sat in the car and talked football. Or listened to us talk about it.

I was heartened and took some relief in it after our hiccup 10 months earlier. Connie said he'd spend hours without saying much, then come back in 45 minutes after sitting in the car and bitch about football opinions. It took his mind off it. God, did I need to hear that. It was absolution, in some weird way.

It always will be with me that I never got a chance to get eye-to-eye with my teenage role model and shake his hand again. Walter Payton was *meaningful* in my life. He was a man who inspired me so much, on and off the field, and that he found an escape from the suffering by listening to a show I was hosting warmed me. Humbled me. Meaningless chatter about football games provided a temporary escape for my sports hero.

Payton was poetry in motion, cliche as those words appear. He was a pillar but also vulnerable. Payton was *the Light* yet much of his time was spent time in darkness. Payton was fire and ice.

Walter was more human than any superhero who ever kicked around the streets of Chicago. It was my good fortune to get to spend some time with the most accomplished Bear in the history of the NFL's charter franchise. He was the greatest player in NFL history. And this was *Payton's Place*.

Nobody ever wanted to be that — and subsequently *earned* it — more than Walter.

CHAPTER 13
Demolition Man
BRIAN URLACHER'S BEARS

> *"That's my darling Luke. He may grin like a baby... but he bites like a gator." – Dragline (George Kennedy) from the 1967 film Cool Hand Luke.*

The final years of the 20th century were marred by some of the darkest hours in Bears history. Most injurious to the hearts and souls of Chicago was the death of Walter Payton in November of 1999. The pride of Bear Nation also was being drained from relentless damage inflicted by the front office and uninspiring performances on the field. The Bears displayed dysfunction in every direction.

They blew a first-round pick trading for Rick Mirer in '97. Chairman Michael McCaskey, who cavalierly thumbed his nose at a rapidly evolving NFL, fumbled the hiring of Dave McGinnis as head coach in '99. The coarse accountant Ted Phillips quickly burrowed under the skin of capable *de facto* general manager Mark Hatley. They screwed the pooch colossally when they drafted Cade McNown 12th overall in '99.

Between '97 and '99, the Bears went 14-34. They beat Green Bay once in six meetings and also went 1-5 against the Vikings. Jesus, Tampa Bay even got 'em five of six tries. The Lions went 4-2 against Chicago in those three seasons. Cellar dwellers.

In some burgs, this is referred to as a drought. A *market correction*. A *bad cycle*. In McCaskeyville, it's called a *lifestyle*.

As coach Dick Jauron was navigating his second year through Bears fog in 2000 — plates spinning all around him — the Bears drafted Brian Urlacher in the first round, ninth overall. Urlacher, an unknown out of New Mexico, was an oversized wrecking ball of a safety at 6-4 and 255. Scouts ogled at the lightning-fast quickness of such a large mammal, who projected as a linebacker.

Hmm. Head scratcher. The ninth overall — not exactly born of a football factory — and they're going to ask him to change positions. Got it. Hatley better really be the smartest guy in the room after pulling the trigger on this one.

The selection of Urlacher wasn't received warmly by many media and fans and the first few weeks of the rook's first training camp only heightened panic. Jauron wasn't certain where Urlacher fit best. Early returns weren't favorable. The converted safety wasn't going to unseat either outside linebacker. Rosevelt Colvin, the weak-side 'backer, and Warrick Holdman, the strong-side 'backer, had a year under their belts with Jauron. Both were fourth-rounders in '99 and had an edge on Urlacher with scheme and terminology.

Before pessimism created mass hysteria, a nagging injury to middle linebacker Barry Minter necessitated moving Urlacher inside. In Week 3, after the Bears had relinquished 71 points in losses at Minnesota and in Tampa, Urlacher got his pro first start against the Giants.

It was baptism by fire for the fresh-faced kid from Lovington, New Mexico. Jim Fassel's eventual NFC champions ran all over the Bears, powered by the thunder and lightning tandem of Ron Dayne and Tiki Barber. Kerry Collins slung it all over Soldier Field, too. Urlacher collected a game-high 11 solo tackles, including a sack, but the Giants prevailed 14-7 and the Bears fell to 0-3. The sky was falling again.

"The ninth pick in the draft for a freakin' safety who can't play middle linebacker" began ringing as the chorus. At 6-4, the challenge of playing with proper pad level never could be "cured." Urlacher, wondered reasonable football minds, may be too tall to be an effective middle linebacker. His frame gave too much target for centers and guards firing out at him.

Meanwhile, myriad long-standing issues remained unaddressed. Jauron had no quarterback of the future on the roster and was battling the exact issues Dave Wannstedt inherited in '93. Offensive voids included quarterback, running backs, wide receivers and tight ends. *"Other than that coach, what's ailing your offense?"* Center Olin Kreutz was the only weapon offensive coordinator Gary Crowton possessed. Build a game plan around that.

Confusion and skepticism prevailed. The Bears rolled dice on hybrid players before and they always flopped. John Thierry, edge rusher or cover backer? Neither. Curtis Enis, fullback or tailback? Neither. Second-rounder Chris Zorich was smallish up front, slowish for linebacker. *Tweeners*. They'll break your heart, too.

"Another project," huffed the majority. Here we go again.

Then we saw the light in his eyes.

It took Urlacher less than a full season to win Chicago's hearts. Maybe he *can* resurrect this thing became the sentiment after Urlacher grabbed defensive rookie of the year honors. Hope became more than dimly visible in '01, when Urlacher matured into the straw that stirred the drink defensively for the next dozen years.

Jauron's defense, on the heels of a 5-11 season, powered an unexpected 13-3 thrill ride and Central division title. Urlacher earned the first of four first-team All Pro selections and Jauron was voted coach of the year. Offensive firepower, the faithful rationalized, could wait. From Bill George to Dick Butkus to Mike Singletary to Brian Urlacher. Quite the legacy.

What was the advice Steven Stills offered when he sang about the one you love not feeling the same about you? *Love the one you're with*. In lieu of a new love from the offensive side of the ball, Brian Urlacher became the *one you're with*. If the Bears weren't adopting new millennium offense (you know, the kind that scores touchdowns), a football "love" would continue to be predicated on a dominant defender.

Urlacher was an unrelenting competitor and enormously skilled player. Brian quickly became the face of the franchise. And his feet firmly were on the ground. Every Bears alum I know who met Urlacher said he thoroughly enjoyed the exchange. Urlacher was respectful, reverential, warm. Those traits had become scarce as salaries escalated dramatically. Urlacher copped defensive player of the year honors in '06, the year the Bears went to the Super Bowl. Over his 13 seasons, many of his most impactful performances were against the Packers.

There were a handful of public missteps along the way, but Urlacher's eventual enshrinement in Canton in '18 was a very satisfying event for many. Count me among them. Urlacher's ferocity, sideline-to-sideline speed, flawless tackling technique and unrivaled ball skills resurrected the teenage football fan in me. He made me want to see the Bears win more than I had in years prior. It wasn't Urlacher's production that elicited the fan in me — it was his passion for the game and his co-conspirators. From his coaches to equipment manager Tony Medellin, Urlacher's Bears were Urlacher's family.

Part of what made this particular Bears badass so unique was his cheerful disposition. Butkus snarled and spat on opponents. Urlacher usually was smiling. *Lack*, as his teammates called him, possessed unbridled youthful exuberance. He *loved* playing football, and it easily was detectable to even casual observers. Of course, there was a deep, dark side to that guy. There must be, in every NFL player whose job — even occasionally — carries a *seek-and-destroy* missive. What they do is, well, kind of criminal. It's violent. It's dangerous. Still, Urlacher's boyish grin, even on the field, and his authentic fondness for teammates and coaches, were rare qualities in a superstar. He was one of the boys. As Walter was.

If you're feeling blue over the absence of football in the spring or summer, seek Bears games from the Urlacher years. They're easy to track and the quality is superior to the games from of the golden era of the '80s.

Watch Urlacher after Lance Briggs, Julius Peppers, Charles Tillman or Mike Brown makes a big play. Pick any teammate who gets to the tackle first, breaks up a pass or hurries the quarterback into a bad throw. Watch how Urlacher responds to their success. Do it for the entire game and try several more games, as I did in the spring. Never have I observed a superstar demonstrate more joy over his teammates' triumphs than Urlacher. He had a visceral connection to "team." He loved his teammates, and they felt the same about him.

What those games also reveal is more than Urlacher imposing his will on opponents with strength and jaw-rattling tackles. Lack put unprecedented speed into the Mike linebacker position in the *Tampa-2* (aka *Cover 2*) scheme. It took many of us a long time to appreciate fully how rare and valuable Urlacher was in the Tampa-2. The safeties share deep coverage responsibility. They defend between the boundary and its nearest hashmark.

The Mike 'backer's responsibility is deep middle. Urlacher defended 40 yards past the line of scrimmage. Now while Brian's body didn't ripple with cuts of a bodybuilder or some linebackers, he was a huge man. Large guys aren't supposed to run like that.

Urlacher also respected his opponents in the fraternity. As Walter did. He occasionally helped the bad guys up off the ground. In Week 10 of the '12 season, after former teammate Danieal Manning intercepted Jay Cutler, Urlacher extended a fist bump to Manning when he jogged back on the field in the Bears' sleepy 13-6 loss to Houston on *Sunday Night Football*.

Some mopes, shallow thinkers who are incapable of unlearning axioms passed along by mindless fathers or bullying big brothers, mocked Urlacher's display of good sportsmanship. Fools, thought I. This is what we call *progress*. In more recent years, Urlacher has been viewed by many as *opposition* to progress. He's a Donald Trump supporter.

HITCHIN A RIDE ON THE NO. 54 TRAIN

In his first training camp, I asked Urlacher in a phone interview "is it er-LACK-er or er-LACK-er?" Wasn't like he played at Ohio State and the world knew. And I'd heard it pronounced both ways. "It's er-LACK-er but I've people say it all kinds of ways my whole life, so it doesn't matter, really." Rhymes with linebacker, was my slick reply to the converted safety. We were off and running.

At the Score, we aimed to get Urlacher to the station's annual celebrity charity golf outing at gorgeous Kemper Lakes. Word circled back he wanted to play but wasn't nuts about cuddling up to title sponsors. Doug Buffone, a station mainstay since its '92 inception, played linebacker here for 14 years and Urlacher reportedly suggested he preferred Buffone or somebody like him (good luck with that) in his group. Lack wasn't well versed in Bears lore and wanted to learn from one who cracked a few heads. Beautiful story, true or embellished.

In late-October of '00, Urlacher's rookie year, I resigned at the Score with the hope ESPN 1000 program director Mitch Rosen could convince his GM to deep-six their amateurish afternoon show and bring me on board. In May of '01, it happened and the *Mac, Jurko & Harry* show launched in afternoon drive. One of my most important missions the first year of *MJH* was to reestablish rapport with Urlacher. He was agreeable on most requests, and I got face time with him in Tampa after the Bears beat the Buc 27-24 to bump their record to 7-2. Jim Miller and Marty Booker were McCartney and Lennon that day.

The unexpectedly fun '01 season ended with a thud in a bad loss to the Eagles at Soldier Field. Hugh Douglas used Miller's head for a seat cushion in Philly's 33-19 divisional-round win. Soon after, the *MJH* show did a Daytona 500 watch party with Urlacher at the ESPN Zone. Urlacher was a playful, engaged participant in a phoner to promote the event and easy to share the stage with at it. The sponsors and listeners all were content, and Urlacher enjoyed his ESPN 1000 debut enough to agree to participate in a black-tie event in May.

Decades Of Dominance was a celebration of the Bears history at middle linebacker. On the dais were honorees Butkus, Singletary and Urlacher. All in tuxes. They sold close to 1000 tickets and the hotel ballroom buzzed for three hours. Former Bears were on hand, some with brief speaking roles. Before the program began, Urlacher had a devilish grin as he approached in the green room.

"I got you clowns again tonight, huh?" he served up. We were the only faces he recognized so he popped over to be among us instead of waiting for the first admirer to kiss his ring. None of us had a significant role in the event. I introduced Dan Hampton (who introduced Ed O'Bradovich, who introduced Butkus). Jurko, former NFL D-tackle John Jurkovic, and sometimes-funny comedian Harry Teinowitz likely did shots with listeners. All in a day's work.

We cracked a beer and Urlacher soon leaned over and whispered, "this is fucking embarrassing." I had no idea what he was referencing so I asked. "I have no business being on the same level with these two. I've played two fuckin' years. Those guys are legends. I'm embarrassed. Wish I would have thought more about it 'cuz I feel stupid."

Perspective and humility at 24. Priceless.

An absence of life experience and his upbringing, however, surfaced not far down the line. I never knew Urlacher remotely well enough to say "success spoiled him" but some erratic behaviors emerged and Lack dropped the PR ball a few times. Taking a few laps around the Paris Hilton track didn't help. I don't remember anybody thinking *that* was cool. A *Sun-Times* article painted Urlacher as verbally abusive to his baby mama via text messages. At a scheduled, mid-week news conference, Lack went asshole in a bizarre but short "give and take" when he didn't want to answer anything. *Anything*. To every question, Urlacher replied "Go to foxsports.com." It was a childish response to what I thought was low-rent reporting by the *S-T*. Are they tracking the lifestyles of Hollywood celebs for *Paparazzi* or football players for a major metro? The trash the paper published was bad form. I expected better from our metros, but I also expected better from Urlacher. For that, I went to foxsports.com.

CROWN THEIR ASS

Devin Hester truly was ridiculous, wasn't he. What a year it was in '06. Urlacher and safety Brown, who came in the same draft 30 picks after Lack, had made a habit of willing the Bears to victory. It went to the next stratosphere in the win over Arizona on *Monday Night Football* in Week 6. Hester joined Batman and Robin for the improbable win, a 24-23 thriller. It was this steal from the Cardinals that prompted Dennis Green's memorable "the Bears were who we thought they were... and we let 'em off the hook" rant. "If you want to crown 'em, crown their ass."

Trailing 23-3 with the third quarter winding down, Lovie Smith's defense took a sledgehammer to the Cardinals and scored twice. Arizona's collars tightened. Brown picked up a Matt Leinart fumble and banged it in from three yards out after rookie Mark Anderson's strip-sacked the left-hander. Peanut Tillman returned a fumble 40 yards for a touchdown with five minutes remaining in regulation. Urlacher ripped the ball violently from Edgerrin James' grasp to set up Nutty. With three minutes left, Hester's majestic 83-yard punt return for a touchdown broke the Cardinals, who also missed chances on two Neil Rackers' field goal misfires.

It wasn't artful but it was perhaps the most exhilarating win of the year. In many years. With it, the Bears improved to 6-0. Thomas Jones, running behind Jerry Angelo's piece-mealed O-line, nicely cloaked Rex Grossman. It was good, old fashioned, hard-nosed football. With Lovie's best-in-the-NFL defense, now led by a sage Urlacher and Brown, the addition of Hester just might be enough to get them deep into the playoffs.

There are few events I've attended that flirt with the air of expectancy of a Super Bowl. After five stellar *Mac, Jurko & Harry* shows on radio row (bacteria alley as I like to call it) during hype week, it finally was game time. The hair on my neck stood as my wife, Sheri, and I walked into Hard Rock Stadium in Miami. I'd been to Stanley Cup Final games. My show went on the road with the Bulls in five of their six NBA Finals appearances. I saw the White Sox in three of their four World Series wins over Houston in '05. The Super Bowl looms over all in anticipation. It isn't a best-of-something series. This is winner-take-all. It's a heavyweight title fight — when those mattered — and the world is watching.

Billy Joel wailed the anthem and military jets roared over the stadium, perfectly synced with the piano man's fading *braaaaaaaave*. Tears rolled down my cheek and not because of patriotism. I suddenly was overwhelmed with gratitude for all I've seen, all the places I've been and people I've met. And that which I was about to experience. Great seats and at face value, a mere $750 each. We were on the sideline behind the Chicago bench, but under the overhang so we stayed dry. Jesse Jackson *and* the Burger King creepy mascot both were a few seats away. Pinch me.

Hester stood nearest the hashmarks on the Indianapolis sideline and bounced up and down, eagerly waiting to unleash his return magic. In less than 12 seconds after fielding the kick from Adam Vinatieri, Hester raised his arms in the air after authoring yet another historic moment. There had been kickoffs returned for TDs in Super Bowls. Even back-to-backers — Baltimore's Jermaine Lewis and Ron Dixon of the Giants traded TD returns in SB 35. Never had a game opened with a kick return for a tuddy. It was surreal. Under rainy skies, Hard Rock was rockin' with Hester's opening number.

Ultimately, the Colts were too much. They beat Team Lovie 29-17. The Bears have not returned to the game with Roman numerals on its masthead.

ONE ON ONE

Several former colleagues and a friend commented favorably after they watched an Urlacher interview I did on YouTube in April. I was eager to reconnect with Urlacher and there was a ton to discuss. Two of his teammates — Hester and Peppers — were on deck for Hall of Fame induction, Justin Fields was traded, and the Caleb Williams buzz was growing. I also wanted his reaction to the many fans who lined up on social media to denounce Urlacher's existence based on political leans. I last interviewed Lack in '18, shortly after he was voted into the Hall, so we were overdue.

I was hoping he'd torch Cutler. Recall how it began for the prickly Cutler? Bobby Wade, a receiver who departed for the Vikings, told a Minneapolis talk show Urlacher thought Cutler was "a pussy." Not a doubt in my mind Urlacher felt that way when Cutler arrived in '09. And Cutler's first night on stage in a Bears uniform was a disaster. He threw four picks in Green Bay on *SNF* — one to fat tackle Johnny Jolly — and the Bears got smoked at Lambeau. I was there for the terribly dispiriting Cutler debut. Urlacher broke his wrist in that game and was lost for the year.

In the NFC Championship game against the Packers, Cutler crapped the bed in the first half and didn't return with an MCL sprain. The Bears lost 21-14 with Caleb Hanie and Todd Collins attempting to rally the offense.

Urlacher deserved better than Cutler. So did Kreutz, Briggs, Nutty, Hester and Peppers — all those players who comprised the heartbeat of the Bears of Super Bowl 41 and again between '09 and '12. Cutler was the textbook asshole teammate. He didn't work hard enough at his craft and his attitude towards teammates and coaches was deplorable. He wouldn't speak to quarterback coach Pep Hamilton. Argue with him and feel free to tell him why he's wrong, but don't sit on the bench staring into the abyss. Urlacher didn't bite on Cutler. Maybe punch-me-face matured behind the scenes and earned some affection. My suspicion is not, but that Urlacher has mellowed.

What I discovered in a half-hour Zoom visit was a former football star who is comfortable in his own skin. It's not that Urlacher wasn't himself publicly as a younger man, but there's an inner peace that's more palpable. He wasn't on guard. A vibe of comfortability seeped into his replies and was evidenced from body language. After watching the conversation in its entirety, I agreed with the others who commented. In the 20ish interviews I did with Urlacher, dating to his first camp, I never recalled him quite this relaxed.

More than anything I'd done with him or heard elsewhere, it was conversational. Just two guys who love football *talking* about it. And the business of it. So, instead of plucking money quotes and bending narratives around them, I invite you to pull up a bar stool and eavesdrop. It was raining that day in San Diego, Urlacher's new home, so golf was scratched. He plays every day "or I'd go ape shit." With little on his docket, Urlacher swapped a Titleist visor for a Trump hat and was sitting in front of shelves adorned with game balls and trophies. He's collected his share.

DM: I heard what you said Super Bowl week about the Bears, Justin Fields specifically, "if you're still asking the same questions after three years, you have your answer." I take it you're a thumbs up on the Fields trade.

BU: Yes and no. He showed signs from time to time where I'd say "damn, this kid is good." And then there's times when you're like, "meh, I don't know." And you could say he doesn't have a good offensive line and doesn't have a lot of weapons around him but I do think he's going to be good. We haven't had good quarterback play in Chicago in a while. That's no secret. They (Pittsburgh) stole him for a fourth- to sixth-round pick. But it you have the number one pick two years in a row and you don't have a franchise quarterback, that's not good for your organization. They had to get a franchise guy... and spend the pick on him.

DM: My wish was they kept Fields *and* drafted Caleb Williams, but people say you can't have those two guys in the building at the same time. I think that's crap. If you have a strong-willed coaching staff, you can, and I don't think they have that. Agree?

BU: I don't agree about the coaches, but I agree about two quarterbacks. Justin was kind of settled in and maybe you give the new guy a year (as a backup). Green Bay's done a great job of getting their young quarterbacks to play. They sit 'em behind these great quarterbacks and then they come in and they're successful. I'm not saying Justin was great but if you gave it one year with the No. 1 pick learning and see what happens.... but it doesn't matter now.

DM: I'd have loved to see them on the field at same time. Put Fields in the slot and have Caleb throw bubble screens to him and let him do what he does best. Mike Tomlin seems the perfect coach to handle the egos of Russell Wilson and Justin and make that work.

BU: I don't feel like Justin's a huge ego guy. I mean he's confident in a good way and doesn't rub people the wrong way. It's going to be a great situation in Pittsburgh. I know people were down on Russell in Denver because they didn't win but his numbers were good and that's what the media *loves* to go on. I think it's a good situation for both of them and Tomlin, he's the freakin' man. He's the one guy in the NFL who I would love to play for.

DM: Not surprised to hear you say that. I like the way you describe Fields, confident but not in a cocky way. Unlike the guy who came here in '09 (Urlacher laughs), who immediately ingratiated himself to Chicago by throwing four picks in Green Bay the night you busted up your wrist and lost the year. What is your relationship, if you have one, with Jay Cutler?

BU: I got no problem with Jay. We speak every once in a while, via social media. I think he lives down in Nashville. I like Jay. I think he's a good dude. He's doin' some media stuff now. I don't watch a lot of NFL media junk. Most of those guys are ex-players I don't know anyway so I don't watch that stuff. I follow Jay on Instagram, but we don't talk that much. I went on his podcast a year or two ago and I had a good time doing that with him. We agree on a lot of the same things, which I appreciate. (smiles wryly wanting a follow up question).

DM: Okay, give me examples of things you agree on?

BU: Politically, we agree on a lot of things. We see eye-to-eye on politics.

DM: So, Jay is a Trump enthusiast like...

BU: Hold on now. I wouldn't say Trump enthusiast. Just because we're on the same side doesn't mean we're Trump enthusiasts. We see things a certain way. Doesn't automatically mean we're big Trump guys. I am but I'm not sure he is. We're on the same side on a lot of issues a lot of people aren't.

DM: Does it bother you there are Bears fans who want to distance themselves from you, forget your career in some cases, because of your fondness for Trump?

BU: I couldn't really give a shit, to tell you the truth. I don't care what people think. At this point in my life, if you don't like me because of what I believe in politically, piss off. I don't care. I've gone through so much shit the last two or three years listening to people "oh, you like Trump. You're this and you're that..." I don't care. I like what I like, you like what you like if that's your thing, do it. I don't care. I don't really give a hell anymore.

DM: That's a good place to be when you arrive at that station in life. You're fortunate you got there quicker than I did. Let's talk about Caleb Williams. A little different than when you came in. You were the ninth pick, he's the first. Different pressure when you're a quarterback. What advice would you give him on handling Chicago and the expectations?

BU: It's a little different, like you said. He's got a lot more pressure on him than I did. He's a quarterback. The number one pick in the draft. It's a big deal. Just go in there and work. Earn the respect of your teammates by working your ass off, going in there and being the first guy in the building. Say the right things to the media. Be humble and put your head down and go to work.

DM: The two GMs who preceded Ryan Poles — Phil Emery and then Ryan Pace — really are the reason they're in this mess. Jerry Angelo did some goofy things, but Jerry also largely built the Super Bowl team roster... (Urlacher wants to talk Angelo and interrupts)

BU: Jerry Angelo was the man. I have so much respect for him. Jerry didn't get enough credit for what he did. He built our team. Lovie was a defensive head coach and that's where Jerry wanted to spend his money and that's what we did. We were great on defense and may have struggled on offense at times but that's the way it was gonna be and we knew that. We were a defensive team. Defensive head coach and our GM knew that so that's how we built. And that's the way it goes.

DM: Jerry did a lot of good things. He rolled dice on Tommie Harris with a bad knee at 14 and for a few years, he was the most disruptive D-lineman in the league. He brought in Thomas Jones. And then on the back end, Jerry botched it and deals him away because he drafted Cedric Benson. Angelo said they couldn't both be in the building. Why the hell not?

BU: If that's the case, then don't draft him. In my opinion, Thomas was not on the decline. He had two monster years, and we were coming off the Super Bowl. Don't draft Cedric the year before. We didn't need him. We had T.J. He was carrying the load for us, and he was awesome. Nothing against Cedric, he did a good job for us when Thomas left but we didn't need him. I think Lovie had a high fondness for what he did in college.

DM: Was that affection you and Lance Briggs had for T.J. behind the rough ride you both gave Benson when he arrived in Bourbonnais after a holdout?

BU: I had no issue with Cedric. No issue with any of my teammates. Business is business, you take care of that on your own and we'll take care of the team until you get here. We had no problem with that. We didn't talk to him a lot. He was just different, real quiet. Some guys are like that, which is fine. But T.J. was a team leader. He said shit that needed to be said, and we all respected him and looked up to him for that. When he left, I was like damn, we lost not only a great leader but a great player, so it was tough.

DM: You're past 45 now so you can be the old man yelling at the clouds. These safeties in the game today... they don't like contact. They don't use their shoulder pads very much anymore and form tackle anymore. What's happened to the Mike Browns of the world? Tony Parrish?

BU: Well, they don't want to get thrown out of the damn game for hitting somebody. That's what happened. The game changed and they're not allowed to hit anybody anymore. I don't know how corners play the game anymore. There's always a holding or an illegal contact penalty. If it's third and 11, there's going to be a defensive penalty so just get ready for it. Maybe it's roughing the passer. How do you get roughing the passer when you sack a guy? I don't understand that. There are so many rules that benefit the offense, it's getting so hard to watch. I don't know how the corners and safeties play defense anymore. The rules changing really impacts these guys on the back end.

DM: With roughing the passer, protecting the quarterback on his way down is the new one I get quite a kick out of. Chris Jones is supposed to control his 300 pounds and facilitate a soft landing.

BU: It makes no sense to me. We could do a podcast on this for four hours and we'd still have stuff to talk about afterwards with these damn rules.

DM: It's customary for NFL teams, for *their* guys who get inducted in Canton, to pick up the tab for the party. That's an expensive party and I know the Bears have been inconsistent with how they've "kicked in" to the party fund. Were they generous to you in 2018?

BU: The Bears were very generous to me for my party, I have to say that. There have been a lot of things said back and forth these last couple years that I don't agree with but they damn sure took care of my party. George McCaskey was great. Mrs. McCaskey came to the party after the game. They definitely did right by me when it came to that.

DM: Glad to hear that 'cuz it was a weird end for you. My read is it would have been hard to be anything but bitter because they basically offered you the league minimum. That's now how you treat 13-year veterans who are Hall of Fame players.

BU: It wasn't about the money; it was the way they handled the situation that bothered me. George could have stepped in at any time. Phil Emery, who's a complete dumbass by the way, and I don't know why they'd fire Jerry to hire this guy, and he screwed up everything for maybe the next five or six years for that organization, maybe even longer. He didn't know what he was doing. He had a stance that I wasn't coming back. You know what, looking back I'm so glad I didn't because they fired Lovie anyway and I didn't want to play for another coach. But it wasn't about the money, it was the way it was handled by Phil Emery. And George could have stepped in and done something about it 'cuz he's the owner, but he didn't. I'm glad now the way it worked out. I'm glad I retired when I did and that I never played for another team.

DM: You've gotten over the bitterness — mostly — you seem like today you are a Bears fan. Am I wrong?

BU: Well, I grew up a Dallas Cowboys fan and that's still my team. I do watch the Bears when they're on TV but if I have to choose a number one team, you know I grew up watching the Cowboys on Sundays. I played for the Bears. I worked for them for 13 years. They're my number two team 'cuz Dallas was my team growing up. Sorry. That's gonna piss some people off but they'll get over it.

DM: Or they won't.

BU: Don't care, either way.

DM: Last thing... it's my contention if Lovie just could have found the right offensive coordinator, there would have been at least one Super Bowl ring. Is that close?

BU: I don't see it that way at all. If we played better on defense, we win that Super Bowl. If we don't give up 200 yards rushing and 300 yards passing against Indy, we win that game. If we had three or four takeaways, if Thomas runs for 115 yards, we win that game. We didn't make enough plays in that game. And then you've got the 2010 NFC Championship game when we lost to Green Bay. Jay gets hurt in the first half. If he stays healthy in that game, who knows what happens. I can't say we'd have won it but maybe get back to the Super Bowl, who knows. I can't blame coaches. I don't blame anyone else. We should have played better. There's no way you can say an OC kept us from winning a game or winning a Super Bowl. I just don't see that as accurate.

DM: Okay. The Colts rushed for 191 yards against you and Peyton Manning got the MVP but ... (interrupted)

BU: Oh, I thought it was more than that. Well, we kept 'em under 200 (sarcastically). That's pretty good for us. Kept 'em under 200 (laughing).

After Urlacher's career, he didn't take to broadcasting as he thought. He gave it a quick whirl, quickly realized it wasn't his flavor or passion and left FOX. If it interested him, I suspect he'd flourish as an occasional host or regularly featured guest on talk radio or a television studio crew. Lack would be bored in a month, if that long. He knows who he is and who he isn't. Right now, he's a dad, golf nut and one of the boys.

Maybe rock and roll radio would do it for Urlacher. The Hall of Famer has a fondness for AC/DC, a band with ample song titles with potential for the title of an Urlacher biography. *Dirty Deeds Done Dirt Cheap* would fit. It'd fit any superstar who worked for the Bears, but Brian Urlacher actually knows the lyrics and riffs. He could belt out even the darkest material from the wacky Aussies with a grin. He's the smiling assassin. From few athletes have I gleaned such enormous joy while watching them work their magic. Urlacher is the most special player the Bears had in a very, very long time.

CHAPTER 14
The Lean Teens
(and beyond)

"Broncos is after me... Broncos so fucked up even the stripes on their socks run the wrong way."
– fictional, over-the-hill running back Gavin Gray (Dennis Quaid), chasing that one last payday, in the 1989 film Everybody's All-American.

My want is to make this section the leanest in the entire diary. That's what it deserves.

Those who steered the Bears between 2013 until the end of the '21 season were conclusive failures and the memories their work produced are mostly unpleasant. In my life, Bears ownership, the personnel department and coaching staffs never bumbled more than they did during this famine. At least we had Walter Payton in the '70s.

The succession of Marc Trestman to John Fox to Matt Nagy was this millennium's answer to Jim Dooley to Abe Gibron to Jack Pardee between '68 and '77. I have a sinking feeling the baton being passed to Matt Eberflus won't be dissimilar to Pardee successor, Neill Armstrong ('78-'81).

The grand slam *of bad*.

For one season, however, the '18 Bears captured the imaginations of their fans and restored civic pride. Reflecting on it should make any fan belt out a full-throated version of *Bear Down*. The economy of words credo must be suspended to characterize Chicago's first meaningful three hours with Nagy.

If you'll indulge me, a few ham-handed war analogies are deployed. At first blush, the '18 Bears possessed enough nuclear weaponry to turn Green Bay into *NFL Hiroshima* when the fuse was lit at Lambeau Field on September 9. Chicago's new commander in chief was the 40-year-old Nagy, a former Andy Reid assistant and University of Delaware and Arena League quarterback.

The opener in '18 was the most dramatic football game I ever watched. The storylines were thick, and the stars came out to play. It wasn't artful, but it was physical, and emotionally charged. Many heroes and many goats. It was a tale of two halves. The Bears won the first.

If you find yourself missing your Bears in the offseason, find *this* game in sparkling high definition and pull up a chair.

The Bears emasculated the Packers for one half, and it produced more euphoria in Chicago than any Bears-Packers game since William Perry steamrolled George Cumby on *Monday Night Football* in '85. Similarly, the nation was watching as Nagy's Bears were embarrassing the Packers on the season's first installment of *Sunday Night Football* on NBC. All of our eyes were getting first glimpses of Nagy's freshly upgraded roster. Battle-tested, proven soldiers.

None were bigger than Khalil Mack. On the evening of Friday, August 31 — nine days before the Bears were in Green Bay — general manager Ryan Pace shocked the NFL world and traded two first-round picks to the Raiders for the 27-year-old Mack. The '16 defensive player of the year was amidst a hold out, underwhelmed by Oakland's offer on his second contract. Stunningly, the Bears gave Pace the keys to the vault and invested in the '16 defensive player of the year. They signed Mack to the most lucrative deal for a defensive player in pro football history. Mack and Nagy quickly sent a message to Green Bay and the country: *Stand back, I'm coming through.*

A relentless pass rush knocked Aaron Rodgers out of the game early in the second quarter. When only 39 seconds remained in the first half, the Bears were mobbing Mack after he punctuated the first half with a 27-yard interception return for a touchdown. The Bears went to the locker room with a 17-point lead. Mack also had a sack, strip and recovery in the first 30 minutes.

There was something refreshingly different in this bombing of the Packers. Bears fans weren't drunk only on defense. Second-year quarterback Mitch Trubisky was sharp. The offense marched 86 yards in 10 plays and drew first blood when Trubisky took it in on the option from two yards out. He went 4-for-4 on the drive. Free agent speedster Taylor Gabriel caught a 31-yard Trubisky bullet to get the Bears to the GB 25. Fellow newcomer Trey Burton, the tight end who was a Super Bowl hero seven months earlier, made a clutch third-down catch that put the Bears in the red zone.

After a second Green Bay punt, it was Allen Robinson's turn to get into the act. The former Jaguar wideout was Pace's biggest offseason move prior to the Mack deal. Robinson made an acrobatic catch on a 33-yard gain to get the offense deep in Packer territory again. Newcomers made plays all over the field on both sides of the ball.

Mack and Co. swarmed Rodgers. Akiem Hicks got to him first on Green Bay's first snap. Rodgers then came up lame after Roy Robertson-Harris swallowed him up on the Pack's third possession. Trailing 10-0, a sour-faced Rodgers was carted into the locker room with a lower left leg injury. DeShone Kizer came off the bench and moved the Packers into the red zone.

It was Mack time again. Wearing jersey No. 52, as he had in Oakland, Mack swiped the ball from Kizer as he was engulfing the second-year Notre Dame alum. Effortlessly, it was as if Mack were snatching a rattle from an infant. The rush linebacker recovered, and the Bears preserved their 10-0 lead.

With only :50 left in the half, Robertson-Harris again was all over Kizer on a drop back from the GB 30. Kizer panicked and lofted a soft toss over Robertson-Harris, towards the offensive line. Mack was the only one there. He snatched it and began sprinting to the end zone. Carrying the ball in an almost defiantly reckless manner in his left hand, Mack beat Davante Adams to the goal line for a 27-yard Pick 6. The Bears led 17-0 at the break.

Pandemonium in Chicago.

TALE OF TWO HALVES

Trubisky dinked and dunked the Bears into field goal range in the third quarter and Cody Parkey's 33-yarder bumped the lead to 20-0 early in the third. On NBC, Al Michaels and Cris Collinsworth were speculating on Mike McCarthy keeping Rodgers parked and take the beating with Kizer. Live to fight another day.

McCarthy and Rodgers thought differently. The Packers found some rhythm and finally scratched with a 41-yard Mason Crosby field goal late in the third. On their next possession, Rodgers hit Geronimo Allison on a 39-yard TD, and it was 20-10 with 14:06 left.

The collars tightened on Nagy's Bears. They went three and out and Rodgers made them pay with a 12-yard TD pass to Adams to make cut the deficit to 20-17. Rodgers was, as usual, distributing the ball to everyone. Allison, in particular, made a splash in the fourth quarter. Randall Cobb led all receivers with nine catches for 142 yards and Adams caught five passes for 88 yards.

With 9:01 left, the Bears appeared to be salting away the win. Starting at their own 25, the Bears chewed up more than six minutes and were 3-for-3 on third down. Jordan Howard smartly stayed in bounds and gave himself up at the Packer 14 after an 11-yard gain around left end. On third and two, Trubisky calmly moved to his right and rifled a spiral to Anthony Miller. The rookie wideout likely would have beaten Jaire Alexander to the marker but Miller couldn't make the catch.

Nagy trotted out Parkey, who belted a fading-right 32-yarder inside the upright to give the Bears a 23-17 lead with 2:42 remaining.

With 75 yards of emerald turf in front of him, Rodgers went back to work. On the first snap, Rodgers was looking for Adams on a short slant to the right. Adams and nickel Bryce Callahan inadvertently collided and the ball sailed into the hands of Kyle Fuller. But Fuller couldn't catch it to seal the win. I suspect Wayne Larrivee, on Green Bay's radio broadcast, suggested it would have been *the dagger*.

The Bears were running out of gas, and it was palpable even on television. They needed Fuller, who had earned a generous new contract in the spring, to come up with the turnover. The pass rush was being neutralized and every defender was a tick behind the receiver. Safety Eddie Jackson lost his footing, and Cobb made an uncontested catch on a crossing route in the middle of the field near the Chicago 45. He was off to the races.

Mack, Adrian Amos and Leonard Floyd gave chase but couldn't catch him. It was a 75-yard score, Rodgers' third TD pass in the fourth quarter, and gave Green Bay a 24-23 lead with 2:13 to go. While Packers fans were squeezing Cobb's glutes upon his Lambeau Leap, Mack collapsed to one knee in the end zone, sucking for oxygen. Without a training camp, Mack was supposed to be on a pitch count but logged 42 snaps. Roquan Smith, who ended his holdout on August 15, also was limited but made his presence felt on several of his eight plays, including a sack of Kizer two plays before Mack's interception return.

The Bears moved the sticks three times on their final possession, but Nick Perry sacked Trubisky on 4th-and-10. The Packers won 24-23.

NFL life is no fairy tale.

After being left for dead, Rodgers finished 20-of-30 for 286 yards, three TDs, no picks and a rating of 130.7. Ownership personified.

The loss was dispiriting after such a dramatically productive first half but there were myriad reasons for renewed enthusiasm. Maybe Nagy really *is* the quarterback whisperer and can fix Trubisky. Mack's presence elevated everybody's game on the defense, which was lightning-fast and youthful.

For some younger Bears fans, the '18 team produced the only satisfying season they *ever have known*. Like generations before them, they learned how to get drunk on defense. Cheers. Nagy's first season remains the only feel-good Bears team in their last 13 editions. They went 12-4 and claimed the NFC North title. Nagy's team lifted the city's spirits more than any Bears' team since the 2010 division champs. There was much to celebrate, and, under coordinator Vic Fangio, Chicago again was elite defensively.

A few quick reflections on '18 must include the 15-6 win over Sean McVay's Rams, the eventual NFC champs, on *SNF* in Week 15. The Bears administered the *Fangioplasty* on the Rams, who were 3-point favorites. They throttled Jared Goff, intercepting the markedly improved quarterback four times and sacking him three more. Nose man Eddie Goldman provided the get 'em up, sacking Goff in the end zone for a safety that gave the Bears an 8-6 lead early in the fourth quarter.

Conversely, eventual defensive player of the year Aaron Donald never touched Trubisky. The vaunted Rams settled for two Greg Zuerlein field goals. Al Michaels' head must have nearly exploded from the absence of splash plays.

The game's lone touchdown came on a Nagy staple — trickeration. I always favored convention over drawin' it up in the dirt, but Nagy never asked me. With the fleshy Hicks lined up at fullback, Trubisky's 2-yard TD pass to tackle Bradley Sowell on play action came with less than 10 minutes left in the final quarter. Prince Amukamara sealed the 15-6 win with a pick of Goff with two minutes remaining.

The '18 Bears were the No. 1 scoring defense in the league, allowing only 17.7 points per game. Mack was a monster with 12.5 sacks and six forced fumbles in 14 games. He was runner-up for DPOY honors. The new Bears catalyst was first-team All Pro, as were Hicks and Fuller, who was becoming an elite corner. Smith also had an impactful first season and led the Bears in tackles. Danny Trevathan was a sure-handed tackler, and Jackson had a productive second season.

They entertained us. Fangio's defense was a joy to watch and '18 was an unapologetically fun year. Who didn't enjoy the many images from *Club Dub* after Ws?

FOOL'S GOLD

Ultimately, Trubisky was who we thought he was. Pedestrian. After the Justin Fields experiment, however, his numbers aren't as unsettling. In four years, Trubisky completed 65% of his passes, threw 64 TDs and 37 INTs. He was 29-21 as the starter and posted a career rating of 87.2 with the Bears. Not second-overall pick material but ask Jets fans if they've seen worse. Ask Clevelanders.

It feels hollow because the Bears didn't score points. The absence of failure doesn't mean success and the Bears habitually were slow starters in most of Nagy's four years. Trailing at halftime every week was not the expectation when they nabbed Reid's top lieutenant.

The 16-15 wild card round loss to defending champion Philadelphia was a gut punch. Most of us thought the Bears could alley brawl their way to the divisional round. All they needed was 17 points. It was too tall an order and Doug Pederson's Eagles advanced.

As was the case when the Bears flopped in the NFC Championship game in January of '11, the fingers were pointed the wrong way on Monday. Parkey took most of the wrath from displeased media and fans. Pay no mind to the offense again failing to bust a grape. The Bears played 51 minutes without a touchdown before Trubisky's 22-yard scoring strike to Robinson, giving the Bears a 15-10 lead.

Pat O'Donnell set up the Philly offense at their own 40 with a shanked 36-yard punt late in the fourth. The Eagles cashed in against a fatigued defense and Nick Foles 2-yard TD toss to Golden Tate broke the Bears' backs.

Tarik Cohen's return of 35 yards afforded Trubisky a chance to put the Bears in field goal range with 56 faithful seconds remaining. The kid completed consecutive passes to Robinson for 25 and eight yards to get to the Philadelphia 25, which landed Parkey in striking distance. Parkey squared up for a would-be 43-yard game winner.

On came the crushing heartbreak of the dreaded double doink. Parkey's kick had plenty of juice and connected with the left upright about half-way to its top. The ball then caromed inward, end over end, and bounced off the crossbar before it fell in Soldier Field's north end zone.

Parkey took a disproportionate amount of the blame. The kicker exacerbated the problem when he showed up two mornings later as a guest on NBC's *Today Show* to lament his psychological torment for America. The nerve of that guy.

It was low hanging fruit for the guys in the cheap seats. Parkey became a punchline and one of the most maligned figures in team history. Burton also took a massive amount of heat. The tight end didn't suit up. It later was revealed Burton suffers from anxiety and the big stage sent him into darkness.

The Bears went 5-for-16 on third down in the loss. Nagy called only 13 runs as the Bears rushed for a skinny 65 yards. The Bears also failed to put substantial heat on Foles, who was sacked only once (Floyd). The Super Bowl 51 MVP threw two picks (Smith, Amos) but played with poise on the game-winning touchdown drive.

We were duped on defense in a points-driven NFL. The thrill ride season ended abruptly. A cast of sports pall loomed for weeks . We all should have known better. Trubisky was a hardworking, mobile quarterback but there was enough evidence he never would be a win *because of him* quarterback. They had to win ugly in '18 and the more Trubisky spoke, the less confidence he inspired.

Remember when the second pick in the '17 draft advocated turning off the televisions at Halas Hall? He was never going to be *the guy*.

Neither was Foles once he put on navy and orange. Neither was Andy Dalton. Or Fields.

Time to move through *The Lean Teens* chronologically with lean copy, commonly referred to as talking points. It's all this era merits. The eight-player band that made the drought possible: Matriarch Virginia McCaskey, 'Ginny's lucky son George McCaskey, accountant Ted Phillips, military man Phil Emery, offensive import Marc Trestman, the boyish-faced Pace, grizzled veteran John Fox and the up-and-comer, Nagy.

MADE IN CANADA

Phil Emery entered the second of his three-years in '13, which brought more purging and pillaging of the roster. As the Brian Urlacher era concluded acrimoniously, Emery thought outside the box and hired Trestman, who was a CFL success. The Minnesota native was a well-traveled NFL offensive assistant before finding his niche with the Montreal Alouettes. Jay Cutler, entering his fifth season with the Bears, and receiver Brandon Marshall enthusiastically applauded the choice. There was guarded optimism from media and fans, primarily because Trestman possessed a quarterback tutor reputation with a background on the offensive side of the ball.

The *Kumbaya*-singing head man won CFL championships in '09 and '10. Still, it had been almost a decade since Trestman lived in an NFL world. He was a Dave Wannstedt assistant with the Dolphins in '04. The new hire wasn't admonished universally but nobody scheduled a parade, either.

Reflections on the two-year Trestman experiment may induce dizziness and nausea. All that salvaged football Sundays in Chicago were the empty calories of a more potent passing game. The Bears scored more points. Trestman got even more out of Josh McCown than he did from Cutler and the receiving tandem of Marshall, opposite second-year man Alshon Jeffrey, easily became the most potent duo in team history.

The Bears finished 8-8 in '13 but averaged 27.8 ppg, which was second in the league. Four offensive starters made the Pro Bowl — Marshall, Jeffrey, Matt Forte and rookie Kyle Long, the 20th-overall pick. McCown completed 66.5% of his passes and posted a whopping 109 rating. The journeyman was 3-2 as the starter and threw 13 touchdowns with only one pick. Forte had a monster season as a dual threat, rushing for 1339 yards (4.6 ypc) and nine TDs with 74 catches for 594 yards (7.0 ypr) and three TDs.

Whatever the Bears accomplished offensively, however, was undone by one of their worst defenses in the modern era. Under coordinator Mel Tucker, the Bears relinquished 29.9 ppg in '13 — 30th in the NFL. Lance Briggs was at the end and appeared in only nine games, Peanut Tillman just eight. Recent draftees — Fuller excepted — weren't good. Neither were free agents. The snowball began rolling down the mountain.

Perhaps most indelibly etched in the minds of Bears enthusiasts is the quirky Trestman's decision to deploy his field goal unit prematurely in a loss to Minnesota. With four minutes left in overtime, Robbie Gould pushed a 47-yard attempt a smidge wide right, which forced overtime. On second down.

Blair Walsh subsequently kicked a 34-yarder and Minnesota won it 23-20.

In '14, the Bears were second from the bottom in scoring defense, relinquishing 27.6 ppg. Strong safety Ryan Mundy, a 30-year-old journeyman, led the team in tackles. Fuller was second. It was a reminder of what John Madden taught us in the '80s: *"When the guys in the secondary are the ones who are making all the tackles, that means your front seven are getting blocked."* RIP to both Madden and the original master of the obvious, baseball announcer Tim McCarver.

Emery's personnel gaffes were obvious misses. Free agent signee Jared Allen was a non-factor. He punched out only 5.5 sacks after taking a big paycheck. Veteran Lamarr Houston wasn't effective, and the Bears began a defensive decline that took several years to rectify. Allen, who was 32, was one of the players I had in mind when choosing the quote from *Everybody's All-American* as an entrance ramp to *The Lean Teens*. The Bears were to Allen what Denver was to Gavin Gray — suckers. Gullible enough to extract one last big payday.

Who can forget, however, that preseason highlight-reel stick by Jonathan Bostic, a second-rounder from Florida. Best August tackle by a Bear ever. I have no memories of Ego Feguson's career. Nothing from Khaseem Greene or Will Sutton. Via draft, Fuller was Emery's only skin on the wall defensively.

The '14 Bears famously had 50+ points laid on them in back-to-back losses to New England and Green Bay. Worse, there was a bye week to lick their wounds after the Patriots slapped them 51-23 in Week 8. The latter was on *Sunday Night Football*. The Packers took a 42-0 lead into the locker room after six TD passes from Rodgers.

After Cutler launched three picks and carded a 55.7 rating in a home loss to New Orleans in Week 15, Trestman benched him. It was amusing, in a twisted way. The Bears were 5-9 and the quarterback guru opted for Jimmy Clausen against the Lions. Clausen's two TD passes weren't enough, and Detroit punched out a 20-14 win. It was the Bears' third straight date at Soldier Field and they lost all of them.

Tresty's Bears fell to 5-10 and played out the string in Minnesota against Mike Zimmer's scuffling Vikings. Cutler went back to work and again guided the Bears to touchdown-free football. Jay Feely's three field goals were all the Bears (Brad) mustered in a 13-9 loss — the fifth straight for Team Trestman.

And just like that, Emery and his coach were gone. George McCaskey and Ted Phillips exiled the GM and Trestman on Monday, December 29. Predecessors Jerry Angelo and Lovie Smith never looked so good. There was more "be careful what you wish for" coming.

20th CENTURY FOX

Fox's arrival marked the first time the Bears hired a skipper with head coaching experience. He was 60 and, even though Fox's forte was defense, it made sense for Pace to trust the acumen of a coach who had taken two franchises to a Super Bowl. Fox was coming off a prosperous four years in Denver. Before Kansas City's dynasty was born, Denver ruled the AFC West and Foxy's Broncos went an astounding 46-18 (.719) in his tenure. Carolina won its first NFC championship under Fox in '03.

The result was three more unsatisfying years. Pace, a former New Orleans scout, inherited Emery's mistakes and quickly demonstrated he also wasn't good as the final decision maker. Pace's shoddy draft ledger debuted with the selection of wide receiver Kevin White in '15. The West Virginia product, picked seventh-overall, rarely got on the field. With White unavailable, 29-year-old Eddie Royal was pressed into nine starts in '15. A trio of young running backs — Jeremy Langford, Ka'Deem Carey and Jacquizz Rodgers — was brought to lighten Forte's load, but none were effective.

In '16, wideout Cameron Meredith was the most targeted receiver on the Bears. Cam freaking Meredith. A 33-yard-old Cutler yielded to Brian Hoyer and Matt Barkley. Jeffrey wasn't as effective. Scrawny Marquess Wilson, a seventh-rounder in '13, made eight starts.

Terrell Freeman, a former Indianapolis linebacker, was the Bears' leading tackler. Harold Jones-Quartey was second. Don't remember him either? Don't feel bad. Jones-Quartey, good old No. 29, was a 23-year-old undrafted safety out of Findlay College. It was his second and last NFL season.

What a mess of a roster. Logan Paulsen. Deonte Thompson. Josh Sitton. Josh Bellamy. Daniel Brown. Joique Bell. Those were the "household names" who played hundreds of offensive snaps. On the defensive side, Hicks was a stud, plausibly the most productive player on the team but the D had personnel problems, too. Too many "depth players" were starters. Tracy Porter. Mitch Unrein. Nick Kwiatkowski. Willie Young. Sam Acho. Callahan.

Long-time sports radio contributor Oak Park Vandy assessed the era perfectly: *"I look forward to a day when the Bears' best player isn't an often-injured guard* (Long)."

The Bears went a sobering 3-13 in Fox's second season. They finished 28th in scoring (17.4 ppg) and 24th in points allowed (24.9 ppg). It was time to move on from Cutler and Pace needed to homer in the '17 draft. Several good ones were there, including Patrick Mahomes and Deshaun Watson, and the Bears had the third pick.

You're familiar with what happened. Pace traded up one slot with San Francisco for Trubisky. Enough already has been said on that in these pages and in every shot and a beer joint in Chicagoland.

As an insurance policy, Pace signed Mike Glennon to mentor the inexperienced North Carolina Tar Heel. On the heels of 3-13, Fox was in save-his-ass mode and opened the year with the veteran. Glennon was dreadful and dropped three of his first four starts before the wheel was placed in the hands of the wide-eyed and overmatched Trubisky.

What's your lasting memory of Fox's three years? If you're thinking it's the challenge he won — only to lose possession of the ball — against Green Bay, we're kindred spirits. The '17 Bears went 5-11 and finished last in the division for the third straight season. Fox was gassed on New Year's Day of '18. His 14-34 record (.292) narrowly escapes *worst Bears coach ever* status. Abe Gibron went 11-30-1 (.272) between '72 and '74.

BACK TO NAGS

Nagy, the '18 coach of the year, joined my Score afternoon show with Danny Parkins in training camp. He did a relaxed 20 minutes and was likeable on and off stage. I asked him if he thought his roster was the best in the league. Defensively, the Bears could stake that claim. The look on Nagy's face spoke volumes on how he really felt about *his* side of the ball. To an even novice face reader, it was apparent the coach wasn't bursting with confidence over his offense. He didn't sell propaganda or get lost in cliches. Nagy complimented those who earned it and pointed to the "hunger for improvement" for players who didn't sparkle in the 12-4 year or have a great offseason.

I liked the team's 16th coach, and it was easy to root for Nagy's success. More than most, his feet were squarely on the ground. He'd been on the outside, training to sell homes when Reid saved his NFL life. He was in a tough spot. Emery's remaining stink and Pace's miscues did Nagy no favors offensively. The challenges of Trubisky, a line that didn't jibe or stay healthy, no credible tight ends on the roster and Nagy's penchant for "the cute" were a recipe for failure. Impassable obstructions.

Nagy soiled the bed on opening night in a 10-3 loss to Green Bay at Soldier Field. At least the Bears had a new kicker. Eddie Piniero's 38-yarder gave the Bears a first quarter lead before three and a half quarters of lifeless, scoreless offensive football. Nagy didn't run it and didn't want to run it. Trubisky attempted 45 throws while running backs David Montgomery and Mike Davis collaborated on 11 carries. There was no offensive identity. The Packers stopped Nagy's crew 12-of-15 times on third down.

Also memorable from the '19 season is the Week 7 loss to New Orleans at Soldier Field. Nagy called only seven runs. Coming off a bye, Sean Payton's Saints thumped the Bears 36-25. Payton was overheard chirping at breakfast downtown at the team hotel. He was atypically cocky and louder than usual. Specifically, he expressed extreme confidence in his offensive and defensive lines. *Men against boys* was the spirit of the Napervillian's forecast.

Coach Kreskin. The Bears rushed for 17 yards on those seven attempts. New Orleans slammed it 35 times for 151 yards. Latavius Murray was the plow horse (27-119-2) as the Saints hogged the ball for more than 37 minutes. Cameron Jordan sacked Trubisky twice. The Bears only got to Teddy Bridgewater once and fell to 3-3 with the loss. New Orleans jumped to 6-1.

A priceless sound bite for sports radio followed when the frustrated headmaster was pressed about his continued lack of consistent commitment to rushing attempts: *"I know we have to run the ball — I'm not an idiot."*

The Bears went 8-8 in '19. There's not much more from the Nagy years that needs to be chronicled. The Chicago careers of Trubisky, Mack and Fields were detailed in Chapters 2 through 6. Same for the decision makers, Emery and Pace. Two final angles on Nagy's last two years, commencing with the '20 playoff game nobody remembers.

It was the first year of *Super Wild Card Weekend* when a seventh team qualified for the postseason in each conference. Nagy's Bears were the NFC's first *seventh* playoff team. On January 7 of '21, New Orleans beat the Bears 21-9 behind Drew Brees' 265 passing yards with two touchdowns. Trailing

21-3, Trubisky threw a 19-yard touchdown pass to Jimmy Graham *as time expired*. The Bears went 99 yards for the touchdown, their second in two playoff games with Nagy running the show.

I do not know if each Bear got an extra dollar at Dairy Queen for the effort.

Nagy wanted Fields desperately in '21 and Pace concurred. Pace again parted with draft equity, forfeiting a first-round pick to slide up nine picks in a deal with the Giants so Fields could rescue the franchise. Rare is the occasion when a GM gets *two* shots to find both a coach and a Messiah quarterback.

When Andy Dalton pulled up lame late in the second quarter against Cincinnati in Week 2, the rookie was forced into action before he was ready. A 53-yard Pick 6 from Roquan Smith gave Fields just enough cushion and the Bears hung on for a 20-17 win. The following week, unfortunately, would be Nagy and Fields' worst nightmare.

In his first career start, Fields was decked nine times and the Bears accrued only six first downs and 47 yards of total offense. The Browns waltzed to a 26-6 win. Myles Garrett had 4.5 sacks. In the 21st century, only twice has a team totaled fewer than 47 yards. It's tied for the seventh lowest output since the merger. Shortly afterward, Nagy lateraled the play calling duties to coordinator Bill Lazor. The Bears lost five straight — for the third straight year — and a coaching change appeared imminent.

The Bears whacked Pace and Nagy in early January of '22 and Ryan Poles and Eberflus took on the wreckage. In the case of the latter, I'm not brimming with optimism the final scene will end with a confetti shower. If he really is this era's Armstrong, the beat will go on and the Bears will continue to book vacations during the first week in February.

'Nuff said. Lean. Like the Chicago offense for most of 105 years.

CHAPTER 15
Team McCaskey
MISERS OF THE MIDWAY

"Christ coach, we're not the team. They're 'the team.' We're just the helmets and the jockstraps. We're the equipment. And they just depreciate us and write it off on tax returns." – fictional NFL receiver Phil Elliott (Nick Nolte) in the 1979 film North Dallas Forty.

George Halas and his descendants have been the only owners and operators of the Chicago Bears for 105 years. Regardless of who sat in which administrative chair — or who played quarterback or what the climate was in the NFL at a given time — the Bears have been a model of consistency.

The team's best players consistently found happiness elusive. The guys who wore helmets invariably had to fight for every dollar and endured poor work conditions. The Bears — since the 1950s — have been called *stingy* by their most productive employees. The last team in the division to upgrade facilities was the Bears.

Those who've worn suits, including Halas, consistently pinched pennies and the bottom line always outweighed the scoreboard. The decision makers were content to find new players when their best fell out of line and asked for reciprocity. The bosses also have sullied success by reneging on promises for rewards. When free agency arrived in 1993, ownership met it with a shrug. It took 17 years in the free market system before the Bears took a meaningful swing and signed Julius Peppers.

Some of the most qualified coaches in America thumbed their noses at the Bears job and sprinted back to O'Hare to escape the front office fumbling and football ignorance of the top dogs. Consistently. Since inception as the Decatur Staleys, the Bears have lacked bedside manner at the highest ranks. Accountants aren't always blessed with people skills. Or football knowledge. That combination of deficiencies resulted in terrible choices, the most crippling being the hiring of ill-qualified general managers and coaches.

Somehow, the Bears continue to be labeled a "storied franchise." *Theirs* is a history steeped in acrimony. Ownership has been so recklessly clumsy; it consistently has elicited contemptuous feelings that burned so hot it cost them longer partnerships with some of the NFL's greatest players. George Blanda, Dick Butkus, Gale Sayers, Mike Ditka, Walter Payton, Jim McMahon and Brian Urlacher all left kicking and screaming. There were medical malpractice allegations and breach of contract lawsuits filed but they settled out of court. There have been many lengthy stretches of estrangements. Some never wanted — or want — to reconcile.

Halas put the nepotism ball in play when he hired his son-in-law to join the family business. Ed McCaskey admitted as much, noting Papa Bear waited 25 years to ensure "the marriage was secure" before Virginia's hubby earned a seat at the big boy table.

The Bears remain homeless, essentially. Less than 25 years after Soldier Field's renovation, they play in the NFL's smallest stadium. Uncertainty looms over a future in Arlington Heights or a new venue on the lakefront.

These are your Bears. And Team McCaskey knows it.

RING IT UP

In February of 1985, San Francisco owner Eddie DeBartolo Jr. rewarded his Vince Lombardi trophy winners with a trip to Oahu to receive their Super Bowl rings and celebrate in paradise. The 49ers historically have been described by their players as first class. Generous. Personable even.

The championship party was a little different for the '85 Bears.

The coldest day of 1986 in Chicago was January 27 when the temperature sunk to -4. It was the day after the Bears drilled New England in Super Bowl XX. A team-record nine Bears who made the Pro Bowl had an all-expenses paid trip to Hawaii in sight but nobody else had plans for fruity umbrella drinks. It's unlikely the Hotel Moraine in Highwood was making them. That's where Team McCaskey huddled to receive their jewelry.

And the '85 Bears didn't get the Super Bowl rings they initially chose. Chairman Michael McCaskey pulled a bookkeeping end-around and it forced the players to scramble and purchase a lesser ring. Here's what *I Bear*

Witness learned:

In the mid-'80s, the NFL made a $5,000 contribution toward each Super Bowl ring. Historically, most owners (DeBartolo among them) dug into their own pockets additionally for customized rings selected by the players. The McCaskey family wasn't kicking in and Bears captains were aware of that. The captains conferred with designers at Jostens Jewelers, and all was set to go for a $5,000 ring.

When the ring's design and production costs were revealed to McCaskey, however, captains were informed of an accounting hiccup. The chairman claimed he'd been misunderstood. Ownership, on its own volition, had customized pendants made for the players' wives. McCaskey said the Bears were deducting the costs of those pendants — $1,500 each — from the league's contribution.

Many players were single and gave the pendants to their mothers. Players never had a voice on the matter. The Bears summarily decided "we're doing this" and then had enough weasel in them to deduct costs from the league's $5K stipend per ring, leaving $3,500 for each ring. If the Bears chose the rings they initially wanted, each player had to cough up $1,500.

Payton was the loudest objector to McCaskey's accounting. He already endured 11 years of McCaskeyian behavior. Oh, to have known these things when Walter was a station mate at the Score in the '90s.

"We just said 'fuck it.' We went back to Jostens and asked for a $3,500 ring as close to that one as possible," one of the principles told me.

What was supposed to be 14-karat gold became 10-karat. The blue sapphire stone was scrapped. It became aluminum with blue enamel paint.

To my surprise, several '85 Bears were unaware of the downsizing when I contacted them in '24.

"Are you fucking kidding me?" said Keith Van Horne, a 13-year Bear.

"Really?" McMahon asked. He paused, then mumbled "Pretty typical. That's McCaskey."

A '90s story from a suburban paper had juicy Steve McMichael quotes on the two-ring circus. "You think it'd be glorious, right? The 49ers got to get their rings in Honolulu so I'm thinking, 'Well, this is going to be a big-time thing.' I get the news we are having the ring ceremony at a Holiday Inn (Mongo embellishment) in Highwood.

"I show up at the dinner and Mike Ditka is already half in the bag. We're sitting there waiting to get the rings and before we get the ring, he's already passed out in his plate of food sitting at the table with the McCaskeys. They start giving the rings out and I look at it — and it's a nice ring, diamonds and gold. But I heard the NFL allocates $5,000 per ring and the owners can put more money into it to make it nicer. How much do you think that ring cost the Bears?"

This isn't the feel-good portion of these diaries. I have not attempted fiction yet.

The Chicago Bears not only have survived themselves, they've proven they can prosper under any threatening climate. War proof. Recession proof. Pandemic proof. With an estimated worth of almost $7 billion, the Bears are a corporate monster, the sixth-highest valued franchise in the league. For their fans, it's hard to accept the possibility profit is all that matters but too much evidence exists to think otherwise.

In my 40 years in Chicago radio, I've conversed with hundreds of former Bears, dating to the '63 championship team. I know things. Words that best describe a player's experience include *disadvantaged, oppressed* (by the contemporary standards in their profession) and *helpless*. Here's a fine zinger from a long-tenured Bear: "Only one group of people the Bears treat worse than their players — their former players."

This NFL charter franchise with "a rich tradition" could use some new ones. Traditions worth keeping is a starting point. Possess more grace. Employ the best people at all levels. Be more generous. Show a little humanity and authentic concern for your own. Those are traditions that lead to trophies, harmony in the hallways and locker room. My hope is for this current administration, which has functioned well in its first two years and change, be given freedoms previously never granted to the football people. Too many non-football people sat in the biggest chairs.

Keep the McCaskeys out of the kitchen. Until this happens, this group will have to win *despite* all the impediments with which management obstructs their path. Just as the '80s Bears did.

MEET "THE TEAM'

Apologies for this delay of game, but a fast refresher is needed so all understand the Halas family tree. With all of the flying McCaskeys, the three Georges and pet nicknames, a Venn diagram is almost requisite to grasp who's who. Please allow me to introduce the devilish cast members entrenched in this real-life NFL reality show.

George Halas, undeniably an American sports icon, founded the NFL in 1920 when he was 25. I'm glad he did. It's my favorite game. It was tremendous vision, but the NFL was a garage-band league for a long time. Halas was a player and a winning coach *some* of his career. As an owner, he was *Mr. Potter*. Before the NFL players unionized in the meaningful way, Halas treated them like livestock.

Halas' 324 career coaching victories, tops in history until Don Shula jumped him in '93, are misleading. Counting stats, I believe, is the phrase. He took breaks periodically to grow the game (launching the college all-stars vs. NFL champions game and writing for the *Tribune* among them) but he kept returning. Halas' teams won games but seldom punctuated good seasons with championships. Following the '46 title (one more chance to say Sid Luckman), Halas' record isn't dissimilar to that of Jeff Fisher or Marvin Lewis. Neither were considered Hall of Fame timber.

Then came '63. The Bears won the NFL championship with an impotent offense, finishing 10th in scoring in a 14-team league. They had a whopping 222 total yards offense in the 14-10 win over the Giants in the title game. How did Halas reward the '63 champs? He reneged on the $5,000 bonuses players were promised. Ditka, on the heels of the Super Bowl win in '86, made sure he got that in his biography, written by the *Tribune's* Don Pierson. Halas' frugality and questionable behavior was public but almost all of it has vaporized as time passed.

Papa Bear outlived his only son, George Halas Jr., more commonly referred to as *Mugs* Halas. The Bears, thusly, were bequeathed to his only daughter.

Virginia McCaskey is the almost 102-year old daughter of Halas. She married Ed McCaskey, and the couple assumed control of the Bears after

Halas' death in '83. Halas' wish was for Mugs be first in line for this football version of *Succession*, but he suffered a fatal heart attack in '79. He was 54. Ed McCaskey passed away in '03, leaving Virginia in total space command.

The Matriarch embraced Papa's maxims and paid it forward. *The Halas Way* survived long after most NFL teams climbed into the 21st century. Virginia McCaskey wants her team to be seen as squeaky clean, respectful, upstanding citizens. There was no chance the Bears were going to sign off on HBO's *Hard Knocks* doing what it had in 18 previous NFL training camps. Swearing and shirtlessness were verboten. All teams have final say on what's used on *Hard Knocks* and the '24 Bears camp was the most sanitized season in the show's history. Why local media appeared so surprised baffled me.

Virginia believed the Honey Bears were objectionable, for God sakes, and had the cheerleaders abolished after '85. Publicly, general manager Jerry Vainisi took one for the team, questioning whether cheerleading is still "relevant." In Lake Forest, Ginny pulled the strings. Her husband, Ed McCaskey, did not attempt to deter her. Today the Bears are one of eight NFL teams that don't have cheerleaders. The Packers bring in cheer squads from Wisconsin colleges.

Ed and Virginia McCaskey had 11 children, two of whom have passed. Of the 11 McCaskeys, Michael and George have had the most prominent roles. Michael assumed control in the early '80s and survived myriad gaffes — not employing a "pure" general manager for 14 years among them — before the botched hiring of Dave McGinnis as head coach in '99 cost him the throne. Like his grandfather, Michael McCaskey went squirrelly about rewarding the '85 *Shufflin' Crew* and was reluctant to spend big on players' salaries, staffing and upgrading the campus.

Ted Phillips was empowered soon after the McGinnis fiasco and immediately put his signature on the legacy of Bears boners with the ill-conceived renovation of Soldier Field in '02. Nobody wearing a suit gave it a second thought, but a year in Champaign gave the guys who wear football gear a season without a home game. That effectively submarined coach Dick Jauron. The Bears went 4-12 and any momentum Jauron's division champs acquired in '01 vaporized. The result was the smallest stadium in the NFL, wrapped by an unsightly combination of old-school colonnades and large sections of comic book spaceships. And now they're gnashing teeth again over the next new house. Phillips retired two years ago, but 20 bucks says he was on the horn with Mama Bear and George to protect Scott Hagel when he learned Warren and Ryan Poles intended to fumigate the malodorous waft of the last regime. It was *Sweaty Teddy* who mentored Hagel.

This has been *The McCaskey Way* since I gained access to the Bears in 'the mid-'80s. Interference from ownership has stunted the team's growth at all levels, not just the suits. It precluded them opportunities to hire qualified coaches — Bruce Arians, Nick Saban and McGinnis — and it severed a relationship with super scout Mark Hatley after four years. Hatley was most responsible for drafting Urlacher, Mike Brown and Olin Kreutz.

To be clear, the medals stand of Bears ineptitude — the trio of terrible that produced the most injurious results — is Michael and George McCaskey, and Phillips, the most over-achieving accountant in American history. This is how the Bears wound up stuck with dead weight hires like Phil Emery, Marc Trestman and Ryan Pace. The Mike and George and Ted effect killed deals for good coaches who yearned to go to the altar with the *storied franchise*. McGinnis was close to a deal, but it bellied up before management crossed the goal line.

COACH REPELLENT

An afternoon news conference was announced at 9:30 a.m. on Friday, January 22 of '99. McGinnis, a former assistant under Ditka and Dave Wannstedt, was going to be presented as Wanny's successor. Coach Mac was furious the Bears leaked the news before the deal was completed. It wasn't. He was Arizona's defensive coordinator and hadn't informed his boss, head coach Vince Tobin. Or his mother.

Shouting and slamming of doors resonated into the early afternoon and the press conference didn't begin as scheduled. McGinnis, a southern gentleman, had groveling to do with his mother, who was hurt she learned of her son's first big-time chance via ESPN. Mac never told her he even interviewed for the job. He was the good soldier and kept his mouth shut, as instructed.

The leak wasn't the deal-breaker, however. What quashed it was Michael McCaskey's response to a McGinnis objection to only two years of guaranteed contract. The standard contract for NFL coaches was four years. The Bears' four-year offer reserved them the freedom to pull the plug at halftime. McGinnis wasn't about to bite. Not for himself and certainly not for his staff.

The TCU alum fumed. As coaches do, McGinnis protected the assistants he'd be bringing, including former Bears cornerback Leslie Frazier, an eventual head coach with Minnesota. There was no way McGinnis was going to ask his guys to pack up with only a two-year commitment. "What do I say to my guys who are willing to move their families about a two-year guarantee?"

"Lie to 'em," was the Michael McCaskey solution.

The news conference never happened. Jauron was hired two weeks later.

Saban was at LSU when general manager Jerry Angelo was hot to get him to succeed Jauron in '04. Negotiations broke off fast. Wish I had more sordid details but what I can report (as I did in '04) is that Saban was so put off by Phillips and his minions, one of the coach's representatives gently pulled him out of the room. Saban needed a timeout before he went too dark on the zero-sum game playing Phillips. My suspicions were — and are — Saban also was being McCaskeyed, haggling over staff, the length of contract guarantees, personnel decisions, etc. Maybe he was asked to be deceitful with his staff, too.

Angelo wryly smiled in July when I broached it with him. Ange said he's too old (he's a very lucid and fit 75) and too mellow to revisit old grudges. He confirmed, however, it was Phillips to whom Saban reacted so strongly but wouldn't elaborate.

In '13, the Arians "courtship" was a laugher, too. The offensive-minded Arians was among the favorites to succeed Lovie Smith. The Bears pushed back on Arians' plan to bring in Todd Bowles as defensive coordinator. The team wanted to retain Rod Marinelli, then didn't believe Arians when he informed them he'd discussed it with Marinelli, who insisted he wasn't returning. The suits persisted, thinking Marinelli would give it another run.

Arians also was irritated by the abundance of suits and absence of football people in the interviews. The Bears included Scott Hagel, initially a public relations and marketing type, in the meetings. Arians is a large man with a big red face, regularly prone to bulging veins, often a result of the naivety of non-football people in football jobs. Front office suits and media clearly never have been his flavor. There also was a mock news conference in which team employees impersonated media and asked Arians questions.

The Chicago coaching candidate was (and remains) the only headmaster in NFL history to win coach of the year as an interim. Chuck Pagano stepped away from the Colts job in midstream in '12 to battle leukemia and Arians deftly landed the plane with an 11-5 finish. Love him or hate him for his bravado, it couldn't have been suggested Arians wasn't battle tested or qualified.

A mock news conference? Only the Bears, who tried this with actual media with candidates in '99. It bit them. Russ Grimm, a member of Washington's legendary *Hogs*, was a candidate years ago and just flopped embarrassingly with Bears media. Grimm was a great offensive lineman but not exactly the board room type. Wearing a crumpled sweater that looked like a gift from Aunt Millie a few years back, Grimm thanked *the McKlaskey family* for considering him.

Bearly believable.

They were up to their old tricks again in the spring. While Bears fans eagerly awaited the Caleb Williams draft, a behind-the-scenes tug-of-war stirred at 1000 Football Drive in Lake Forest. It's the kind of interference from ownership that's been an ever-present malignancy.

George McCaskey, the 68-year-old son of Virginia McCaskey, stone-walled president Kevin Warren on a front office personnel shakeup clearly within Warren's "jurisdiction." As reported in Chapter 1, Warren wanted *his guys* in the marketing and digital media departments. Who wouldn't. The ability to operate freely with full autonomy isn't his privilege — it's something Warren earned by building an impressive resume.

Warren has been termed a politician. So what? Why push back against a Bears executive finally comporting himself in a *presidential* manner? I don't know if the Bears ever employed a top-of-the-food chain leader with people skills. Warren's background in the front office with the Vikings and as Big Ten commissioner unequivocally makes him qualified to assess what happens with digital media distribution, partnerships with sponsors, community and media relations.

Still, Warren had to wrestle for it when Boy George protected *their own*. After several months of behind-the-scenes give and take, Warren brought in Ted Crews as a special advisor in April. Crews has built an impressive NFL resume and with several organizations, most recently serving as director of communications for the Chiefs.

It never should have gone that way. That was a five-minute conversation. But these are the Bears, and don't assume the fallout from these things doesn't have the potential to spill on down to the coaching staff or roster. It's representative of a management style that has precluded the Bears numerous chances to hire football people with far more skins on the wall than the Topps trading cards collecting son of Virginia McCaskey, George. Or his late big brother, Michael.

A FEW McCNUGGETS...

- Butkus died on October 5 of '23. This spring, Butkus' son, Matt, received a letter informing him the team was rescinding his father's annual ticket allotment. Word was Matt Butkus was seething over the correspondence.

- November 1 marked the 25th anniversary of Walter Payton's death. Connie Payton, Walter's widow, received a form letter from the Bears a couple years ago, scolding her for violating the team's quirky rules regarding tickets. Bears alumni can request two complimentary tickets to one home per season but the former player (in this case, widow) must use those seats. Connie had given the tickets to son, Jarrett, now a veteran WGN-TV sports anchor.

Alarms went off when a team employee noticed the Payton seats were empty in the second half. After being spotted by friends, Jarrett Payton accepted an invitation to join them in a luxury suite. The Bears resent all empty seats but the few they comp even more. And the McCaskeys bristle when their guidelines aren't followed in entirety. Via form letter.

Survivors of two of the greatest players in team history and the Bears send form letters. A little charm school would be a good idea for this outfit. Some public relations touch around the greens would be a welcomed change.

- "What a nice gesture," thought a veteran Bear in the late-'80s. At each locker stall were boxes of Chicago Bears Christmas cards for players to send. Still on the buzz of the Super Bowl victory, which Bear wouldn't be proud to snail mail those to family and friends.

On the next pay stub, the player noticed the team deducted charges incurred for production of the greeting cards. If a sleepless player sucked down a Mountain Dew or had a bag of chips from the minibar in his hotel room, those charges also appeared as deductions on his next game check. A few players made it a game, invariably taking something from the minibar. Every time, their game checks reflected crisp accounting.

- NFL new ownership approvals usually are unanimous. Nobody wants to be on an island alone or with one or two other dissenting votes. The Bears were skittish in '99 when Daniel Snyder put in a bid to purchase the Washington Redskins from the estate of Jack Kent Cooke. It's an uncomfortable conversation to have, even for the Bears, when trying to dissuade fellow owners from approving a bid. How do you say, *"the league is Jewish enough already,"* even to the old boys' club? That was the sentiment expressed by one of the biggest suits in Lake Forest.

- As Phillips' star ascended, so did his ego. And his resolve to keep the worker bees compensated as little as possible. In the mid-'90s, he objected to press releases, crafted to promote a player's accomplishments. Peering over the shoulder of a public relations staffer, Phillips cracked "Tone it down a bit with the glowing praise. I'm the one who has to pay these guys."

The accountant actually said, *"I'm the one who has to pay these guys.*" That's rich.

In his 24-years as team president, Phillips' Bears won three playoff games. Not even enough for each wife to experience the rush. The postseason wins over Seattle and New Orleans came on back-to-back Sundays in January of '07. Even Phillips doesn't operate that quickly when he's recruiting the next former Mrs. Phillips. Sometimes, it didn't necessitate leaving Halas Hall.

- Colin Kaepernick taking a knee in '17 was more nightmarish for the McCaskeys than the Mike Glennon-Mitch Trubisky experience. The family historically has been Republican. Conservative. Catholic. And the Bears hate when their employees express a thought (or gesture) on anything flirting with a political lean or a religious bent. I question its authenticity, but George McCaskey publicly expressed dissatisfaction with Urlacher's social media posts that "leaned right."

Robert Quinn stayed in the locker room during the anthem in his '20 one-hit wonder year. Jaylon Johnson remains indoors until the anthem concludes. Oh, to have been a fly on the wall for those conversations at Halas Hall then, or *today* if the topic were renewed. If Warren and Poles went to G-Mac and said several players requested going back to the knee, and we support them, the reaction from the chairman would be fascinating.

The old boys' club (and mom) prefer the rank and file just go play football. Don't pick a lane and risk the flow of business. In a different era, management's stance might have been radically different and less passive. And those views wouldn't fly in today's climate.

- Covid-19, as it was called in '20, postponed Jimbo Covert's Hall of Fame induction to '21. I called a few '85 Bears to get reviews on the big weekend.

"It was a great party, but the Bears jacked him over," said two teammates who went to Canton. I asked them to elaborate and was informed the Bears weren't as generous with their contribution to Covert's party as they were for Richard Dent's 10 years earlier.

Covert isn't a whiner, but he confirmed the team's contribution to his weekend party was light — around 10% less than what Dent received in '11. Expenses for a weekend of hotel rooms and a banquet blitz past $100K. Some teams cover all of the costs.

The Raiders threw the biggest bash in Canton in '21 and that was for Cliff Branch, the receiver who died in '19. Historically, the Raiders cover all costs for *their* guys. So do the Buccaneers, Patriots, 49ers and Cowboys (maybe more). The Bears seem to contribute whatever dollar amount strikes their fancy that day. Seems random.

- The first blush reaction from a Bear of renown when I called about an interview for a book about the Bears was telling. Before I described the mission statement or tone, he belted out "Ha! You should call it *Random Acts of Cheapness.*"

- I knew George Blanda was a Bear before his AFL days with the Oilers and Raiders, but I never heard the Hall of Famer left Chicago with enormous contempt for Halas. Blanda "retired" in '59 after 10 seasons with the Bears. He was fed up with Halas, whom the game "had passed by" according to Blanda. The colorful Blanda was relegated to kicking duties and accused Halas of favoritism toward Johnny Lujack after Blanda outplayed him in camp. Blanda also accused Halas of demanding the return of a $600 signing bonus after he made the team.

This, however, is the money shot. Blanda saved a receipt for a special kicking shoe he had made and kept it in his wallet for decades. Halas refused to pay $32.51 for a custom made squared-toed shoe. Over a long career as a compelling public speaker, Blanda would whip out the old receipt when he sensed the audience fading on him.

"Lemme tell you about that cheap sonofabitch George Halas," Blanda began. And he regaled crowds with tales of Halas' cheap, mulish ways. When Blanda retired, he was the NFL's all-time leading scorer and a shoo-in for the Hall. (No additional charge for that one).

- An e-mail the Bears sent to their still-included alumni was forwarded to me. It was an invitation to a sponsored event. There was a $40 discount coupon for a hotel room. In the same e-mail, at the same hotel, it was noted overnight parking is $53. No coupon.

- I don't absolve Halas of his stubbornness on social change because "that's how people thought back then." Halas played pro football and with the New York Yankees before he founded the NFL in '20. If there's a culture that dissolves racial barriers more than athletics, I never experienced it.

Halas required a push on white and black players rooming together. It's played out in the '71 ABC film *Brian's Song*, which was based on Sayers' biography *I Am Third*. Defensive captain J.C. Caroline and Ed McCaskey poked Halas enough to green light a change in team traditions. The players were Sayers and Brian Piccolo, and the year was 1965. Halas was 70 when he finally let go of the axioms taught to children of white parents for centuries.

Sayers and his biographer suggested the film grossly exaggerated his friendship with Piccolo but he and other '60s Bears told me that dramatization was, in fact, the truth. Other truisms included a distrust for the team's doctors, stupidity at the quarterback position (specifically, Jack Concannon) and Halas' son-in-law Ed McCaskey having a voice in football operations. Nepotism is a family thing.

If players were designated separate water coolers, which was a thing in America into the '60s, none of them mentioned it. Maybe it wasn't near the top of the list of their concerns regarding "amenities." The Bears were busy pleading for hot water for a shower after practicing at Wrigley Field.

A request for something more user-friendly than one-ply toilet paper also was denied. Doug Buffone years ago, told me coach Abe Gibron laughed at him when Buffone pleaded for better toilet tissue. *You'll get nothing and like it.*

BRING IT ON HOME

If the Bears were a restaurant, you'd never eat there. The food's been bad. Unsightly aesthetics. I've suffered the emotional pangs of divorce from two steakhouses after ownership or staff changes sent them spiraling. Most people, I assume, don't give many mulligans to establishments.

We give our teams a long leash, however. Loyal to a fault. Historically, only the White Sox and Blackhawks learned they can't serve crummy "food" in Chicago. The Bulls' "experience" fills the United Center and the appeal of Wrigley Field, and the neighborhood afford the Cubs unlimited freedom to stink.

Bears fans go even further. They have defined the dynamics of enabling. This Bears market has granted Team McCaskey a license to fail. Michael McCaskey spotted it and pounced on the opportunity to kick up the heels and reap the spoils. A fan base that craves the product ensures profitability.

The logo. The roaring Bear. All the *"remember when"* conversations. Regardless of the stench, we've continued to line up for it.

In the inaugural year of the Score — Chicago's first sports talk station, then on AM-820 — McCaskey quickly learned the kid gloves with which he was treated on other stations were a thing of the past. Midday host Mike North held the owner's feet to the fire on August 28 of '92 after the Bears traded perennial Pro Bowl center Jay Hilgenberg, who was holding out for a new contract, to Cleveland for a fourth-round pick (Todd Perry, Kentucky). North peppered McCaskey with pointed questions and harsh criticism of the team's frugality and indifference about results.

"Say something else silly, Mike" McCaskey responded sheepishly after North projected a dismal '92 season. North was right. The Bears went 5-11 and fired Ditka.

Michael McCaskey lost his battle with cancer in May of '20 during the first few months of the pandemic. After keeping a low profile since his demotion 20 years earlier, McCaskey's death received little fanfare. He was 76.

The eldest of the lucky 11, McCaskey was hugely unpopular. Most owners are but McCaskey chronically rubbed players, coaches and fans the wrong way. Some of the '80s Bears weren't the kind of guys who'd mask their contempt for ownership. McMahon was among the most vocal critics.

"He (Michael McCaskey) told me flat out, as long as Soldier Field is full and ratings are good, that's what matters most," McMahon told me on the Score in the summer of '20 when we I asked for a belated eulogy. McMahon's willingness to push back publicly against McCaskey (and Ditka) resonated with Bears fans in the '80s. Jimmy Mac just didn't give a damn about consequences, and it was refreshing. McCaskey wasn't amused. He grew tired of the rebellions and collaborated with Ditka on McMahon's trade to the Chargers in '89.

A well-intended suggestion from your humble storyteller is to create a befitting role for the late Michael McCaskey's little brother, George. Give the chairman a chance to dazzle. Boiled down, George is a team historian. He possesses the most impressive collection of Bears memorabilia on the planet. Valuable sponsors who love the team would cherish a tour of the ultimate mancave for Bears fans. Put George in his natural habitat.

The weapons he always has on patrol would be lied down and the usually socially awkward McCaskey would let down his guard. The team's benefactors would discover a more relaxed chairman, a personable football heir. George McCaskey, the manchild, would beam as he flaunts his favorite figurine, Clyde *Bulldog* Turner, good ol' no. 66. Flash that Polaroid of the wide-eyed grandson, sitting on the lap of receiver Johnny Morris after the Bears won the '63 championship.

George McCaskey can't do much harm staying in his lane. He's a super fan. The Bears have a whole bunch of those.

Man, don't they know it.

CHAPTER 16
Bears Say the Darndest Things
HELMETS TO HEADPHONES

"Before we take our next caller, we'd like to remind you folks calling in to please keep your questions within the boundaries of good taste."
– Jim Carr (Andrew Duncan) in the 1977 film Slapshot.

Devin Hester's Hall of Fame induction speech in August made me grin from ear to ear. With the same confidence he possessed when waiting for Adam Vinatieri's opening kickoff in Super Bowl 41, Hester sparkled.

Full disclosure, I was nervous for Hester and his family and friends. My 31-year-old son has autism and making speech is complicated for him. Speaking never has been Hester's strong suit. People who use social media (yes, I've looked in the mirror) can be cruel. When I was ignorant to neurology, I also took easy shots at Hester from the cheap seats. Hester, now 42, is a decidedly more confident communicator than he was in his eight years with the Bears. It didn't happen accidentally. The game's most electrifying return man clearly has benefitted from his life's experiences and success as an athlete helped grow his personal skills and self-esteem. It's a beautiful thing, really.

Since I've been watching the NFL, former Bears have been prominent in the broadcast booth and other arenas that kept them in the public eye. Johnny Morris was a fixture on Bears' games on CBS in the 1970s and beyond. In 2024, nobody with Bears roots has a brighter star than Greg Olsen. The '07 first-round pick cut his teeth in the studio briefly before FOX made him an analyst and Olsen quickly crushed it, ascending to the network's top crew with play-by-man Kevin Burkhardt.

It was short-lived, however, and Tom Brady swiped the top job at FOX, which drew the ire of a football-crazed nation when the outgoing Olsen dazzled during the NFC Championship game in January. Olsen's insight to the 49ers-Lions was so keen, casual fans lined up on social media to sing his praises and rip Brady, whose FOX deal is worth $375M. Tony Romo also was abused by thumb tapping critics after a rough postseason as the No. 1 at CBS.

America finally grasped what I was saying about Romo since he jumped right into the seat next to lead salesman Jim Nantz. While his enthusiasm and play calling predictions get high marks, Romo is thin on content. He regularly forgets (or doesn't know) all the rules. He rarely does homework on the big uglies or defensive players. Kansas City defensive coordinator Steve Spagnola might be the only defensive coach in the league Romo knows. He's not good with rosters or names. In Week 18, he curiously heaped bouquets at Luke Getsy, whom he called "*Getzsky*" (like Gretzky) three times. The stats CBS popped on the screen didn't support Romo's thesis on the improvement of Justin Fields or the Chicago offense.

Olsen will continue to prosper. He's only 39 and he's working, and the former tight end's playing career soon will be a Hall of Fame debate. Olsen produced nine consistently productive seasons with Carolina after he and the Bears failed to see eye-to-eye on his role and was traded. Both sides remained unshakably devoted to their positions (see Ch. 4) and Olsen was gone after four years. There isn't a prize given for it, but the New Jersey native is the biggest media star of any former Bear.

This chapter sprays to all fields on talking Bears. Talking as players or former players. Coaches or ex-coaches. Broadcasters by vocation, side job or just picking up the phone and yapping on good old terrestrial radio. The arrival of Chicago's first full-time sports talk station is a good place to begin. I was on the ground floor.

DITKA LAUNCHES THE SCORE

Mike Ditka was a somebody. We were nobodies. Diamond Broadcasting, which also owned rocker WXRT 93.1 FM, purchased the dormant frequency AM-820 and signed on as WSCR, the *Score, Sports Radio 820* on January 2 of '92. After almost four years at the Loop as a producer, sidekick and weekend host, the Score hired me to be the lead host in afternoons. I was 30.

An inexperienced air staff wasn't the station's only handicap. The

820 frequency was a daytime-only operation. At sundown, we went dark after rolling Sinatra's *My Kind of Town*. At dawn, the station was back. Additionally, the collection of hosts was an odd mix of newspaper and television guys with little talk radio experience. The Score initially was intended to be a "niche outlet," a boutique fraternity house, if you will. It was purchased for only $800,000 in '91 and management went bare bones on everything that extracted cash from under the mattress.

Seth Mason, Diamond's big boss, then swiped Ditka's weekly show from the Bears' flagship and once-dominant WGN. Score management had operated similarly to Bears management — reluctant spenders for even the most essential tools, like computers and monthly fees for Associated Press wire services. The shorty history made the Ditka show acquisition staggering. Ditka didn't get out of bed without getting paid for it. It was huge for the station economically and for morale. The Score quickly became relevant.

Ditka undeniably helped put us on the map.

The timing for getting the coach's show was fortuitous because his Bears went 5-11 and, along the way, Ditka lost his mind. Usually, it was on our air. Uptight Ditka was appointment radio Tuesdays at 4. Our first football season was Ditka's last with the Bears

Mike often failed to handle even success well. How was he going to hold up with his '92 team's blemishes even more glaring than those in the 6-10 season of '89? It ensured the Score a maniacal Ditka. In October, the 11th-year head coach grew so fatigued explaining bad losses, he punted his required weekly news conferences at Halas Hall. In an era when newspapers, terrestrial radio and television news were essential, the Score was the only source for fresh Ditka. Bears media were forced to listen to AM-820 if they wanted to have the latest piping hot Ditka quotes. And quotes he gave.

Nothing was more eye-popping — and em*bear*assing — than Ditka threatening to beat up an unhappy Bears fan who called and accused him of "acting like a baby." It was the infamous Neal from Northlake who summoned *Bully Ditka*. "Well, what you are Neal, I can't say on the radio, but I'll tell you this: I'm 52 years old. I work at 250 N. Washington (*Worshington*).

Anytime you wanna meet me there, pal, you tell me what time and when and I'll whip your ass."

In the audience, beefy, hairy men wearing gold chains barked and jeered. I couldn't wait to get with my audio producer, John *Shakey* Siuntres to discuss accompanying bells and whistles for the launch of an *I'll Whip Your Ass* feature. *Whip it* real *good*, and thanks to techno-poppers Devo for the lively music bed underneath the content.

Ditka's nightmares became a treasure trove for the ants in the afterbirth who make sports radio. A caller told Ditka he was a joke, to which steel country Mike replied, "I may be a joke but I'm a rich joke."

Pyle, who was Ditka's accomplice at WGN, had been the driver of the Ditka show and resident apologist for years. He continued to drive the show and our "starting five" alternated as co-pilots. Ditka was okay with morning man Tom Shaer and he liked the midday team of Dan Jiggetts and Mike North. The Score's afternoon tandem — Terry Boers and I — brought out *Dark Ditka*. The coach pushed back against Boers after a September loss and the bit *Who You Crappin'* was born.

Boers: One of the things that was mentioned after the game, Mike, was that you don't have the fire anymore, that you're... are you resigned to that fate? Are you...

Ditka: (interrupting): Well, you're the same guy who said about me when I did have the fire, that it was the wrong thing to do, so who you crappin'.

Boers: Well, I'm just askin'. Do you...

Ditka: (interrupts again) Don't crap me now, no, no, no.

Who You Crappin' gave callers a shot to cut loose on any athlete or media type they thought was serving up bullshit. It was a station feature for 20 years.

Ditka was leaving the reservation on a weekly basis, and it was ours *exclusively*. Every TV station in town had crews camped on the restaurant terrace and in parking lots. Ditka never stopped or acknowledged them when he walked into the NW side establishment. Every Tuesday night for two months, the 6 and 10 o'clock newscasts led with *Mt. St. Ditka's* most recent eruption. The Score's original logo — an orange baseball with Coca-

Cola style font over a black backdrop — was splashed all over Chicagoland.

Selfishly, for a few dozen people trying to launch a radio station, it was perfect. For Chicago, the fall of Ditka was palpable. The roster had rotted and the '85 Bears were going to remain a one-and-done. One could *feel* the end of Ditka's time.

Ditka's drinking buddy in the '60s was defensive end Ed O'Bradovich, who was Ditka's choice to present him for HOF induction in '88. The duo had 30 years of history of being teammates and running mates. As a guest with *Jiggetts & North*, O'B was critical of Ditka: "Do I think he's forgotten where he's come from? Yes. Yes, I do." Hot stuff was coming up on the next Ditka show if that week's co-pilot dared to share it with Mike. It was my turn.

Me: I'm sure you heard or heard about Ed O'Bradovich's comments. Last week with Dan and Mike, he suggested you've lost perspective, you've forgotten where you came from. You've known O'B forever. What's your response to that?

Ditka: (long pause) I don't know O.B.

Me: (waits, waits) The guy who presented you at your enshrinement in Canton.

Ditka: (longer pause this time) Biggest mistake I ever made.

Sound byte gold. I wanted more and was content to lay out until he started back but Pyle sensed the tension (you can't slip one past an Ivy Leaguer) and mumbled "Dan... we can't have dead air, now, can we?" Actually, I do hate dead air. *This* wasn't. It was a natural pause in a conversation turning emotional, as people do when they're weighing their words. Ditka was a volatile man and arguably the biggest sports figure in Chicago. He was about to come off the top ropes and barbecue his best friend. Yeah. I'll live with a few seconds of quiet. I debated with Pyle. Ditka grew tired of it and removed his headphones.

Ditka took off the cans whenever he wanted. As he did 15 years later on ESPN 1000. Ditka did whatever the fuck he wanted almost all his adult life. *Good, Dolphin.*

More of the lava spilled on me the next time I hopped in with the Mikes. I was talking about the Bears not getting pressure from their front four when

Ditka interrupted bizarrely with a non-sequitur. "Vince Tobin doesn't know you. And if he did know you, he wouldn't like you. And if Greg Landry knew you, he wouldn't like you either." Sideswiped, out of nowhere. I hadn't even mentioned Tobin, who was the defensive coordinator. (Actually, we did know each other. I never got the impression he disliked me, but I've been wrong before).

I hadn't met Landry, but I learned how the Bears offensive coordinator felt about Ditka before the Bears went to Houston for a Dec. 7 *Monday Night Football* date with the Oilers. A Ditka habit was berating Landry on the sideline while the Bears OC just stood with a vacant expression. Until he couldn't take it anymore. A tipster told me Landry wasn't going to call plays on the sideline for the *MNF* game against Houston. The OC's intention was to operate upstairs in the coach's box to avoid the nationally-televised scoldings under Ditka spit spray. North and I did Saturdays between 10 and 2 in the Score's first year and I broke the story. It first required a reaction, so I called Ditka in his office at 8 a.m. before the Bears met and boarded their charter.

Ditka answered. "Well, if that's his plan, I haven't heard about it yet. I guess we'll just have to wait and see Monday night." He didn't jump my ass as I was expecting. Ditka was more matter of fact about it. Maybe he already was *resigned to his fate*. Sure enough, Landry called plays from the box in the Astrodome. The Bears lost to the Oilers 24-7, their sixth straight loss.

As the Bears played out the string during Ditka's final year of a wild ride of a career, the Score established itself as a brand. All of us were grateful to Mason for loosening up the purse strings and popping for Ditka. "He was a Godsend," North reflected. Near Christmas in '92, I asked Ditka to sign the famous picture of him flipping off the camera during pregame warmups. "And can you write '*Who You Crappin*' before your signature?"

I was fascinated by the uncertainty of his reaction. The coach knew *WYC* had become a weekly segment. He likely was aware of the goofy "radio play" we did — *Thanksgiving at Ditka's* — mocking the estrangement with O'Bradovich. Sybil didn't flinch about the request and signed it as I asked.

Over the years, our interactions were more amicable and cordial. Ditka was a weekly contributor on the *Waddle & Silvy* show on ESPN 1000 during my eight years there and I regularly attended shows at Ditka's restaurant in the Tremont Hotel. A double win, supporting station mates and entertaining key sponsors and contributors to the *Mac, Jurko & Harry* show in the cozy nest of Coach Red Face.

ERIK KRAMER'S SMILE

I reconnected with Kramer early in the '23 season to get his read on the current Bears and Lions, as well as the single-season records he set in '95. Those numbers remain franchise highs. It was the first time we talked in 24 years. It was connective and we got deep in a 55-minute Zoom. Before the blow-by-blow on a confrontational on-air exchange in '97, a note he never shared before regarding his Bears experience. Kramer first realized he suffered from clinical depression during his best professional season. During the best season by any quarterback in team history.

"There were days when I didn't think I could go to work," he reflected. "Going to work means being around people and that means having to talk to people."

He carried himself with the confidence of an All American. He dripped "California cool" and Erik was a good-looking guy. It would have been easy to assume Kramer had enjoyed a charmed life. Those who did were dead wrong. It took Wannstedt and Turner to say, *"Here are the keys to the Cadillac."* Kramer was freaking 30.

As the '97 season quickly unraveled, the Bears had Detroit at Soldier Field in Week 3. They were 0-2 with losses to the Packers and Vikings so they couldn't lose this game. Mirer started and did the things that made him among the all-time NFL busts. He was awful. Kramer wasn't much better, but it wouldn't have mattered because of the hole they dug and their inability to put Barry Sanders. Sanders went for 161 yards and the Lions scored 32 unanswered points in a 32-7 runaway.

Late in the game, FOX had a shot of the sideline where quarterbacks were conversing. Mirer, after his 39.8 rating performance, looked as he always did — like a deer in headlights. Kramer, conversely, had a huge smile on his face. Amidst disaster, find humor perhaps? It didn't agree with some of us, and I chose to represent the meatheads. We got Kramer on to discuss it.

E.K. had been on our show and with *Jiggetts & North* and was one of the more thoughtful interviews on the team. It wasn't my intention to ambush him with anger over it but when it started to go sideways, I was willing to engage and suspend a genteel relationship for a few minutes of deliciously uncomfortable radio. I was a 36-year-old host still desperately seeking the attention and admiration of dudes.

Kramer had just taken a beating for downplaying the importance of the Green Bay game before Week 1. "To me, it's just another game" was the Kramer comment that offended many. I wasn't put off by his comment, but I wished he used the qualifier "divisional" before "game." It still would have upset some because there's supposed to be some visceral need to hate Green Bay every chance you get. I bitched about Kramer's smile at least once an hour for three days. It was an immature reaction on my part and even more juvenile was my edgy response to Kramer.

We talked about the game to warm him and then I pivoted to *the smile*. This is my paraphrased recollection of how it went:

Me: What was the reason for that big grin Sunday in the fourth quarter?

E.K.: What are you talkin' about?

Me: In the fourth quarter. Game out of hand. You were talking to Mirer and had a huge grin on your face. I'm just wondering what made you laugh in those circumstances.

E.K.: I have no idea what you're talking about.

That agitated me. Either he doesn't want to talk about what was said or he's being passive-aggressive with me. My suspicion was he knew we'd been knocking him. From a teammate or public relations staffer. A reporter or his mailman. No way the great Score afternoon show didn't penetrate public consciousness. I told him that.

E.K. Who's this?

Me: I'm talking to you.

E.K. Hey, easy pal.

Me: How about answering the question?

E.K. How about (interrupted)

Me: How about 'to me, you're just another quarterback.'

Nothing I had done in media ever received the volume of reaction. There must have been 250 voicemails and the Barrett's Home Theater sponsored fax machine ran out of every other hour for two days. I didn't keep score but it likely was close to split down the middle. Half of the respondents said they had no desire to hear my voice again and the other half thought I should be the mayor of Chicago.

When I told Kramer that last fall, he said "Well, you did your job then, right? The oddsmaker's goal is to get people split right down the middle."

Erik's life after football took a catastrophic turn. His marriage disintegrated. His son, Griffen, was an accomplished prep athlete whose fondness for heroin led to a fatal overdose in '11. Kramer attempted suicide in '15 but the bullet that ripped through his tongue, crushed his palate and met his brain didn't kill him. After many months of treatment and rehabilitation, Kramer found his way again. His autobiography *The Ultimate Comeback* brings his humanity to its fullest. He again is living with purpose and is an exceptionally qualified advocate for mental health awareness.

It's safe to say there are few people I've met in Chicago sports who are easier to root for than Erik Kramer. Even more so after learning about his plight and openly discussing depression, addiction and suicide. It's been uplifting reconnecting with him several times in the past year, once for just a lengthy life conversation.

EDDIE JACKSON'S BREAD PUDDING

On a lighter note, one of the rarest treats in sports radio is when the legend of Yogi Berra is resurrected. The malaprop. Merging cliches — by accident or by ignorance — always tickles me. When one can laugh at himself, it's even better.

In '19, Bears safety Eddie Jackson was a weekly regular on my Score afternoon show with Danny Parkins. I have no memory of what Jackson was talking about, only what happened when he tried to say, "the proof is in the pudding."

"The bread is in the pudding," Jackson said. He recognized his own mistake, huffed, then trailed off with a whisper "or whatever it is they say."

Since he left it open-ended, I pounced.

"Actually, it's the *proof* that's in the pudding, Eddie."

"That's it. That's what I meant to say."

I joked about having a fondness for bread pudding, even though it's not often a menu item here in this part of the world. And it was worth noting the cliche originally could have included bread as a modifier for pudding.

"The proof is in the bread pudding actually sounds better," I said. Jackson was giggling hard. What else could he do?

- The standard for Bear malaprops belongs to quarterback Moses Moreno, who got his first NFL start late in his rookie season of '98. Moreno was a seventh-round pick out of Colorado State and Wannstedt decided to give him a shot in Week 13 in Tampa. Man cannot live on Steve Stenstrom alone. The new quarterback guested on my show and exuded a quiet confidence and an authentic expression of nothing-to-lose mentality.

  "Now it's my turn to go claim my stake," Moreno said. My partner and I quietly snorted, covered our mouths and let it go.

  For a short while, the kid's claim was earning a big juicy steak. Moreno's 21-yard scoring strike to Curtis Conway gave the Bears a second-quarter lead. It would be the only TD pass in his career. Trent Dilfer threw three TD passes and Sam Wyche's Bucs cruised. Wannstedt went back to Stenstrom the next week. Moreno made two more starts for the Chargers before his career concluded. San Diego lost them both. No stakes claimed there, either. No steak for you.

- Self-reflection revealed something I said a couple years ago worth noting: "He plays to the *shadow* of the whistle." I was looking for the whistle's echo, but only found the slight shadow it cast.

- In '98, the Bears drafted tight end Alonzo Mayes out of Oklahoma State in the fourth round. Mayes was AWOL on the first day of camp after missing three flights. Once he got to camp in Platteville, I asked him how in the world that could happen. His answer was perfect.

  "Sometimes, it's notch-yo day."

- For the life of me, I can't recall which '90s Bear liked our show's idea of running a gadget play for him with more frequency. He confirmed it in an interview with us.

  "You guys are right. We should call that more often. When I go back to work tomorrow, I'm gonna have to put a bug in the coaches' eyes about that." After plowing through every roster in the decade *twice* I still can't recall which part-time contributor wanted to be an eye bugger. Somebody like Eddie Kennison, but it wasn't Eddie Kennison.

- The '90s, for my money, marked the best years of sports talk in Chicago. There were many Bears players and coaches who were regular contributors. Chicago Vocational's Chris Zorich was a fan favorite and quickly became a friend of the Score. Say it with me, long-time Scoreheads: *"When are dey gonna move Zorich to linebaaacker?"* Chris, who was 100% a Ditka draft pick, was a terrific guy with a big smile. At a grass roots level radio promotion, Zorich agreed to race North in a 40-yard sprint in the street on the northwest side by the original Score's home. A throng of listeners showed up to watch Zorro win the challenge. Jiggetts did the play-by-play (step-by-step?) on the air.

  It was an exciting time in all our careers. We made good radio, enjoyed each other (usually) and many Bears — before stations paid regular active players to be consistent contributors — helped make it happen. The day linebacker Joe Cain signed a free agent deal in '93, he was on our afternoon show and quickly was a regular. Joe was funnier than any Bear and occasionally belted out a wild cackle that got everybody laughing. Cain was a better player than people thought, too. He was a Bear for only four years but bashed his way into the top 10 all-time tacklers in Bearsville. Joe loved music — all genres — and still embraces the riff we did as an intro theme. Eric Clapton's *Cocaine* was turned into *Joecaine*.

Cain starred at Oregon after growing up in South Central L.A. and returned to the Pac Northwest shortly after his career. His passion is cooking and he's skilled. The topic of Amish chicken was broached in an interview he did with us on the Score in May of '20. With his deep voice and fast reflexes, Cain meandered. "You know, I was thinking about the Amish the other day. And it occurred to me, do you think they know we're in a pandemic?"

- Ron Rivera, now a regular on NFL Network's *Game Day Preview* and *Good Morning Football*, was toying with a career in broadcasting before he took his first coaching apprenticeship on Dave Wannstedt's staff in '97. Rivera did whatever the Score asked him to do. In '94, Chico co-hosted with Boers and me from his National Hispanic Scholarship Fund golf outing at Tamarack and Rivera remains a champion of several charitable endeavors. He's as loyal to Chicago as any city at which he stopped and Rivera remains loyal *to me*, personally and professionally. He never asks for anything in return. Ron and his wife, Coach Steph, built a home in Las Vegas recently.

- Jay Cutler was among the 21st century Bears who cashed checks for weekly appearances on local radio while they were playing. Cutler was a Tuesday regular on *Waddle & Silvy* on ESPN 1000 and refused to wear headphones. The excuse: beautiful hair. Cutty spotted television cameras more easily than he did double coverage. He wanted to look his best when cameras rolled on his indifference. *You dick* (Spicoli).

- In 2024, Tom Thayer and Olin Kreutz — a pair of 57s — are excellent sources for meaty Bears conversation on the radio. Thayer has been an ally since the '80s and makes regular appearances on ESPN 1000, now in its second year as the Bears flagship. Joliet's pride and joy has been a fixture on Bears radio since the late-'90s and cut his broadcast teeth with Steve Dahl, the most talented and compelling radio talent in

Chicago history. No former professional athlete has given more positive reinforcement on my work than Thayer. My favorite Thayerism: "He needs to be more decisive in his decision making." Away from football and broadcasting, Thayer is among the most selfless guys I know. True blue.

Kreutz remains a mainstay on the Score's pregame Bears programming and also appears on the *Spiegel & Holmes* show. I was heartened to see the Score give him a second shot after his unfortunate loss of composure at *CHGO* in '22, when he roughed up co-worker Adam Hoge a smidge. I didn't condone Big O's behavior, but I understood it. Better than my brethren in the yap community, for sure. Since he was a teenager, Kreutz was tasked with demands requisite of a leader in a football locker room. The rules there are different. Radically different. It is not essential you understand. Kreutz was "a victim" of cognitive conditioning. Expecting a football player to magically *turn if off* once they take off the gear is a tougher ask than people realize. Kreutz, in the moment, failed to un-do a lifetime of learned behaviors that not only were accepted, but they were also rewarded. Olin is a solid dude. Mahalo, my Oahuan pally.

MILLER TIME

For any readers who spend hours commuting and favor non-stop NFL content, I confidently recommend Jim Miller's show on Sirius/XM. *Movin' The Chains* is on the afternoons on the NFL's channel 88. The former Bears quarterback's knowledge of personnel around the league is unrivaled. Miller watches freakin' practice tapes. Nobody outworks him and sidekick Pat Kerwin has grown on me. A little.

In '99, when Miller initially was acquired midstream to backstop first-rounder Cade McNown and Shane Matthews, he guested on my show — then with Jiggetts — for the first of what would become 101 visits. For a game manager, Miller put some skins on the wall in his three years. I was at the Week 11 Bears-Chargers game in San Diego as a fan. Miller passed for 357 yards in a 23-20 overtime win over the Jim Harbaugh-led Chargers.

Miller's big day came the week after he threw for 422 yards and three TDs in a loss to the Vikings. Almost 800 passing yards in two games from a Bears quarterback? Wow. And I was at Jack Murphy Stadium to bear witness.

Miller reflected on the McNown experience when talked in April. In 2000, Dick Jauron's second season, the 4-10 Bears were going to San Francisco, which was 6-8. The 12th-overall pick in '99 wasn't dialed in during practices before departing for the Bay. When they arrived, McNown was more interested in talking to actor Scott Caan. James Caan's son, for my money, was at his best in *Varsity Blues* as *Charlie Tweeder*, the beer-guzzling, panties-chasing wide receiver for the West Canaan Coyotes.

"When they drafted Cade, he was very immature," Miller said. "He had a lot of growing up to do. For me, I was fine with it because I knew I'd beat him out. Dick Jauron wanted me to be his roommate before games. And we'd be downtown at the Hilton, and he'd be on the phone with all his actor friends. He says to me 'do you want to talk to Farrah Fawcett?' I said 'no, Cade, I think we should be going over all your checkdowns. We kind of need to go over these plays because I don't think you're prepared to play tomorrow.' That when on for about six weeks and I finally called Dick Jauron and said 'coach, I'm not doing this anymore. This kid's not serious.' It was embarrassing.

"In the second year ('00), I was starting. I tore my left Achilles up in Buffalo. Two weeks later, we had a game in San Francisco. Coach Jauron asked me to go and the night before the game, John Shoop was our OC, and he wanted to go over the top 15 plays. About half of the plays have check-with-mes where you're going to run one play or the other. Coach Shoop says 'alright, Cade, you're gonna run so-and-so... they line up in a 4-3 under, what's your check?' And Cade gets it wrong. We go through this entire script, and he got everyone of his checks wrong. And Shane Matthews whispers in my ear 'dude, we're gonna get our fuckin' ass kicked tomorrow.' I said 'yeah, you're God damn right we are.' "

McNown's performance against the 49ers might have been the worst day of Bears offense since the '70s. They went 3-of-13 on third down and squeezed out eight first downs. McNown was 9-of-29 for 73 yards with no touchdowns and a pick. He laid a 26.1 rating, and the Bears lost 17-0. They had 104 yards of total offense. Miller continued.

"That's the game when T.O. set the record (20 receptions for 283 yards). Our offense? We never crossed the 50. That's how bad we were. I had the headsets on during the game and John Shoop is begging coach Jauron to take Cade out. 'We need to pull him and put in Shane.' And Dick says, and I only heard him swear one time, says 'No. They (management) wanted him, they're gonna get every fuckin' awful bit of him.' They kept him in the entire game to prove he wasn't the guy. And we got the shit kicked out of us."

Miller's work on preseason Bears telecasts is a must-have for fans who want to learn the back end of the roster. He works hard at his craft. His career was highlighted by the 13-3 divisional championship team he orchestrated in '01. Philadelphia smoked the Bears in the playoffs, but it was an unexpectedly satisfying year in Chicago. Jauron won coach of the year, then got to stare at a 16-game road schedule in '02 when the Bears played in Champaign.

But at least McNown was gone. Nobody ever offered him a radio or television gig.

CHAPTER 17
Dearly Departed
BEARS WE'VE LOST

> *"Whatever it takes to keep them in the game to keep the whole thing going... Tape. Needles. Vicodin. Toradol. Lidocaine. Percocet. Lexapro. Zoloft. Have I left anything out? It's tires and oil." – Pittsburgh Steelers physician Julian Bales (Alec Baldwin) in the 2015 film Concussion.*

As I neared a September 30 deadline for final edits, Steve McMichael remained late in the fourth quarter in his nearly four-year struggle with amyotrophic lateral sclerosis — ALS. In the past couple years, few days have passed when my thoughts didn't drift to McMichael's plight. I suspect your experience has been similar.

With heavy hearts over Mongo's terminal illness, Bears fans found some comfort in the images of Misty McMichael, accompanied by Steve's teammates, presenting the Canton bust and gold jacket No. 376 to her emaciated, helpless husband. It was August 3, 2024. The day before, former Bears tackle Keith Van Horne and I spent three hours with Steve and his younger sister, Kathy, at Mongo's home in Homer Glen.

In a year replete with sad days, that first Friday in August probably stung the most. Keith and I discussed our mission on the backyard patio when Steve was asleep. Our visit was to say both congratulations and goodbye.

"He's trying to talk to you," Kathy said as she and I joked about her brother's heroics as a kicker at Texas. I looked to my left, where McMichael lied in his bed, kept alive by a respirator and attached to several devices that monitor his vitals. Steve was able to turn his head just a little and could move his mouth slightly. I knew what ALS does and had given myself a pep talk on the commute. An ALS patient (*victim* is more appropriate) cannot move or speak. Mongo lost use of his arms shortly before his ability to speak left him. That was many months prior to Hall of Fame weekend.

I attempted to understand what part of the conversation might have intrigued McMichael, what he might be wishing he could share. At the minimum, we knew the content interested him enough to attempt speech. So, I circled back to Texas football, the one game I saw in Austin in '02 and Kathy's story about her big brother once practicing kicking *on her*.

McMichael lit up around those he enjoyed. Van Horne and I were among those. We knew we had to bury all that sorrow deep inside, look our friend in the eye and offer laughter and small talk. Mongo sleeps all the time, but never for long. His full-time medical aides try to keep him comfortable but not overly sedated. Teammates have kept Misty amply stocked with dissolvable THC for Steve to "change altitude," which he enjoyed. Since '01, McMichael and I regularly swapped quotes from *North Dallas Forty*, so I went with that. Kathy said she'd add the '79 satire to his playlist for the 85" television that's on 24/7 and provides him some escapism.

It was difficult to "stay in" a one-way conversation for long. It's impossible to not be distracted and deeply disturbed by an ALS victim's helplessness and appearance. McMichael's muscular atrophy already had been advanced. He essentially was a skeleton wrapped by skin. There wasn't much left of this once-powerfully built athlete.

Mongo has been comforted by a legion of former teammates and friends who consistently have shown up in Homer Glen to offer support for Steve, Misty and daughter, Macy, who's 17. McMichael's running mate since '81, Dan Hampton, has been among them. I talked to Hampton at length on February 8, the day the world learned Mongo was getting into the Hall.

"Every time I go, I walk out and say, 'I can't come back.' I just can't see him like that," Hamp admitted. "But after a little bit of time, I realize I *have* to go. I *need* to be there. I *will* be there." Dan's contention is McMichael was beloved by everyone who ever played with him. In my conversations with at least a dozen of those former teammates, that assertion was validated.

Tom Thayer, who demonstrates selflessness most days of his life, assisting family and friends, was at the front of the line encouraging Steve to deploy the technology available to assist otherwise helpless ALS communicate. It's called "augmentative and alternative communication devices" (AACs), and it spares an ALS victim the emotional torment of not being able to communicate. "Eye gaze devices" allow users to "write" words and sentences. The eye muscles are among the last to fail. McMichael initially was reluctant to deploy the technology but eventually warmed up to it. Mongo was eager to demonstrate his newly-developed skills upon Thayer's next visit.

It's inspiring and heartwarming, really. More than 40 years after football brought them together, they still push each other, even if it means a little tough love now and again. For those who roll their eyes at the suggestion "football is family," this is my middle finger for the snark.

Steve McMichael was a football player I admired enormously. He's been a hang-out buddy. His was a life of endless adventures, misadventures, victories, setbacks, glory and pain. How he *lived* needed to be the *Mongo's share* of this diary, which is why I parked ALS until *Dearly Departed.*

The day before Mongo's enshrinement, I looked him in the eye and told him how much he earned the award, that it wasn't a sympathy recognition. I told Steve I didn't think there was any other star — from any team in town I covered — who was more universally respected than he was. He also was loved and was appreciated by his co-workers at ESPN 1000. I acknowledged him for being a *Dangerous Dan* supporter once upon a time and, eventually, a friend. I told Mongo I loved him and thanked him for loving me back.

CHRONIC TRAUMATIC ENCEPHALOPATHY (CTE)

It took several years before I finally watched *Concussion.* Call it willful ignorance, which truly is bliss. Not understanding the truth precluded me the internal conflict that came with the knowledge playing football isn't a good idea. I cheerfully bloviated about the game's *divinity* my entire adult life.

What's revealed in the film (and explained skillfully for the layman) is the absence of a natural defense system for blows to the head. The human brain possesses no shock absorber. Unlike a woodpecker, whose tongue wraps around the brain to form a safety belt of sorts for repetitive poundings, no anatomical defense mechanism exists to keep the human brain from banging against the skull. Repetitive "sub-concussive blows to the head" exacerbate trauma. When trauma (bleeding) occurs in the brain, killer proteins are released. Ultimately, they entangle the brain and cause radical shifts in mood, depression and mental instability. In *Concussion*, the dynamic is likened to pouring wet cement down the drains in a kitchen sink. Eventually, it hardens and "chokes out" its functionality.

Many CTE sufferers hear voices. Some are prone to violent outbursts. Suicide becomes the only "sensible" solution. CTE is real, not imagined. Former NFL players die from it. Some of them were household names, like Junior Seau.

Ex-Bears who've died from their profession's risks include Dave Duerson, a smart and tenacious safety between '83 and '89. It's been almost 15 years since Duerson took his own life and several other former Bears have done similarly. They also were determined to have CTE.

While these are not all recent obituaries, it's important to me to include each. The gravity of CTE and football's role in the disease hasn't penetrated public awareness deeply enough yet. I mourn the passing of all young men and women who never grow old, but it's particularly disturbing when symptoms of CTE are perceived to be character flaws or weakness. These guys are sick. Knowing this, the Aaron Hernandez jokes at the Tom Brady roast this past summer didn't agree with me. It was a terrific event, tossing political correctness out the window and talking dirty the way a roast should, but I have zero appetite for humor at the expense of a CTE sufferer. Hernandez's brain was studied and confirmed to be an absolute mess.

The obits below include CTE victims, as well as historically significant Bears I covered or with whom I spent time. Rest In Peace, dearly departed former Chicago Bears.

Avellini, Bob (b. Aug. 28, 1953. d. May 4. 2024)

The Bears quarterback between '75 and '81 lost his battle with pancreatic cancer in the spring. He was 70.

A sixth-rounder out of Maryland, Avellini was a fun-loving, beer-drinking, trash-talking New York sports fan. He occasionally threw golf clubs in anger — once through a Lincoln Park bar window after getting tossed for being overserved. Bob was a tough dude. He just wasn't very good at playing quarterback at the professional level.

Avellini threw 33 touchdown passes in his career and was intercepted 69 times. He posted a career quarterback rating of 54.8. Often a punchline, Avellini typically possessed a good sense of humor about his shortcomings. He was a regular at celebrity roasts and charity golf outings. Bob enjoyed debate and wasn't afraid to express himself. At an outing a dozen or so years ago, I chided Avellini for his role in the 37-7 playoff loss in Dallas in '77. "You were more accurate with that 9-iron you fired through the bar's window" was the spirit of the playful insult. Avellini answered with a friendly flip off.

We had cigars and beers on the patio after the round. Bob was a pleasure to get to know a little bit and I wish our circles had intersected more frequently in the new millennium. I should have put him on the air more. Avellini was user-friendly and entertaining.

Benson, Cedric (b. Dec. 28, 1982. d. Aug.17. 2019)

Benson and a female passenger died at the scene when his motorcycle crashed with a minivan in Austin, Tex. He was 36.

The Heisman trophy winner, picked fourth-overall in '05, went 5-11 and 225 with tremendous burst and cut-back quickness. Benson never got out of second gear in Chicago and was shown the door in '08 after two alcohol-related arrests in a month. His rap sheep grew considerably as his NFL career devolved. He muscled out a few respectable years with the Bengals before one final season with the Packers.

Weed. Criminal trespassing. Boating under the influence. Punching a bartender. Cedric Benson lived recklessly.

I admired Benson's college career at Texas. He was a four-year starter and finished with 5,500+ career rushing yards, second only to Ricky Williams in Austin. He was my kind of back. Low to the ground. Powerful, but sleek. Elusive, but tough. At training camp in Bourbonnais, Benson pulled up a chair in the air-conditioned RV to do a segment on my ESPN 1000 *Mac, Jurko & Harry* show. We were just beginning a long commercial break when Benson entered the trailer, so I attempted small talk and apologized for the lengthy wait before we got started.

"All good," Benson said softly. "I got nobody else to go talk to." He was serious. Teammates paid him little or no mind. The beatings Benson endured following his 36-day holdout (defenders tackling him at full speed during *thud* time when tacklers don't take ball carriers to the ground) were only rookie hazings but proved detrimental. An already bashful guy pulled away even more. Ced never closed the distance from teammates and was a football tragedy.

Buffone, Doug (b. June 27, 1944. d. April 20, 2015)

For several years, Buffone suffered from health issues, including cardiac problems, high blood pressure and inconsistent blood sugar levels. He neither drank nor smoked for decades, but Doug ate like a college freshman and didn't exercise. He was 70.

The Bears drafted Buffone 60th overall in '66. He became a fixture for 14 seasons and his 20 career interceptions are the most by any linebacker in team history. Doug was a heady player and an effective tackler. In his final season in '79, the Bears came up short in the postseason and lost a heartbreaker in Philadelphia. Buffone concluded his career without tasting a playoff victory. Two years earlier, Dallas punched out Jack Pardee's team in the first round. Buffone concluded his career without tasting a playoff victory.

Shortly after his playing career, the happy-go-lucky Western Pennsylvanian slipped on headphones and embarked on a 30-year run as a Chicago radio personality. *Uncle Fuzzy* gained enormous popularity hosting postgame shows with former teammate Ed O'Bradovich on the Score, 670-AM. The tandem — loud and loutish as they were — became a must-listen for Bears fans, especially after lousy performances. One never knew which former Bear would blow out his larynx or pop a vein first. I was Doug's pregame co-pilot in the station's first several years.

It was early on New Year's Day, 1995 and Buffone sat alone in the kitchen at the Score's humble first facility on the Northwest side. The Bears were at Minnesota for a Wild Card round date with the Vikings at the Metrodome. Dennis Green's Vikings were six-point favorites over Dave Wannstedt's Bears, who milked nine wins out of a thin roster. The affable Buffone looked up from the newspaper to greet me. Always the optimist, he was on his second cup of Kool-Aid.

"Ya know, I think I've built a pretty good case for these guys today, little buddy," he beamed. Of course he did. Doug always schemed a way for the Bears to win games in which they were overmatched.

Comfort over fashion always has been the sports yapper's maxim and Buffone took it to unprecedented levels. He was wearing tan corduroy pants with a hole in the knee. Under what appeared to be a flannel he owned since college; he wore a red thermal long sleeve with a mustard stain below his left breast. Doug's old work boots were untied, and the laces loosened to the point he might trip on them. One sock was blue, the other black. From his pores loomed a waft of salami. Buffone often smelled of deli meats. He was unshaven and wore a baseball cap over his long, still-dark hair. In the teens, Doug's thinning hair was completely white.

We fired up the show at 9:00 and he espoused his recipe for a Chicago victory. On this day, he was prescient. The Bears upset Minnesota 35-18. The victory remains their last road win in the postseason.

More than any former professional athlete I got to know well, Doug Buffone was grounded. He was every man's man. Doug grew up humbly in coal mine and steel country and didn't have a pretentious bone in his body. Buff looked and acted like your favorite uncle — the one who laid carpet for a living. His greatest gift was making people feel good. Never once did Buffone look over a stranger's shoulder for somebody "more important" to acknowledge. He belonged to Chicago and spread good cheer at station events that canvassed Chicagoland. I spent many hours with Buffone, professionally and socially, and his death in '15 rocked me. I loved him. Dana and Doug's sister insisted he felt similarly about me when I wept with them at Doug's wake.

Perhaps Buffone's most endearing quality was his self-deprecating humor. Doug shared a story of embarrassing his parents when he spelled *apple* "A P L E" in a grade school spelling bee. He once put kerosene in the gas tank of his lawnmower and almost blew up the garage. Doug knew exactly who he was *without* being cursed by it. He laughed at himself. And when he recognized he possessed the ability to make others laugh, he began to carve out a successful second career as a personality.

I think my favorite Uncle Fuzzy anecdote is from a Christmas shopping adventure in '94. We did the standard 9 a.m. to noon Sunday pregame shift but the Bears didn't kick until 3:00. The station aired an NFL game via Westwood One at noon, which gave us a window to shop for toys for boys before the Bears game. Doug's son, Ryan (with second wife, Dana), was close in age to my first son, Van, so we hit Brickyard Mall, not far from the Score's studio.

Buffone's eyes met a mid-level race car and track set. The flashing bright lights and sirens intoxicated the manchild. He had to have it for Ry-Ry. Buffone enlisted a saleswoman with the wide-eyed excitement of a five-year-old.

"I want this one," he bubbled. "Terrific. They're right here," the woman said, pointing to the shelves below the table on which several tracks had been assembled for demonstration. "No, I mean *this* one. I want *this* track, so I don't have to put it together."

The sales associate recoiled, then glared at Doug like a disappointed teacher might have when he was a challenged grade schooler in Rural Valley, Penn. "That one's not for sale. That's the floor model we use as a demo," she said. Buffone returned volley. "I can pay a little bit more since it's already assembled," he volunteered.

"Mister, you look like a capable daddy. Don't be so lazy." To her assessment, No. 55 had the perfect comeback. "I'm not lazy — I'm stupid. Lazy I can control, but there's nothing I can do about being an idiot."

Everybody who ever worked at the Score or knew Buffone from other associations lost something that April day when we learned Doug had passed. I think of him often and reflect on our friendship with gratitude and fondness. In the teens, while sharing sadness over his morning show partner Norm Van Lier's passing, Buffone and I had several therapeutic phone visits. The former Bulls star of the '70s died in February of '09. Like me, Doug was decidedly more emotionally attached to the first iteration of the Score in the '90s'.

Butkus, Dick (b. December 9, 1942. d. Oct. 5, 2023)

Several medical conditions, including A-Fib, caused the stroke that took Dick Butkus' life as he slept in his Malibu home. He was 80.

The Bears never stopped inviting Butkus back to Chicago for games and alumni events. And he obliged. Taking bows never bothered the former *Most Feared Man in The Game* (*Sports Illustrated* cover in '70). Taking checks didn't, either. Butkus did television shows. He pitched products. He made movies. He was the Bears radio analyst in the mid-'80s. I think WGN paid him by the grunt.

Butkus made a fortune and his was a life filled with riches and doting admirers, men and women. Not bad for the youngest of eight children, son of Lithuanian immigrant John Butkus. Papa Butkus was an electrician in the Pullman district and spoke little English. Dick Butkus had to grow up tough, but I can offer no explanation why he felt the need to be such a prickly, unapproachable grouch after decades of plucking grapes from the vine.

Of all Chicago's sports obits in '23, nobody received more RIP good vibes than Butkus. The U of I's Butkus, however, was a cold fish by most accounts — including some of his friends. Butkus mumbled. He was aloof and didn't maintain eye contact. He was a grumpy old man long before he was old. *"That's just Dick being Dick"* didn't fly with me. That's just anybody *being* a dick. On rare occasions, Butkus hit comedic home runs with the same authority he knocked down ball carriers for most of nine NFL seasons. Typically, however, he was a stick in the mud who didn't muster up many original thoughts. Worse, he couldn't be cordial to people — young kids and little old ladies alike.

Duerson, Dave (b. Nov. 28, 1960. d. Feb. 17, 2011)

A self-inflicted shotgun wound to the chest ended Duerson's life. Before he pulled the trigger, he texted his family to request his brain be tested for chronic traumatic encephalopathy at the University of Boston medical center. Tests confirmed Duerson had CTE. He was 50.

After initially pushing back against the medical community's concern over CTE, Duerson admitted he was suffering CTE symptoms, like mood swings and rage. After police were called for a domestic dispute in a South Bend hotel room, Dave's marriage to Alicia dissolved and he was forced to resign from Notre Dame's Board of Regents. Duerson's food companies (he was a bright guy with business acumen) began to suffer.

Duerson withdrew and retreated to his home near Miami. *Doo Doo* was a third-round pick out of Notre Dame in '83 and quickly earned the respect of coaches and teammates. He was 6-1, 210 but played much bigger. Dave loved contact and seamlessly followed the team tradition of projectile safeties like Doug Plank and Gary Fencik. Between '85 and '88, Duerson recorded four straight Pro Bowl selections.

Tasked primarily with run support, Double D also had good ball skills and bagged a career-high six interceptions in '86 (he also had seven sacks that year). He collected 20 picks in his Bears career. Duerson signed with the Giants before the '90 season and earned another Super Bowl ring with Bill Parcells' SB XXV winners.

Doo Doo returned to Chicago following an 11-year pro career and immediately threw his hat in the ring in sports radio. *Concussion* painted Duerson as a staunch detractor of Dr. Bennett Omalu (Dave's family found that off-putting), the pathologist who "discovered" the disease, gave it a name, then had the audacity to ask the NFL to investigate CTE and player safety more aggressively. When the film got to Duerson's suicide, depicting Dave crying as he penned a heartfelt good-bye to Alicia and their four children, I had to hit pause and take a lap. It was too disturbing. I wept. What price victory?

On the Score in the '90s and at ESPN 1000 in the aughts, No. 22 was a regular contributor on my shows. He was always punctual and always well prepared. Doo Doo was a staple at *Mac, Jurko & Harry* charity golf outings for autism and consistently was personable and agreeable with an admiring public. I really liked Duerson, and it appeared reciprocal. He grew up in Muncie, Ind., where I attended what I like to call *Thee* Ball State University. Double D got a kick out of that handle. I met him in his hometown when I was working a club that melded townies with gownies.

I was vacationing in San Diego in '11 when news of Duerson's death broke. My head and heart sank as I slumped in a chair, staring at text messages flooding my phone. "What's wrong?" my wife, Sheri, asked. "Dave Duerson put a shotgun to his chest and killed himself." Sheri is a Notre Dame alum, a Bears fan and had met Dave at one of our golf outings. She was jarred, too.

Double D was a good man, a credit to his parents, teachers and coaches. Duerson wasn't only smart; he was a tireless worker and team-oriented. I know Dave would appreciate the Bears' growth in the secondary in recent years. He was proud of his place in the lineage and had enormous reverence for the traditions worthy of keeping alive.

Gedney, Chris (b. Aug. 9, 1970. d. July 3, 2018)

After several years of experiencing depression, erratic behavior, alcohol abuse and subsequent failed marriage, Gedney fatally shot himself in the neck. The autopsy at the Boston University brain bank confirmed the suspicion Gedney had Stage 2 CTE. He was 47.

A pleasant-natured guy from Syracuse, the tight end was a third-round pick in '93. *GET-nee*, as Dave Wannstedt called him, was supposed to be Jay Novacek, the Cowboys tight end with whom Wannstedt was familiar. All the Bears were missing was Troy Aikman, Emmitt Smith and Michael Irvin to make that happen. Gedney's career never gained any traction in three years with the Bears. He only made a dozen starts before fitting in a little more comfortably for four more NFL seasons with Arizona. Chris returned to his *alma mater* Syracuse to work in athletic administration and with the 'Cuse broadcasting network.

Robinson, Bryan (b. June 22, 1974. d. July 11, 2016)

Medical examiners said Robinson died from hypertensive heart disease after he was found dead in his Milwaukee hotel room. He was 41.

Despite going undrafted out of Fresno State, Robinson authored a 14-year NFL career, six of them with the Bears ('98-'03). *The Big Dog* suited up and went to the post often. He was a large mammal at 6-4, 315 and played with good technique. Robinson's signature moment with the Bears was in Green Bay in early November of '99. The Bears and all of Chicago had heavy hearts that week following the death of Walter Payton. The Packers trailed 14-13 in the final half minute when they trotted out the reliable Ryan Longwell for a chip shot field goal to win it. Robinson jumped, extended his long arms and blocked the kick.

Naturally, many were quick to suggest it was Sweetness himself *whose spirit lifted up Robinson to preserve the victory*. I was not among those voices.

Sayers, Gale (b. May 30, 1943. d. September 23, 2020)

Sayers, and family and friends, struggled badly the past couple years of his life. The NFL legend was felled by complications from Alzheimer's. He was 77.

Drafted fourth-overall in '65, the *Kansas Comet* exploded on the NFL like an atomic bomb. In his rookie season, Sayers rushed for 14 touchdowns and immediately was a first-team All Pro selection. He also caught 29 passes for 507 yards — a ridiculous 17.5 yards per catch for a running back — and six more TDs. Throw in an 85-yard punt return for a score and a kickoff return for another. *Black Magic* indeed ("*I love Brian Piccolo*").

Sayers had swivel hips and changed direction similarly to Barry Sanders. *Mercurial* is the most accurate adjective. He had an explosive first step as well as breakaway speed. Vision. Patience. And uncanny body control. I know these things because I saw none of it. Born too late. What I *did* do is watch a ton of "tape" on Sayers and talk to a lot of his contemporaries over the years. I missed out on "good Sayers" and "good Butkus."

In Week 9 of the '68 season, Gale's knee infamously was blown out in a clean-but-vicious tackle by San Francisco defensive back Kermit Alexander. Sayers returned in '69 and was productive, but he didn't possess the same explosion. He led the league in attempts and rushing yards but his average yards per carry dipped precipitously, from a whopping 6.2 to 4.4. How could Sayers ever be the same after serving up his flesh, bone and tendon to team orthopedist, Dr. Theodore Fox. The universally shared opinion from the guys who wore those uniforms had been that Doc Fox was *NFL Kevorkian*. Buffone once told me players took a magic marker and circled which knee or appendage to fix and which not.

Sayers played in only 68 NFL games — not one in the post-season — to get to Canton. That's the fewest games for any player who received Hall induction. After his career, *Black Magic* was a bitter man. He resented the money players were earning (Sayers claimed he earned $275,000 in his career) and many perceived Gale as resentful of the affection Chicago threw at Payton.

I'm glad I met and interviewed Gale Sayers a few times. He didn't drip warmth but was far more cordial than reputation suggested. Not seeing him wear the cape, however, remains among my top sports regrets.

Salaam, Rashaan (b. Oct 8, 1974. d. Dec. 5, 2016)

Salaam died from a self-inflicted gunshot wound to the head. He was 42.

The Colorado running back was the first Heisman trophy winner ever drafted by the Bears, who plucked him with the 21st-overall pick in '95. Salaam put his head down and grinded as a rookie but his 1074 rushing yards and 10 touchdowns weren't exactly a harvest. Salaam averaged only 3.6 yards per carry and had fumbling issues. He went backwards in his second year, starting only six of the 12 games for which he dressed, rushing for 496 yards and three TDs.

Salaam incurred a horrible ankle injury and subsequently smoked his way out of town and, eventually, the NFL. His career as a Bears ended after the '97 season. Three teams employed him in '99 — Cleveland, Oakland and Green Bay. Salaam never found his way, on or off the field. His family chose not to donate his brain to the Boston brain study group. It conflicted with their Muslim faith and burial rituals.

Tobin, Bill (b. Feb. 16, 1941. d. April 19, 2024)

The Bears long-time scout and eventual director of player personnel died of natural causes. He was 83. Plausible arguments can be made Bill Tobin is the most unheralded contributor to the great teams of the '80s. He began his career with the Bears as a Jim Finks lieutenant in '75, serving as a scout. In '87, following the dismissal of GM Jerry Vainisi, Tobin was promoted to director of player personnel, a title he held through '92. After his outstanding service with the Bears, Tobin took the GM job in Indianapolis in '94. He quickly gained national notoriety for blasting ESPN's Mel Kiper, who'd criticized the Colts for drafting linebacker Trev Alberts. No surprise to anyone who got to know Tobin during his 12 years in Chicago. When I approached him as a guest for Chet Coppock's radio show on the AM Loop, Toby often asked what *"those two smartasses in the afternoon"* were saying about the Bears. The *Steve & Garry* show was not a sports show and wasn't on a sports station. I explained that to Tobin and assured him of *S & G*'s fandom. I suggested *S & G* "just wanted to see you guys win all the time." "Well, they should come to a practice to learn a little more. Talk to some people, ya know?" I didn't know. My loyalty was to my station mates. And I couldn't wait to get back to the Loop studios to tell Steve Dahl and Garry Meier about their show getting under the skin of the personnel guru again.

Tobin, Vince (b. Sept. 29, 1943. d. July 3, 2023, 79) He was 79.

Two years junior to Bill Tobin, Vince got the defensive coordinator job after Buddy Ryan split for Philadelphia. The volume of defensive players who hurled verbal bouquets at Ryan likely was responsible for disproportionate concern for the defending champs navigating through the world without the great James David Ryan. Vince Tobin answered skepticism right out of the gate. In fact, the Bears relinquished fewer points than they did in the *Woof Woof* season of '85. Dull but cordial, Tobin later became the head coach of the Arizona Cardinals, '96-'00, 28-43 (.394). Vince was a quiet but thoughtful guy. He was a solid teacher and schemer. Though not dynamic, Tobin was approachable and easy to like.

CHAPTER 18
The Postgame Show
WE'LL HAVE TO LOOK AT THE TAPE

> *"The postgame show is brought to you by... Christ, I can't find it. The hell with it!" – fictional Cleveland Indians announcer Harry Doyle (Bob Eucker) in the 1989 film Major League*

If your suspicion was this final section would unpack amusing anecdotes from Dan Hampton, Ed O'Bradovich and the late Doug Buffone, your humble narrator has bad news. Even if their emotionally charged content did comprise these words, there's no way to capture the spirit of those boys without audio accompaniment. You'd would miss the 1960s Bears slamming their fists on the table. Wheezing, as they blurt outdated terminology like "red dog" and "flanker." You'd miss Hamp's farm animal analogies, crystalized by a sarcastic producer inserting animal noise sound bytes. What time *do* the cows come home?

Bears fans who went to WGN for Danimal and O'B after Team Eberflus finally got its act together offensively in the Week 4 win over the Rams were furious. Seething. As 61,000 fans filed out of Soldier Field, 'GN was shadowing the historically-bad White Sox for ESPN 1000, home of the Bears. Baby boomers stomped and swore. The Score also was Bears-free with its Cubs commitment. Meaningless baseball play-by-play filled playlists and denizens of this Bears-crazed community felt slighted. I attempted to calm them and noted Hampton and O'Bradovich are far more entertaining after losses, and more were coming.

This chapter begins as a partial postgame for the 2024 season. Best I can offer to make deadlines. As I leave you, the Bears were 2-2, readying for David Tepper — *NFL Genie* — to roll into town with his Carolina Panthers. My wish was for *NFL Aladdin* — Ryan Poles — to request more wishes from his benefactor. Tepper may be vacant enough upstairs to forget Poles was granted his three already.

As we expected, the Bears still have a Matt Eberflus problem. He doesn't think on his feet, and he made bad decisions — the kind that cost you wins — in every game they played. Eberflusian boners included the peculiar need to see more evidence Velus Jones Jr. can't field a punt cleanly. His lost muff on opening day was costly. Flus was coerced into blowing a challenge against the Texans in Week 2. A gesticulating Kyler Gordon persuaded the Flus to toss the red flag. Without conversation with staffers assigned to look at replays, the coach placated his player, who was convinced he had both hands under a C.J. Stroud pass. Gordon didn't and it took five seconds to get the "call on the field stands" announcement. In the loss to the Colts, Eberflus wasted a timeout, uncertain over kicking the PAT or going for the deuce after Caleb Williams' first NFL touchdown pass. They were in the fourth quarter, when there never should be doubt. Nobody on the staff was in the head coach's face to insist for two. And in Week 4, Flus burned a timeout in the final minute when he didn't need it. It followed an unsuccessful (and uninspired) attempt to get the Rams to jump offsides on fourth down.

The following morning, the head coach did his weekly shot with ESPN 1000 and talked himself into a pretzel on the *Kap & Hoody* show. The ball's placement was damn near perfect to punt and pin L.A. deep. Eberflus flapped about "the sweet spot" for punter Tory Taylor. He said he expected the Rams would take a timeout if he didn't. The word salad was dissected deftly by *Waddle & Silvy* later that day. The "sweet spot" for a punter you drafted in the fourth round? And if Flus anticipated Sean McVay was going to take a timeout, why did he waste his own? Taking a five-yard delay of game was an easy call but not for the Bears head coach.

I predicted 11-6 and a playoff appearance but my confidence waned after four games. Eberflus is the biggest reason. If the Bears are going to win this year, they must overcome their coach. He's done a fine job with the defense, but Eberflus proves each week he turns left when he should go right. Every game. I'm waiting for the Bears to win the coin toss and *not* defer, as Flus did in Week 18 against Green Bay last season. This head coaching job... it's not for him.

Also as anticipated, the offensive line was in disarray in September and

Williams spent the first three games running for his life. Poles acquired new players, not better ones. The year began with expected starting center Ryan Bates on IR and Coleman Shelton was worse than Lucas Patrick. Matt Pryor is a jag (just a guy). Pre-snap penalties vexed the Bears. Of those who weren't new to the group, Darnell Wright proved to be the only trustworthy starter. And Wright had three false starts after four games. He only had five all season in '23, when he didn't miss a snap. Teven Jenkins is a credible player but remains dinged up every week. Nate Davis again was unavailable. Braxton Jones' decent rookie season in '22 looks an outlier. An offensive line crisis rarely is fixable during the season. Former Bears offensive coordinator Mike Martz told me after Week 3 Poles needed to deal for *two* better players up front if the Bears were going anywhere this year.

And then there's the quarterback position. I haven't felt the panic of *"Head for the hills! The sky is falling!"* in Bearsville but alarms sounded after an underwhelming September. For the next 10 years, Williams and Jayden Daniels are going to be measured against each other. They were the first and second players chosen. Daniels roared into October with the edge. The Commanders QB was 3-1 and completed 81% of his passes. He threw three touchdown passes with only one pick. Daniels' rating was near 100. Williams was 2-2 and completed 61% of his passes. He threw three touchdown passes with four picks. Williams' rating was near 72.

It was only four games, I continued to remind the torches-and-pitchforks crowd. The two will go toe-to-toe and trade punches, by proxy, for 13 more games and maybe 13 more seasons. That said, the Shane Waldron era opened with a resounding thud. When the ball went in the air against Tennessee, Waldron's offense displayed no identity. All too familiar. Had it not been for a generous Will Levis and a blocked punt returned for a touchdown, the Titans would have beaten the Bears. Waldron wasted August. Eberflus oversaw it. Again.

The always energetic and opinionated Herm Edwards brought the heat on my BetRivers podcast and let the Bears have it for letting Kliff Kingsbury slip away to join Dan Quinn with the Commanders. K.K. had a positive connection with Caleb at USC (we all were told) and the Bears had him in for interviews and let him get away. Kingsbury helped pave a smooth entrance ramp for Williams' NFL career. Waldron's running game stunk for three weeks and the decision to enlist D'Andre Swift for all of two snaps in preseason games offended Edwards' football sensibilities.

PHONE LINES ARE OPEN

In this section of *The Postgame Show*, the emotions of Bears fans and Bears media — this season and historically — are on the docket. I consume sports talk as much as I can during football season. I'll stay for good "guy talk" but when conversation moves to anything but the skin of Buffone's pig, by British companions are a voice command away. *"Play* album *Sticky Fingers."* Dopey callers — not all, but most of the callers — are a sure-fire way to break a nail punching the button.

For years, I thought the obsession with former Chicago players succeeding elsewhere was a local problem. Technology came and gave us all a chance to hear idiocy from every area code in North America. It's not just here. I knew the *told you so!* crowd would be loud and proud before the second set of games kicked off opening day.

Justin Fields played a clean game in a surprise start for the Steelers. Chris Boswell kicked six field goals and Pittsburgh upset Atlanta 18-10 in Kirk Cousins' Falcons debut. "The first puffy-chested call from a member of *Justin's Army* in 3-2-1." In Week 2, Darnell Mooney caught three passes for 88 yards and a touchdown and Atlanta upset Philadelphia. Here come's *Mooney's Army*. I coveted Bears conversation, but the Fields debate was a wrap for me after the Bears moved him. Mooney had four years to distinguish himself and didn't. The Moon Dog made 49 starts and never proved worthy of the bloated deal he got in Atlanta. In his second year in '21, Mooney had 81 catches for 1055 yards and four TDs, but his production was halved in years three and four. Who was impeding Mooney's path to become *the man*, Dante Pettis, Chase Claypool, Byron Pringle or Equanimeous St. Brown?

Fields was a good soldier when he was here and good luck to him. When he bumped the Steelers to 3-0, I was happy for Fields, but it made me sheepish about punching into sports gab. Let Mooney go, kids. He had his chances. End of story.

An argument worth exploring is James Daniels, the Steelers center. Like Mooney, Daniels had four years here and made 48 starts. From the moment Ryan Pace took the Iowa O-lineman 39th overall in '18, the Bears talked about changing his position. Is he a center or a guard? Injuries and uncertainty forced another spin of the broken record *Musical Bears*. Daniels never settled in after playing center and both guard spots. Two coaching staffs couldn't figure out where he fit best. It stunted the Bears' growth and was unfair to Daniels.

Another inevitability in September was the always deep thinking *"why can't you just be happy with the win"* community. I'm not sure why a listener requires happiness from the gatekeepers who do the analyzing but it appears to be a requisite ingredient for some. This sentiment has brought shows to a screeching halt since Wally Phillips was giving away pantyhose to a suburban housewife after providing directions to the Shedd Aquarium. These calls never should clear screening, but they do. The show stalls and hosts invariably play nice and explain the "film doesn't lie" credo to a *narpian*. That's Boomer Esiason speak for "non-athletic regular person." Condescending as hell. And spot on.

No more delay of game penalties. Send them away, producers. Or find a postgame show in which Marc Trestman leads *Kumbaya* after ugly wins. The win over Tennessee was unsatisfying. They were gifted a victory and the high-decibel hype machine ringing out all over Chicagoland had it stuffed up its backside. *"Why can't you just be happy with the win"* didn't fit. It never did. It's called analysis.

SUFFERING FOOLS GLADLY

Throughout almost 40 years of doing Bears media, it's been my want to be kind to listeners and to those who read my columns in the *Tribune*. I view my audience as customers and, in retail, the maxim is "the customer is always right." But he isn't. In my business, I've been tasked with looking in the eyes of some grown men who view the world with the maturity of an 8-year-old. What did I expect in sports talk, you may be thinking. Not this.

I didn't suspect I'd find willful ignorance in every direction. And listening to their complaints challenges my emotional sobriety.

There are Bears fans who never — and I mean never — want to hear a compliment to a Green Bay Packer or anything flattering about the village of Green Bay. Man, I've heard hosts say it. This is Chicago, not Topeka. When I canvass Chicagoland to promote *I Bear Witness*, some listeners will approach and warn me "I may not buy it if it's *Danny Green and Gold* shining through." If you're gonna sing the praises of that dump *Scam-beau* Field or Mike Holmgren, especially since you hate Ditka, I won't buy it."

It's difficult, you know. You understand the guy will listen regardless (and you really don't care if one man doesn't). You know the Bears and Packers, while a rivalry that stirs the juices like no other, is a small percentage of your menu. You know you're with the shallowest end of the gene pool. And you still want to smack him. At the minimum, shout at him. What are you, 12? But, I bite my tongue and try to be gracious. Unless I don't. I'd love to tell all of them, in monosyllabic words, how their willingness to be fat, lazy and stupid is no way to go through life (sky point to *Dean Wormer*).

If one of those Packerphobes could open his mind to *why* the evil enemy has dominated the series for more than 30 years, *Dairyland Drought* might blow his hair back more than any chapter in this record. I admire what the Packers pulled off with Lambeau's reconstruction and consider it a palace. A listener literally demanded an apology from me "before I come back" after I accepted invitation to a VIP tour of Lambeau during the facelift. President Bob Harlan guided the tour, and it was fascinating to learn the differences between the approaches of the Pack with Lambeau and the Bears with Soldier Field. Looks like Green Bay won that one, too. An apology? Hardly. Insight gained remains valuable. Maybe the guy was a NASCAR fan (I am not) and was jealous I watched a game in Harlan's suite with the King, Richard Petty, while *"stuffin' your fat face with free shrimp and slurpin' Jack Daniels."* Some in the sports radio congregation lacks bedside manner more than those of us who write the sermons. The unclean. And unevolved.

Holmgren earned respect as a coach but even more as a man. The former Packers coach is a glaring Hall of Fame omission and should be applauded for his integrity as much as his record. How many NFL coaches have an authentic concern for their players' betterment as men? For sportsmanship and developing life skills? Holmgren, more than any coach in any professional sport, reminds me of my high school coach, Dave Shelbourne. My coach provided a needed compass and was a meaningful influence in my life, as Holmgren has been with hundreds of NFL players if they chose it. His values system wasn't tweaked by the trappings of money or fame. The same cannot be said of Ditka but I did not *hate* him.

I didn't even *dislike* Ditka. He bullied me publicly a long time ago and I was grateful for it. The Score was a start-up radio station, and I was a 31-year-old with a very small following. Ditka helped make the radio station and I've given him enormous credit for that, historically and again in these memoirs. I felt bad for Mike, truthfully, when I listened to some of the biggest stars from '85 still burning hot with resentments. Nobody more than Richard Dent, with Otis Wilson not far behind. Even guys who loved Ditka like to poke. The Chicago Six, as recently as 2020, performed their parody to Pink Floyd's *Another Brick in the Wall*. "We don't need no education" flipped to "We don't need no I-formation." It was rich. "Hey! Ditka, leave the plays alone." Hampton and Steve McMichael sang back up and belted it out with grins. And both are huge Ditka disciples. Still, in 2024, there are a few guys from that '85 team who will die convinced Michael McCaskey should have fired Ditka and retained Ryan after the Super Bowl. My responsibility is to report what the Bears think but I never *hated* Ditka. To my surprise, Jim McMahon mellowed and takes a mature approach to Ditka. Jay Hilgenberg, who always respected Ditka, may even have gained some regard for the 85-year-old coach. "We wouldn't have won a Super Bowl without him," Hilgy said.

BRING IT HOME, MACKER

Man, it felt so good to do this. I want to use these final pages to illuminate how *I Bear Witness* rejuvenated my spirits and reconnected me to the most fulfilling experiences in my work life. The benefits I extracted from doing the book — as a football fan and as an opinionist — were gifts I never saw coming. There also were days when reflection or swapping heart-felt emotions with Bears alums led to tears. I grew to care about a lot of these guys many have been unshakably loyal to me. Friendships were forged, some nearing 40 years.

It was tricky finding the right tone with a projected release date between six and eight weeks after *I Bear Witness* was put to bed. Initially, I wanted *IBW* available in the middle of August. What I didn't consider was the possibility of a Caleb Williams holdout. He finally signed two days before camp started. I moved the goalposts several times. Once the Messiah was in the fold with a deal, it was wise to consume the Hall of Fame inductions on Aug. 3. With *Two and A Half Bears* getting gold jackets, we needed to make sure nothing important was missed. It was too personal to too many of us.

When Williams didn't suit up for the scrimmage against the Texans in Canton, we (Rick Kaempfer, my editor, publisher and Shaman) agreed to let the rookie get his snaps in without damage. Rex Grossman missed the '04 season from a dress rehearsal. If a prop existed, which of the six first-round QBs loses his rookie year from an August mishap, Caleb would have been the prohibitive favorite. Bears karma being the reason. Instead, the "first-year grim reaper" shelved J.J. McCarthy. How about the Purple getting out of the gate clean at 4-0. Sam Darnold, your comp pool suite at the Sybaris is ready.

Don't reach for your radio because it's time to roll credits. They include you. If you devoured this book because the content *means* something to you, gimme a few more minutes so you can learn a thing or two about guys for whom you rooted. The gratitude I have for former Bears players, coaches and media is enormous. My champions included many of *our* only champions. Almost 40 years with the Super Bears brought me to admire many of them far more for what they are and have become. The football stuff is incidental.

I've seen some good daddin'. Jimbo and Penny Covert — college sweethearts — were blessed with three children. Daughter Jessica, in the middle, arrived with spina bifida, a birth defect that sometimes requires surgery for infants. Spina bifida can be extremely serious. Treatable but terrifying. When I did a live auction at a spina bifida fundraiser Jimbo chaired, my heart sank but also was warmed. Young Jessica's extremities had braces, and her strength and mobility were challenged. Exhausted from all the stimulation in a loud lively room, Jessica nestled in daddy's chest. Jess got better. Lots better. She's lived with pain, but Jessica excelled academically and is a successful woman, joyful mother and wife.

Covert's always been a solid interview but an even better speaker. With a chronically troublesome lumbar spine, driving challenged the big guy. The Pitt in him, having been taught reciprocity, the big left tackle schlepped 150 miles round trip to speak at my high school's football banquet. For free. He wouldn't take even a small gratuity to cover expenses or take Penny out for a steak and a few Iron City tall boys.

In more recent years, some of us have shared the pangs of aging parents, suffering and expiring parents. Here's an oddity: Tom Thayer, the most tenured friendship I enjoy from this cast, was born 11 days before I was in August of '61. His dad, a COM-ED lineman and nurturing father, died 11 days before my dad died in the fall of '19. Thayer's parents raised their own children and more who needed parents. Tom was his dad's nearest caretaker in '19 when it got ugly (I'd like to believe the same of me and my dying pops) and is a devoted brother to his siblings. Few people on the back nine of life — let's say 50 and beyond — don't have physical issues of their own or sibs with serious complications. Thayer takes care of his people.

All of us in our 60s now and math isn't on our side. It was heartening to see McMichael's teammates rally around him so universally and compassionately. I've witnessed humanity, an authentic generosity of spirit. I wanted to get together via Zoom with William Perry before it's too late. The Fridge is reclusive and off the grid. I'm best served jumping in the SUV and just showing up at his ranch in Aiken, S.C. with a case of Pabst Blue Ribbon and tub of chicken livers for catfish bait. Would love to see Neal Anderson and Shaun Gayle again, too. Neal was so damn underappreciated in this town.

I don't keep score, but I'm asked regularly, "who's your closest friend" from this team or that team. I'd have to say I'm closest to Jim Morrissey, the rookie linebacker in '85 and eventual successor to Wilber Marshall.

Morrissey and wife, Amy, make all my weddings. Mo grew up without the silver spoon in Flint, Mich. and has a much different perspective than those of many high draft picks. Often, the guys who put the most skins on the wall and make the most money end up the most bitter along the way and after it's done. Morrissey was headed back to Michigan State to complete his degree before the final preseason game in '85. Ditka summoned him to return and play the entire final dress rehearsal due to an injury to Brian Cabral. *Judge Smails* played, earned a roster spot and was a valuable special teams ace his first year. After his career concluded with the Packers in '92, he began a career with AXA Equitable and we've done business together for more than 25 years. Not a pretentious bone in his body.

I'd say the two Bears who appreciated being Bears and sticking in the NFL against big odds were Morrissey and Tom Waddle. Perspective is easily accessible to those who show up in Platteville in a "fecal remnant brown Buick" as Waddle described his ride. Like Covert, Waddle commuted to be keynote speaker at a prep football banquet I chaired and didn't take a fee. And WGN wasn't paying huge money to Waddle for working evenings with David Kaplan in '97. Morrissey is one of those guys. So was Jim Miller when I asked him to speak after the 13-3 season in '01. "Put this into the weight room," Miller said as he returned the check. Later, he showed up at the local bar, Traditions, to visit more with the grown-ups after devoting his time to the athletes at the banquet. Miller said no to a limo when I offered. "Not my style." Perspective comes fast for those who cling to NFL opportunities every time they step on the practice field. Mills almost had his arm amputated late in his career. Infections following surgery.

Keith Van Horne and I always got along, but the last 15 years or so years our friendship has added depth. It's hard watching the big guy try to get around and, knowing a thing or two about isolation, see him bunkered down. Zooming in on 70, I witness the broken bodies and remind myself of the ownership group so arrogantly underpaying the players who were most responsible for the ascent from the rubble in the early '80s. One would think, over time, Team McCaskey would recognize the '85 crew never tasted the big money that arrived when *White vs the NFL* came down in

'93. But no. Never. I'm reminded of the philosopher *Rust Cohle* (Matthew McConaughey) in *True Detective: "People incapable of guilt usually do have a good time."*

Jay Hilgenberg was an ally early on and remains a guy I try to hit golf balls with or maybe eat red meat. My hope is Hilgy gets hooks in a musky's jaw for the first time if tentative plans to hit the Chippewa flowage in November come to fruition. It'll be fun to get him on my turf. Hilgenberg's short game precludes me a fair shot at competing with him on the course. Being a single parent is not an easy putt and Jay and Lisa did a terrific job with Mara after they went their own ways long ago. Hilgy is one of the guys I think of first when friends ask, "who was a great player who's just a normal dude, fun to have a beer with?" Jay pulled up in front of a saloon where we were doing an appearance 10 years ago in a dusty, dingy Ford F-250 with 350,000 miles on it. "Ain't she a beauty?" The answer to the question is Hilgenberg. Of the Iowa Hilgenbergs.

Warmest thanks to these '85 champs, supporters in the past and some still to the present: Thayer. Covert. Perry. Gayle. Van Horne. Morrissey. Ron Rivera. Hilgenberg. Gary Fencik. Dan Hampton. Dent. McMahon. Wilson. McMahon. Steve, Misty and Kathy McMichael. Emery Moorehead. Kevin Butler. Maury Buford. Kurt Becker. Mark Bortz. Mike Singletary. Mike and Diana Ditka. Steve Kazor. Dick Stanfel. Bryan Harlan. Ken Valdisseri. Tony Medelin. John Bostrom. Doug Green. Barb Allen.

Bears alums who didn't earn that *McCaskeyed down* version of a Super Bowl ring have been equally loyal and helpful. Thanks for the time and friendship historically and for my book, players and coaches: Waddle. Miller. Dan Jiggetts. Al Harris. Glen Kozlowski. Mark Carrier. Dave Wannstedt. Tony Wise. Ron Turner. Bobby Slowik. Joe Cain. Erik Kramer. Bryan Cox. Todd Burger. Curtis Conway. Greg Blache. Brian Urlacher. Jerry Angelo. Mike Wells. James Allen. Olin Kreutz. Patrick Mannelly. Alex Brown. Russ Reiderer.

Posthumously, I'm grateful to Bears who were friends of the show. I think so fondly and so often of my friendship with Buffone. I was his "little buddy," like Gilligan to the Skipper. Sky points to my friends, Buffone, Dave

Duerson, Bob Avellini, Vince and Bill Tobin and Dick Stanfel.

It's been my good fortune to work in radio with some guys who really love the game I find the most compelling. Thanks to Terry Boers, my first partner at the Score. Boers went against his judgment and joined Wanny's Army with me. The Score's original midday team of *Jiggetts & North* were an absolute blast to do football with, be it in Lacrosse to see their beloved *Da Coach* guide his Saints to another bad season or in the hallways. Dan Bernstein, now with 30 contiguous years of service at the Score, always had an authentic third for the game. Returning to the dorm from a night at the Hoist House in '97, I found Bernstein and suburban scribe Joe Stevenson shirtless and, in their boxers, demonstrating a particular hand-fighting technique they observed that day in Platteville. Those are memories that keep Platteville close to my heart. *We were young and we were improvin'.* On Saturdays, I've become a *Wake & Bake* regular. *Sunshine Stevie* Rosenbloom has had the sharpest blade on the dial for Flus, and we park our cars in the same garage on the issue. "He shouldn't be here." Economy of words from the ink-stained hockey scribe.

Laurence Holmes was a producer for *Dan & Dan* when Jiggetts and I did our show in camp in '00. It was his first training camp, and the H-F Viking was wide-eyed and into every bit out of it. Holmes recently was paired with my former midday partner, Matt Spiegel, in afternoons on the Score. I make the duo the favorites to produce a parody to mock the Bears' inability to get the center position settled. Pearl Jam, anyone? *"Can't find a center, maaaan. Can't find a center, maaaan."* In the fall of '09, Spiegs and I produced more hit records in three months than the sports radio community has collectively in its lifetime. *Who'll Stop the Run?* (Credence Clearwater Revival), *I Blame the Line* (Johnny Cash), *Maynard and Gould* (Burl Ives) and *The 12 Days of Bearsmas* sent Bears fans into the holidays laughing, even though the wheels were coming off the bus. How could I forget *Santa Claus is Cutler's Hometown! "He's throwin' a pick and fumblin' twice. Didn't like Martz, now he doesn't like Tice. Santa Claus is Cutler's Hometown."*

At ESPN 1000, I enjoyed an amazing eight years with former Packer John Jurkovic and occasionally funny comedian Harry Teinowitz. Beginning in the summer of our first year in '01, we buzzed all over the country for Bears programming and Super Bowl hype week. Many forecast doom for the show, particularly Jurko, since he was a hated Packer. *MJH* did a few things. We ruled the aughts. Looking forward to sharing sordid details soon in my next project. And Jurk's done okay since it was blown up in '09. *Waddle & Silvy* were good teammates, and I'd like to believe they'd say the same of me. Carmen DeFalco is a solid football man and shares my contempt for antiquated Bears receiving records. Jonathan Hood was a '90s teammate at the Score and I was thrilled to see him get another shot in a big chair when they paired him with Kap two years ago. Bring back *Jivin' Hal McRae*, Hoody.

It was an honor to share space in press boxes, locker rooms and bar rooms with Bears media who passed. I miss them all: my mentor and biggest early advocate, Chet Coppock (*Dangerous, wave to the whole section at Soldier Field, not just to the one guy who recognized you*). My loyal and sweet mentee, the selfless Jeff Dickerson (*Pass! Ball! Bison!*). Les Grobstein, who I first heard when I was in 7th grade (*Stop talking all the time about cybermetrics!*). John *Moon* Mullen, the deep-watered scribe who held me up when our mutual friend, Gene Seymour, columnist for Copley News, passed in '96. (*I love 'looms.'*). Tommy Williams, Score teammate in the '90s and fellow Regionite (*I don't like Lavell Edwards. The man is arrogant!*).

NFL alumni have been generous to me over the years and I'm grateful for should-be Hall of Famer Mike Holmgren, who was available and enormously insightful for this record. NFL alums who contributed to *IBW* included: my former show mate Jurkovic. Jarrett Payton. Warren Moon. Rodney Peete. Lomas Brown. Scott Mitchell. Tony Dungy. Herm Edwards. Pete Bercich. Joe Klecko. T.J. Houshmandzadeh. Amani Toomer. Over the years, it's been my good fortune, and beneficial to my audiences, to have warm acquaintanceships with Matt Millen, Terry Bradshaw, Howard Griffith, Nolan Harrison, Jack Youngblood, Fred Smerlas, Jim Grabowski, Chuck Foreman, Jim Grabowski. Larry McCarren, Mick Tinglehoff, Bill Brown. Posthumously, I salute Franco Harris, Todd Christensen and Leroy Selmon. The kindnesses those three great players extended me will be detailed in a forthcoming radio autobiography (working title is *Just Me And The Boys*).

Most importantly, thank you for reading. There's nobody for whom I crafted this more than those of you who were with me since the Coppock days, and the early days on Belmont Ave., when the Score was an adolescent. It was before I deserved a microphone. If you were one of those readers who couldn't wait to play *"remember when"* with me, my hope is your expectations were exceeded. Thanks for letting me take you home. I miss being in your vehicles and your headphones during the football season.

Your loyalty to the Bears is both admirable and disturbing. We all enable Team McCaskey. Supply and demand, *my friends*. Keep demanding the product and they'll keep supplying the rhetoric and dysfunction. A time will come soon when the McCaskey heirs assemble to vote on selling the Bears. Today, there are nine surviving children of Virginia and Ed McCaskey but only eight have voting rights. Whichever way it goes, my hope for future generations is for the Bears to resurrect the buzz. For Caleb Williams to put an end to Sid Luckman jokes and give Bears fans under 50 a chance to experience what I did once.

As committed to this outfit as you've been, you've deserved a better product. If the Bears were a restaurant, you'd never eat there. Here's a wish they serve better food consistently soon and at a full-service sports and entertainment playhouse in Arlington Heights. Make my burger with American cheese and erect my stadium with a retractable roof. Milwaukee has one, for f___ sakes.

Whatever vocation one chooses, when work doesn't feel like work, our lives become less complicated. The result is a better employee and happier human. Hitching my work wagon to the Bears and NFL — beginning in 1985 at the flagship when the skies were sunny every day — was the easiest and most satisfying thing I ever did. In radio, we're instructed to play the hits. The Bears have been the No. 1 song in the city since I can recall and I'm good with that. Just how much those at the top deserve the spoils is a different conversation.

This book was designed to be a combination of reporting, feature writing and columnizing. It had to be biographical, stuffed with facts, dates, scores and stats. I wanted a meaty, definitive look at how Poles built this

Bears unit, as well as the team's history since '85 when I joined the party. All through the eyes of a radio host and a columnist, but a football fan first and foremost. That means bringing it from the toes, having a strong opinion. *This was about the Bears.* Their biggest triumphs, their most insufferable losses, their most unspeakable tragedies.

If you felt like you were listening to one of my shows most of the time, I did my job. That's how it was supposed to feel. More than that, I hope you felt something *deeper*. Be it during this armchair psychologist's take on Walter Payton or McMichael's plight, I hope your heart strings were tugged. If it was the joy you experienced when your dad or big brother turned you onto the Bears, I hope *I Bear Witness* resurrected that feeling a time or two. If you read it almost cover to cover and *felt* something, then I scored a touchdown and made the two-point conversation. Without Flus burning a time out.

"If it suddenly ended tomorrow, I could somehow adjust to the fall. Good times and riches and son of a bitches, I've seen more than I can recall."

– Jimmy Buffet, from *Changes in Latitude.*

Thank you for inviting me to talk football with you. Bear Down.

.

ABOUT THE AUTHOR

Dan McNeil, 63, is a Chicago sports radio titan, podcaster and writer. Known best for his fast paced, no holds barred approach, McNeil became a Chicago brand in his early 30s at Chicago's first all sports talk format, the Score. Danny Mac's knowledge and passion for Chicago sports, particularly football, coupled with a quick wit, playful manner and hair-trigger temper, ingratiated him to listeners. An ex-high school jock, Mac talked about quitting restaurant jobs to go see rock bands or a hockey game. He partied a lot and he was relatable.

Drama and controversy, however, became McNeil's calling card. Disagreement over creative control caused him to resign the Score in 2000 and in May of '01, the *Mac, Jurko & Harry* show launched on ESPN 1000. McNeil's star skyrocketed and the *Afternoon Saloon*, as it came to be known, reset the standards for ratings and revenue in a sports format. The Disney owned station, however, regularly disciplined the trio for racy content and their own combustible relationships. The *Saloon* became "soap opera for dudes" and McNeil was the straw that stirred the drink. Despite *MJH's* popularity and earnings power, ESPN fired McNeil in January of '09.

McNeil's mercurial career included two more returns to the Score ('09-'14 and '18-'20) and a brief stint at the Drive, an FM rocker that hired him to co-host mornings in '15. "Yeah, I took $150K less to get out of bed at 3:30, drive downtown and say, 'Here's Aerosmith.' What about it?" The Score wanted him to return in the summer of '14 to continue in middays with Matt Spiegel, but Mac needed a change. "I wanted to write a love letter to rock and roll," he says.

The son of a manufacturing warehouse foreman, McNeil grew up in Highland, Indiana, about 25 miles south of Comiskey Park. Though his first love was baseball, McNeil contends he "found his way" through the weight room and success as a high school football player. At 8, he began writing about sports on a manual, dated Smith-Corona. His hero was *Oscar Madison*, the beer-swilling, disheveled sportswriter played by Jack Klugman on *The Odd Couple*. At 10, he turned down the sound on Blackhawks game and did his own play-by-play into a cassette recorder. "I was lucky. I knew what I wanted and started training for it before I knew the difference between the boys and the girls."

McNeil's credits include Chicago *Tribune*, weekly guest columnist '09-'13. Chicago *Sun-Times*, weekly columnist '07-'09. The Hammond *Times*, weekly guest columnist '05-'07; prep and college reporter '86-'87. WXRT 93.1 FM, "*Athletes Feats*" commentary '95-'99. The Loop, AM 1000, executive producer/weekend host '88-'91. WGN 720-AM, intern producer '85-'86.

McNeil trained formally at Ball State University, where he majored in radio/television with minors in journalism and sociology. In his senior year, he won an Associated Press award for sports reporting but also tasted his first disciplinary action. Testing boundaries, pushing the envelope and confrontation became as present as McNeil's best attributes.

The father of three sons, McNeil's is an autism advocate and has chaired a dozen celebrity golf outings to raise money and awareness. His middle son, Patrick, 31, is severely autistic. Van, 34, is Mac's "fishing soulmate" while Jack, 29, shares his passion for classic rock. "My drummer son," says McNeil, who took Jack to see AC/DC in the second row for his first concert experience.

Danny Mac and his wife, Sheri, reside in Northwest Indiana.